Dash
diet COOKBOOK

THE DASH DIET IS PERFECT FOR YOU AND YOUR HEALTH, MORE THAN 300 RICH AND HEALTHY RECIPES YOU WILL FIND IN THIS BOOK

KATHERINE FIELDS

Table of Contents

Introduction

Scientists have been studying the effect of diet on blood pressure for some time. The time has come to put this knowledge into practice. The researchers also observed that diets rich in calcium and potassium and, to a lesser extent, magnesium had helped lower blood pressure. Logically, it seemed that taking these dietary supplements would lower blood pressure.

The menu was rich in plant foods such as fruits, vegetables, beans, nuts, seeds, mainly whole grains, and heart-healthy oils. Low-fat dairy products were an essential part of the diet, as were limited quantities of lean meat, poultry, and fish. It was based on the knowledge acquired in vegetarian diets. The first research on the DASH diet was published in 1997. It is a study that aimed to evaluate the effect of the dietary pattern on blood pressure, and it did it very effectively.

The DASH diet reduced blood pressure and first-line medications in just fourteen days. Surprisingly, the rise in blood pressure occurred even though researchers did not allow participants to lose weight. It contained many carbohydrates, mainly to prevent weight loss because if the participants had also lost weight, the researchers would not have known if weight loss or diet would have been helpful. As reported and stated by the New England Journal of Medicine "DASH is particularly effective in people with hypertension (variation of SBP and DBP -10.7 and -4.7 mm Hg, respectively)." In the late 1980s and 1990s, most heart specialists recommended replacing saturated fat. (SFA) with so-called complex carbohydrates.

Another study (Omni-Heart) was conducted to evaluate whether the results of measuring blood pressure in the DASH diet would be better if, instead of replacing SFA with carbohydrates (particularly refined), SFAs were replaced with monounsaturated fats (MUFA) or protein. And actually, they have seen better results. Both approaches reduced total cholesterol, but MUFA did not increase triglycerides (TG) or "good" cholesterol (HDL). Maintaining a higher HDL value and a lower TG is very beneficial for heart health. It is a vital sign that you are successfully managing the risk of metabolic syndrome. A particular advantage was that appetite seemed to be much easier to control. Instead of needing drugs with very unwanted side effects, participants can have very positive "side effects." Wouldn't you like to check your blood pressure with food instead of medications Have you ever heard of the DASH diet before reading this book Many people don't. So why isn't DASH adoption universal Why didn't it explode

Most educational material, including the National Heart, Lung, and Blood Institute (NHLBI), makes monitoring DASH difficult. Based on the complex information in this literature, many doctors believed that it would be tough for patients to follow them, so they did not. Don't even bother to it recommend what a pity! I thought this food model was too important to be a research curiosity. I made this cookbook about the DASH diet to show people how easy it is to take a life formula. And it worked. People have found that they can continue with this and that their health has improved significantly. So, lets follow the latest DASH improvements and include all the recipes here to make it the best plan in the world! And the best flavor!

The basics of the DASH diet are pretty simple eat whole plant foods, stay away from packaged foods. It may sound ridiculously easy but what s underneath it is a deep understanding of human physiology and a careful appraisal of well-conducted medical research.

Do you know how French fries taste so good That s because they are fried in trans-fat (AKA partially hydrogenated oils). This is one of the worst types of fat you can consume. Stick to healthier cooking methods like grilling or baking your food instead.

Sugar-sweetened drinks are loaded with calories and have no nutritional value.

The DASH diet recommends filling half of your plate with fresh fruits and vegetables, a quarter with protein, and the rest with low-fat carbohydrates (such as beans or whole grains).

The DASH diet is not just about food, it's also about variety. That's because your body needs different nutrients to function correctly, and eating the same foods all the time can cause deficiencies in certain nutrients.

Your body doesn't need large amounts of sodium, and most of what you consume comes from processed foods.

If you are eating a healthy variety of food, you can skip the supplements and still be on the DASH diet. However, they can be beneficial to some individuals. For example, if you are pregnant or nursing, then take a calcium supplement. If you have osteoporosis an extra 000,1mg of calcium per day is recommended. If you are looking for minerals in your diet, consider taking a multi-mineral supplement like magnesium andor zinc (which can both cause mild flushes).

Pure protein sources such as fish, poultry, eggs, and lean meat. Eggs are a staple of the DASH diet and can be cooked in so many different ways. Canned fish is also great because it's easy to add to salads or even pack for lunch on the go.

You can select from fresh fruits and veggies, dried fruits, beans, whole grains, and nuts. For example, you can have sweet potatoes with all your meals. You can also have berries or bananas for breakfast followed by a mid-morning snack of raw nuts.

Fresh fruit is always allowed but otherwise, look for low-sugar alternatives such as dried fruit or berries. If you are cooking something at home, then you know exactly what goes into it.

Avocados are one of the Holy Grail foods when it comes to fats. They're packed with healthy monounsaturated fat, and they are a great source of plant-based protein too! You can also include olive oil in your diet, which is rich in omega-3 fatty acids. An omega-3 supplement is also recommended if you don't eat fish, especially if you have a family history of heart disease.

The vitamins and nutrients in nut foods such as almonds and cashews are great, but they're also high in calories and fat. If you are counting your calories, then choose nuts in moderation because they can quickly add up.

All dairy is off-limits except for unsweetened almond milk and rice milk. If you are lactose intolerant then the only way to get enough calcium is through supplements. Also, be careful about pairing this plant-based milk with lots of sugar which can cause unnecessary calories.

Fresh fruit, veggies with hummus or guacamole, air-popped popcorn, baby carrots, and even a small handful of nuts or seeds can be eaten as an on-the-go snack.

Chapter 1

DASH (Dietary Approach to Stop Hypertension) Foundations

Unlike the regular diets out there, DASH is a tad bit different. It means Dietary Approaches to Stop Hypertension. Yes, you read that right. Finally, a diet that focuses on one of the greatest killers of the 21st century- hypertension. According to recent studies, one out of three adults suffers from hypertension or high blood pressure. It keeps increasing with age, with almost two-thirds of the population suffering from it from the age of 65. High blood pressure is not a single stroke disease- it brings heart trouble, kidney diseases, and even diabetes.

Our sedentary lifestyles, coupled with unhealthy eating habits, have fueled several hypertension-related diseases. Most can be corrected by following a healthy diet, which is what DASH aims at. This diet comprises foods and recipes that promote lower sodium levels and higher potassium, calcium, fiber, and magnesium levels in the body. It can also help achieve optimal general blood pressure levels without damaging the bodily processes. When this happens, the likelihood of hypertensions-related disorders is lowered, such as osteoporosis, diabetes, and kidney failure.

The original diet plan aimed to lower blood pressure through natural foods and without medication aid. It was sponsored and endorsed by the US National Institute of Health. When the trials of the first DASH diet came out, it was found that lowering the blood pressure helped maintain the level even with some excess sodium in the blood. Not only this, but the diet was also found to be beneficial in keeping the extra lb. off and prevent many disorders related to hypertension.

WHO SHOULD FOLLOW THIS DIET

Is the diet for me? Or is it only for people with existing hypertension problems? According to the Dietary Guidelines for Americans, the DASH diet is a healthy eating model that anyone can follow. Of course, since the diet's primary objective is to lower blood pressure, people suffering from hypertension become the primary beneficiaries of the diet. But anyone who wishes to get healthy and scientifically lose weight can follow it, children included.

This diet works while other diets fail miserably because the body is kept full of the required nutrition. The fundamental nutrients, such as calcium, magnesium, and potassium, are elevated in the body through a wholesome diet plan, and sodium levels are also kept in control. And it is all done in a controlled, scientific, and disciplined manner without any crashes or spikes in the metabolism, ensuring a healthier you.

THE IMPROVED DASH DIET PLAN

When research into diet plans for hypertension began, they did not focus too much on weight loss. They were more concerned with getting the blood pressure levels regulated. But soon, the researchers realized that healthy weight loss was the need of the hour, and therefore there was an additional need to create a systematic weight loss plan and reduced blood pressure levels. So, after a lot of deliberation, the DASH diet for weight loss was also formulated, including nuts, cereals, whole fruits and vegetables, and seeds.

Unlike other flyby diets, which are more word of mouth than scientific, the DASH diet is primarily based on scientific principles of good health. The research on DASH diets indicates that it is not merely a tool for reducing your blood pressure by eating a low-sodium diet. The plan is designed for each person, keeping their specific needs in mind, and comprises wholesome foods, such as fruits, vegetables, grains, fresh produce, etc., which keep the body in fighting fit condition. Top rung research institutes such as the American Heart Association, Dietary Guidelines for Americans, the National Heart, Lung, and Blood Institute– all endorse this diet plan.

Several more corroborating research reports after, the DASH diet was further improved to optimize health and contrast hypertension by increasing the protein intake and cuttingdown on empty Carbohydrates and bad fats. The DASH diet's primary hypothesis is based on sound scientific principles of attainable and sustainable weight loss. The meals and snacks prescribed in the diet plan comprise bulky, fibrous foods, which keep you filled for hours and do not let you snack mindlessly. They are designed to keep your blood sugar levels regulated instead of the spike and crash cycles, as seen with other diets. By following this diet, you keep your blood sugar levels on an even keel, contrast other diseases like diabetes. You also aim to reduce your triglycerides, melt your stubborn belly fat, lower your LDL, improve your HDL numbers, and generally feel healthier on average. Of course, a significant portion of the diet is protein-rich, so you promote muscle growth and body fat loss, and in the process, you avoid slowing your metabolism, which aids in sustaining your current weight.

Even if you're is not suffering from hypertension, you can adopt the DASH diet to keep your internal systems healthy and robust. In this part of your journey, you will learn how you can make this diet work for you.

Rome wasn't built in a day. Similarly, your body will not take too kindly to change if you do it suddenly. It will protest, and you will soon return to square one. To avoid that discomfort, take baby steps. Do not jump into the diet headlong. Try the meal plan for two days a week, then increase it to three times, and when you are comfortable with it, adopt it ultimately. You might already be eating some DASH diet foods and snacks and not be aware of it. Make a list and see which food items correspond to the diet s meal plan. And do not be under the impression that the DASH diet goes for a toss while dining out. There are plenty of options and strategies you can adopt while eating out. You need to be careful and select healthy choices.

BEGINNING THE DASH DIET

Now that you are supplied with the necessary background information on the DASH diet let us see first what it entails. This meal plan is rich in vegetables, fruits, dairy products, whole grains, lean meats, poultry, fish, and legumes such as peas and beans. Additionally, it contains low fat from natural sources and high fiber from sweet potatoes, cabbage, and leafy vegetables. It adheres to the US guidelines about sodium and potassium content. It is a flexible eating plan designed to meet the needs of a variety of people and keep in mind their food preferences. There is a healthy alternative to almost any kind of food craving. It is what a typical DASH diet comparises:

TYPE OF FOOD	NUMBER OF SERVINGS (1,600–3,000 CALORIE PLAN)	NUMBER OF SERVINGS (1,500–2,000 CALORIE PLAN)
Whole grains or meals made out of whole grains	6–12	7–9
Fresh fruits (not fruit juice)	4–5	4–6
Farm fresh vegetables (try avoiding store bought ones)	4–6	4–6
Dairy products (low fat)	3–4	2–4
Poultry, fish, lean meats	2–3	3–4
Legumes, seeds and nuts	3–5	4–5
Desserts, natural fats	2–3	2

DASH Diet meal plan helps people to be healthier already for more than 20 years. Last few years, the diet is top-rated among other popular diets. It is already proved the beneficial abilities of diet to fight high blood pressure (hypertension). Let's give a few numbers for more conviction. According to the National Institutes of health, the effectiveness of the diet in weight loss is 3.3 points out of 5 and 4.8 points out of 5 in normalizing and lowering blood pressure.

One of the main causes of high blood pressure is the high sodium content in the human body. The salt which we usually consume is high in sodium. Excessive concentration of sodium leads to the fact that it is deposited in the walls of blood vessels. Sodium "attracts" water, and the blood vessels start to swell and narrow. Consequently, the blood pressure rises, and the man feels bad.

For 70 years of life, people eat approximately half a ton of salt. This is the only mineral that we eat in its pure form. It doesn't mean that salt is harmful to our body, as every mineral, it has benefits and vital for regulating the water-salt balance in the body, the formation of gastric juice, and the transfer of oxygen in blood cells. However, its excess in the diet is a time bomb for us.

DASH diet allows you to reduce the amount of sodium in your body thanks to its limitation and striking out the high sodium-containing products from your diet. The amount of sodium in day meals should be no more than 2,300 mg. Some research proves that decreasing the sodium amount to 005,1mg can help to get rid of high blood pressure faster.

Simple restriction of sodium in the organism will not bring the desired result. The diet is balanced in the content of substances vital for normal blood pressure, such as potassium, magnesium, calcium, protein, and plant fibers. Only the right combination of these substances will give the needful effect.

The diet involves the perfect combination of different food groups such as fruits, vegetables, grains, dairy products, meat, fish, poultry, eggs, nuts and seeds, legumes, and oils. Therefore, the organism is balanced in the content of many important nutritional components.

Besides this, you start consuming less salt, sugar, and fatty junk foods, which cause high blood cholesterol. If you follow the diet strictly and do sport every day, it is possible to lose .shtnom 4 rof .bl 917 1

The biggest advantage of dash eating is that such a diet is not as fast as most radical methods, but it is natural and correct. And the lost kilos don't return back if you make such a diet as a lifestyle.

The dash diet is considered one of the most beneficial for health. Although it is created for hypertensive patients, such a diet will improve the well-being and health of everyone.

The advantages of the dash diet are that it is recommended by doctors and is not harmful to health. The dash diet forms the habit of eating properly.

Proper diet and health care that is what matters. And this diet is a healthy meal plan that fits this philosophy perfectly.

TOP 10 TIPS FOR DASH DIET

WALKING IS IMPORTANT

Simple sports activities, walking, or riding the bike will enforce the effect of the dash diet and will help in weight loss too.

The perfect combo for stabilizing the blood pressure is a minimum of 2 hours walking and 30-minute sports activities per week. If it looks complicated for you, start from 1-hour walking and 10-minutes sports exercises increase the load till you reach the aimed time.

DON'T CHANGE YOUR LIFE DRASTICALLY

To not make stress for your body, change your eating habits step-by-step until you adjust them according to the dash diet plan totally.

CREATE A FOOD JOURNAL

It will help you to realize how much food you eat per day and if it is dash diet-friendly. Follow such a journal should be regular. Be sure, in a week, you will see a significant result in your attitude to food.

MAKE EVERY MEAL GREEN

Make a rule to add some green vegetables to every meal. By doing this, you will provide much fiber and potassium for your organism.

BE A VEGAN ONCE PER WEEK

Limit your meat consumption and avoid eating meat totally once per week. Eat more beans, nuts, tofu, which are rich in proteins too.

FRESH BOX

Make a box with fruits, vegetables, and rice cakes for your snack time. Such a box will help you to avoid the consumption of high-sodium fast food.

FOOD LABELS ARE USEFUL

Always read the food labels before buying packaged or processed food. By doing this, you can control the level of sodium amount better.

Notice that the low-sodium canned food should have less than 140 mg of sodium per serving.

ADD SPICES

Such spices as rosemary, cayenne pepper, chili pepper, cilantro, dill, cinnamon, etc. can saturate the taste and make more delicious even non-salty meals.

MAKE YOUR SNACK DELICIOUS

People prefer different types of snacks, not all of them adore fruits and vegetables. For them, it can be a difficult step to switch on healthy food immediately. That's why make a list of your favorite products and eat them during the day like a snack. The food list will be appropriate until you get rid of all junk food from your diet.

MAKE A BODY EXAMINATION EVERY 2 MONTHS

Some health problems can't be changed just by changing the food plan. The doctor's participation in your diet is important. Make the full body examination before starting a diet and then consult a doctor about any discomfort in your body or health every 2 months it will allow following the diet in the most comfortable way for your health.

Chapter 2
Benefits of DASH Diet

Although you're likely to go for the DASH diet because of a slimmer waist and better health, there are more reasons to consider the DASH diet. They include the following

WEIGHT LOSS

DASH advocates for much less fat than you'd find in a typical American diet. It means that it's lower in calories. This diet eliminates and reduces unhealthy fats, fast food, fried foods, as well as foods that are highly processed. Instead, it emphasizes healthy fats like saturated fats and healthy saturated fats like omega-3 fats that are good for your body and help weight loss. These are mostly present in foods with lower calories. The high fiber content in most of the foods recommended under the DASH diet is another great contributor to weight loss because fibers help you have a feeling of satiety while also aiding digestion so your body can eliminate wastes while slowing down the absorption of sugar and fat. It promotes efficient regulation and response to insulin, contrasting the risk of and symptoms of metabolicsyndrome.

The high absorption or consumption of fresh vegetables and fruits translates to high vitamin c and antioxidants levels. Vitamin C is instrumental in reducing the stress that reduces the amount of stress hormone, cortisol, produced. This hormone is also responsible for the storage of fat in the area around the abdomen. Therefore, what you eat will not be stored as fat in your abdomen. Additionally, vitamin C is a building block of L-carnitine that is instrumental in the transportation of fat. When your body receives a signal or cue that you no longer need the fat, it is turned to glucose for use as energy. The body needs sufficient amounts of vitamin C to make L-carnitine naturally. It means you need to consume vitamin C daily to contribute to weight loss because the primary role of vitamin C is fighting infection and rebuilding damaged cells.

The DASH diet also advocates for caloric intake that differs from one person to another, considering your weight loss goals, current weight, body shape, and activity level. This diet avoids consuming very few calories that eventually puts you at risk of losing lean muscle tissue instead of fat while ensuring you re getting enough nutrients to support your level of activity.

HEART DISEASE

When you have a combination of high blood pressure, metabolic syndrome, and type 2 diabetes, you re likely to end up with heart disease. The fact that the DASH diet addresses all these conditions means that it can also strengthening the body's resistance to heart disease. This diet is an excellent option even when you re not already experiencing any of these conditions. Heart disease records the most significant number of deaths among Americans. Health professionals recommend a diet low in unhealthy fats and high in healthy fats, and fiber will positively influence your heart health. The American Heart Association recommends DASH because it s a heart-healthy diet. Apart from improved heart health,this diet has also a beneficial effect on the colon and digestive system.

METABOLIC SYNDROME

The term metabolic syndrome is used for a group of symptoms associated with insulin and obesity. This syndrome is sometimes known as pre-diabetes because when not checked, it results in type 2 diabetes. Some of the typical metabolic syndrome markers include high blood sugar, large waist size, elevated HDL, and high triglycerides. The DASH diet aims to contrast these unwanted symptoms. The DASH diet consists of reduced amounts of bad fats and an increase in the consumption of good fats and fiber, aiming to reduce the levels of triglyceride and HDL cholesterol. The nutrients you obtain from the DASH diet with the potential fat loss experienced around the abdomen, counteract the metabolic syndrome, helping you experience optimal health.

TYPE 2 DIABETES

The DASH diet was rated as the best diet for battling type 2 diabetes and for anyone facing the risk of developing diabetes by the U.S. News and World Report. It has been demonstrated that this diet is capable of lessening the symptoms and the severity of diabetes significantly. In some cases, the dietary change associated with this diet has helped in reversing the condition. The reason behind this is simple. The foods incorporated into the DASH diet help in improving the health of people who have diabetes. For instance, nuts help controlling glucose in people with diabetes. Simultaneously, the high fiber content will slow down the absorption of sugar, which helps calm blood sugar levels. All the vegetables and fruits in theDASH diet are packed with antioxidants that help contrast complications related to type 2 diabetes. TheDASH diet could positively affect type 2 diabetes by promoting weight loss, especiallyabdominal fat that triggers insulin insensitivity.

CONTROLLED BLOOD PRESSURE

It is the main benefit of the DASH diet and the reason why nutritionists and physicians recommend it. Following DASH lets you keep your blood pressure in check. This diet is ideal for anyone who is taking medication to control blood pressure and those with prehypertension symptoms and are looking for better ways of managing these symptoms. DASH is specially designed to help tame blood pressure and has been scientifically proven to work.

HEALTHY EATING

Let's face it. One of the grounds or reasons why most people experience high blood pressure is that being overweight or obese is associated with poor eating choices. Following the DASH diet helps you make a lifestyle change to healthy eating. Thus, you will be spending more time in the kitchen preparing fresh food instead of grabbing processed food on the go. You will also enjoy your mealtimes because your plate will be filled with more nutritious foods. DASH also stretches you a little to try out new vegetables and fruits and experiment with various seasonings that are salt-free to create meals that you will enjoy.

EFFECTS ON THE RISK OF OSTEOPOROSIS

The majority of dietary approaches to preventing and treating osteoporosis include increasing your intake of calcium and vitamin D that is found in abundance in foods recommended for the DASH diet. It, coupled with reduced sodium intake, is proof that the DASH diet is quite beneficial for bone health. Some studies found a notable decline in bone turnover for people who followed the DASH diet. When sustained over a more extended period, the DASH diet is instrumental in improving bone mineral status. Other nutrients inabundance in the DASH diet are excellent at promoting bone health over time include vitamin C, antioxidants, magnesium, and polyphenols.

HEALTHY CHOLESTEROL LEVELS

Since most of the fruits, beans, nuts, whole grains, and vegetables recommended under the DASH diet have high fiber content, you can eat them alongside fish and lean meat while limiting or regulating your intake of refined carbohydrates and sweets. It goes a long way in improving your cholesterol levels.

HEALTHIER KIDNEYS

The DASH diet is recommended for kidney health because of the abundance of magnesium, potassium, calcium, and fiber present in the foods encouraged. The focus on reducing sodium intake is also an advantage if you face developing kidney disease. Even then, the DASH diet should be restricted to patients who have chronic kidney disease and those undergoing dialysis without close guidance from qualified health care professionals.

EFFECTS ON CERTAIN CANCERS

Researchers have studied the relationship between the DASH diet and certain types of cancers and found a positive association that relates to reducing salt intake and monitoring dietary fat consumption. The diet is also low in red means that it is linked to cancer of the rectum, colon, esophagus, lung, stomach, kidney, and prostate. Eating plenty of fresh produce helps contrast the onset of various cancers while emphasizing dairy products that are lowin fat contributes to a healthier colon.

BETTER MENTAL HEALTH

The DASH diet will boost your mood by counteracting symptoms of mental healthdisorders like anxiety or depression. It is associated with various lifestyle changes that include avoiding cigarettes, moderating alcohol consumption, and exercising regularly. Moreover, the inclusion of nutrient-rich foods in the diet also helps balance hormones and chemicals in the brain and body, thus contributing to improved mental health and overall well-being.

ANTI-AGING PROPERTIES

Many people who follow the DASH diet have attested to the fact that this diet helps avoid some effects of aging so that they keep them feeling and looking younger. Increasing your consumption of fresh vegetables and fruits that are full of antioxidants will rejuvenate your hair and skin, revitalize and strengthen your joints, muscles, and bones, help you lose weight, and leave you feeling healthier.

EFFECTS ON THE RISK OF DEVELOPING HEART DISEASE

The DASH diet's ability to keep your blood pressure in check is instrumental in strengtheningthe body's resistance to heart disease. According to a 1 study, DASH can be ofconsiderable help in heart health. It is particularly remarkable given the persistent andenormous burden of coronary heart disease. It is attributed to the fact that lowered blood pressure lets the heart function efficiently and effectively. Moreover, it can also be beneficial for those who are not struggling with hypertension but are particularly attentive to the health of their heart.

WHAT TO EAT AND AVOID ON DASH DIET

GRAIN PRODUCTS

Use only whole grains because they are richer in fiber and nutrients. They are low-fat and can easily substitute butter, cheese, and cream.

WHAT TO EAT	EAT OCCASIONALLY	WHAT TO AVOID
Brown rice	Whole-wheat pasta	White rice
Whole-grain breakfast cereals	Whole-wheat noodles	Regular pasta
Bulgur		White bread
Quinoa		
Oatmeal		
Popcorn		
Rice cakes		

VEGETABLES

Vegetables are the richest source of fiber, vitamins, potassium, and magnesium. You can use vegetables not only as a side dish but also as a topping, spread, or meat-free main dish substitute.

WHAT TO EAT	WHAT TO AVOID
All fresh vegetables and greens	Regular canned vegetables
Low-sodium canned vegetables	

FRUITS AND BERRIES

Fruits and berries have the same vital benefits as vegetables. They are rich in minerals and vitamins.

One more advantage of fruits and berries is their low-fat content. They can be a good substitution for desserts and snacks. Fruit peels contain the highest amount of fiber and useful nutrients in comparison with fruit flesh.

WHAT TO EAT	EAT OCCASIONALLY	WHAT TO AVOID
All fruits and berries (pineapple, apple, mango, pears, strawberries, raspberries, dates, apricots, etc.)	Grapefruit Orange Lemon	Sugar added canned fruits Coconut

MEAT AND POULTRY

Meat is rich in zinc, B vitamins, protein, and iron. There is a big variety of recipes that will help you to cook meat in different ways. You can broil, grill, bake or roast it but anyways it will be delicious.

Noté avoid eating skin and fat from poultry and meat

WHAT TO EAT	EAT OCCASIONALLY	WHAT TO AVOID
Skinless chicken breast	Lean cuts of red meat (pork, beef, veal, lamb)	Fat cuts of meat
Skinless chicken thighs	Eggs	Pork belly
Skinless chicken wings		Bacon
Skinless drumsticks		Fat
Chicken fillet		

FISH AND SEAFOOD

The main benefits you will get from the fish which is high in omega-3 fatty acids. All types of seafood and fish are allowed on the dash diet. You will find the best fish choice for the dash diet below.

WHAT TO EAT	WHAT TO AVOID
Salmon	High sodium canned fish and seafood
Herring	
Tuna	

NUTS, SEEDS, AND LEGUMES

This type of product is rich in fiber, phytochemicals, potassium, magnesium, and proteins. It can fight cancer and cardiovascular disease.

Nuts, seeds, and legumes are high in calories and should be eaten in moderation. Add them into your salads or main dishes, they will saturate the taste.

WHAT TO EAT
All types of seeds
All types of nuts
All types of legumes

FATS AND OILS

The main function of fats is to help in absorbing vitamins nevertheless, the high amount of fats can lead to developing heart diseases, obesity, and diabetes.

According to the dash diet, your daily meal plan shouldn t include more than 30% of fats of daily calories.

WHAT TO EAT	EAT OCCASIONALLY	WHAT TO AVOID
Margarine	Low-fat mayonnaise	Butter
Vegetable oils	Light-salad dressings	Lard
		Solid shortening
		Palm oil

SWEETS

It is not necessary to cross out all sweets from your daily diet but it is important to follow some restrictions that the dash diet provides choose sugar-free, low-fat fat-free sweets or replace them with fruits and berries.

WHAT TO EAT	EAT OCCASIONALLY	WHAT TO AVOID
Fruit berries sorbets	Hard candy	Biscuits
Fruit ice	Splenda	Crackers
Graham crackers	Aspartame	Cookies
Honey	Agave syrup	Soda
Sugar-free fruit jelly	Maple syrup	Unrefined sugar
		Table sugar
		Sweet junk food

ALCOHOL AND CAFFEINE

You should limit alcohol to 2 drinks per day for men and up to 1 or fewer drinks for women.

Note alcohol and caffeine consumption can be forbidden totally if it is required according to a medical examination.

DASH DIET PHASE 1

DASH Diet Phase 1 is an eating plan that is low in fat, saturated acids, and sodium. It may be the world s most effective diet for reversing disease. DASH for weight loss has been proven to help reduce obesity and lower cholesterol levels even in those who have not had any other weight-loss programs.

Phase 1 of the diet is truly amazing. It works for people suffering from various health conditions. It also boosts energy levels and speeds up metabolism.

Adherence to DASH Diet Phase 1 makes you feel full of energy every day and this helps you concentrate on your everyday tasks without feeling weak or tired.

DASH Diet Phase 1 has several components like

LOW-FAT, HIGH FIBER, AND MONO-PROTEIN DIETS

This proves to be a great way of losing weight and reversing diseases including diabetes as well as heart conditions.

HIGH IN WATER, LOW IN BAD FAT (SATURATED FATS), AND SODIUM

As stated above it helps in reducing the levels of bad fat in the body by decreasing the intake of saturated fats. On eating this diet you will also feel full all day long which an added advantage is for those who are struggling with their weight loss goals or even trying to keep their weight under control.

BALANCED MEALS WITH LOW-GLYCEMIC INDEX FOODS

This is one of the most beneficial parts of DASH Diet Phase 1 and is an important component for the success of the diet. The reason behind this is that it helps to decrease the levels of bad cholesterol, triglycerides, and improve overall health.

HIGH IN ANTIOXIDANTS

The diet also helps in boosting your immune system and preventing you from diseases like heart conditions and diabetes by increasing your resistance against them. It reduces the number of free radicals in your body which leads to an increase in longevity.

MODERATE USE OF SODIUM AND SPICES

The diet does not allow an excess use of salt in any form. They are however allowed to the extent specified by the diet, which means a maximum of 2,300 mg per day. The diet also allows you to consume 3 different types of spices (Black pepper, paprika, and basil) in moderate amounts for better taste.

LOW-GLYCEMIC FOODS

The food items that you consume should be those that have a low glycemic index as it helps in regulating your blood sugar levels and reduces the risk of you suffering from high blood pressure or even getting diabetes later on when you are older.

HIGH IN VEGETABLES AND WHOLE GRAINS

One of the key aspects of the diet is that it contains a high percentage of vegetables along with fruits to reduce the risk of diseases like cancer, heart conditions, and diabetes as well as to increase your longevity.

HELP ON LOSING WEIGHT

The diet helps you in dropping weight by increasing your energy levels as well as reducing your appetite. It also may help you in improving the way you look or how you feel about yourself without really taking any additional effort on your end.

DASH DIET PHASE 2

Phase 2 is a food-based diet plan that s comprised of vegetables, fruits, whole grains, low-fat dairy products, and protein foods. The diet phases are divided into three parts in order to ensure that you have the necessary nutrients for your body. You can have two servings per day from the DASH diet phase 2 list and one serving from the DASH diet phase 1 or 3 lists as well as unlimited water. Fresh vegetables and fresh fruit options are just what your body needs to stay physically healthy during this point in time.

Phase 2 is a part of the DASH diet plan which is created by working with eating habits and physical activity levels. Phase 2 of this diet consists of healthy fats, low-fat dairy, protein foods like fish and seafood, nuts, seeds, and beans. You can consume two servings a day from the phase 2 list and one serving from the phase 1 lists. This will ensure that your body receives all the essential nutrients that it needs without overconsuming calories. It is important to have a variety of food sources while you are in Phase 2. The diet should include fresh vegetables and fruits, low-fat dairy products, protein foods like fish and seafood, nuts, seeds, and beans. You can have unlimited water for the whole day. Your weekly goal is for you to be at a healthy weight for your height. If you are overweight or obese (BMI is over 25), then you can calculate your goal based on the percentage of fat mass which you want to have in your weight (see chart below). For example if you are overweight at 235 lb. with 15% body fat then your desired weight loss goal would be 150 lb.

Chapter 3
Breakfast Recipes

1. Greek Yogurt Pancakes

10 MIN

COOKING TIME

5 MIN

SERVINGS

2

INGREDIENTS

- 1 cup all-purpose flour
- 1 cup whole-wheat flour
- 1/4 tsp. salt
- 4 tsp. baking powder
- 1 tbsp. sugar
- 1 1/2 cups unsweetened almond milk
- 2 tsp. vanilla extract
- 2 large eggs
- 1/2 cup plain 2% Greek yogurt
- Fruit, for serving
- Maple syrup, for serving

DIRECTIONS

1. First, you will have to pour the curds into the bowl and mix them well until creamy. After that, you will have to add egg whites and mix them well until combined.
2. Then take a separate bowl, pour the wet mixture into the dry mixture. Stir to combine. The batter will be extremely thick.
3. Then, simply spoon the batter onto the sprayed pan heated too medium-high. The batter must make 4 large pancakes.
4. Then, you will have to flip the pancakes once when they start to bubble a bit on the surface. Cook until golden brown on both sides.

NUTRITIONS

- Calories: 166
- Carbohydrates: 52 g
- Fat: 5 g

- Protein: 14 g

2. Egg White Scramble With Cherry Tomatoes & Spinach

PREPARATION TIME

5 MIN

COOKING TIME

8-10 MIN

SERVINGS

4

INGREDIENTS

- 1 tbsp. olive oil
- 1 whole egg
- 10 egg whites
- 1/4 tsp. black pepper
- 1/2 tsp. salt
- 1 garlic clove, minced
- 2 cups cherry tomatoes, halved
- 2 cups packed fresh baby spinach
- 1/2 cup Light cream or Half & Half
- 1/4 cup finely grated parmesan cheese

DIRECTIONS

1. Whisk the eggs, pepper, salt, 1 tbsp. olive oil, and light cream. Prepare a skillet using the med-high temperature setting. Toss in the garlic when the pan is hot to sauté for approximately 30 seconds.
2. Pour in the tomatoes and spinach and continue to sauté it for one additional minute. The tomatoes should be softened, and the spinach wilted.
3. Add the egg mixture into the pan using the medium heat setting. Fold the egg gently as it cooks for about two to three minutes. Remove from the burner, and sprinkle with a sprinkle of cheese.

NUTRITIONS

- Calories: 142
- Carbohydrates: 4 g
- Fat: 2 g

- Protein: 15 g

3. Feta & Quinoa Egg Muffins

20 MIN

COOKING TIME

45-50 MIN

SERVINGS

12

INGREDIENTS

- 1 cup cooked quinoa
- 2 cups baby spinach, chopped
- 1/2 cup Kalamata olives
- 1 cup tomatoes
- 1/2 cup white onion
- 1 tbsp. fresh oregano
- 1/2 tsp. salt
- 2 tsp. and more for coating pans olive oil
- 8 eggs
- 1 cup crumbled feta cheese
- Also needed: 12 cups muffin tin

DIRECTIONS

1. Heat the oven to reach 350° F. Lightly grease the muffin tray cups with a spritz of cooking oil.
2. Prepare a skillet using the medium temperature setting and add the oil. When it's hot, toss in the onions to sauté for two minutes.
3. Dump the tomatoes into the skillet and sauté for one minute. Fold in the spinach and continue cooking until the leaves have wilted (1 min.).
4. Transfer the pot to the countertop and add the oregano and olives. Set it aside.
5. Crack the eggs into a mixing bowl, using an immersion stick blender to mix them thoroughly. Add the cooked veggies in with the rest of the ingredients.
6. Stir until it's combined and scoop the mixture into the greased muffin cups. Set the timer to bake the muffins for 30 minutes until browned, and the muffins are set. Cool for about ten minutes. Serve.

NUTRITIONS

- Calories: 295
- Carbohydrates: 3 g
- Fat: 23 g

- Protein: 19 g

4. 5-Minute Heirloom Tomato & Cucumber Toast matoes & Spinach

PREPARATION TIME

10 MIN

COOKING TIME

6-10 MIN

SERVINGS

1

INGREDIENTS

- 1 small Heirloom tomato
- 1 Persian cucumber
- 1 tsp. olive oil
- 1 pinch oregano
- Kosher salt and pepper as desired
- 2 tsp. low-fat whipped cream cheese
- 2 pieces Trader Joe's Whole Grain Crispbread or your choice
- 1 tsp. Balsamic glaze

DIRECTIONS

1. Dice the cucumber and tomato. Combine all the ingredients except for the cream cheese. Smear the cheese on the bread and add the mixture. Top it off with the balsamic glaze and serve.

NUTRITIONS

- Calories: 239
- Carbohydrates: 32 g
- Fat: 11 g

- Protein: 7 g

5. Greek Yogurt With Walnuts and Honey

5 MIN

COOKING TIME

0 MIN

SERVINGS

4

INGREDIENTS

- 4 cups Greek yogurt, fat-free, plain or vanilla
- 1/2 cup California walnuts, toasted, chopped
- 3 tbsp. Honey or agave nectar
- Fresh fruit, chopped or granola, low-fat (both optional)

DIRECTIONS

1. Spoon yogurt into 4 individual cups. Sprinkle 2 tbsp. walnuts over each and drizzle 2 tsps. honey over each. Top with fruit or granola, whichever is preferred.

NUTRITIONS

- Calories: 300
- Carbohydrates: 25 g
- Fat: 10 g

- Protein: 29 g

6. Tahini Pine Nuts Toast

PREPARATION TIME

5 MIN

COOKING TIME

0 MIN

SERVINGS

2

INGREDIENTS

- 2 whole-wheat bread slices, toasted
- 1 tsp. water
- 1 tbsp. Tahini paste
- 2 tsp. Feta cheese, crumbled
- Juice of 1/2 lemon
- 2 tsp. Pine nuts
- A pinch of black pepper

DIRECTIONS

1. In a bowl, mix the tahini with the water and the lemon juice, whisk well, and spread over the toasted bread slices. Top each serving with the remaining ingredients and serve for breakfast.

NUTRITIONS

- Calories: 142
- Carbohydrates: 13.7 g
- Fat: 7.6 g

- Protein: 5.8 g

7. Feta - Avocado & Mashed Chickpea Toast

PREPARATION TIME

10 MIN

COOKING TIME

15 MIN

SERVINGS

4

INGREDIENTS

- 15 oz. can Chickpeas
- 2 oz. and 1/2 cup diced feta cheese
- 1 pitted avocado
- 2 tsp. lemon (or 1 tbsp. Orange)
- 1/2 tsp. black pepper
- 2 tsp. honey
- 4 slices Multigrain toast

DIRECTIONS

1. Toast the bread. Drain the chickpeas in a colander. Scoop the avocado flesh into the bowl. Use a large fork/potato masher to mash them until the mix is spreadable.
2. Pour in the lemon juice, pepper, and feta. Combine and divide onto the four slices of toast. Drizzle using the honey and serve.

NUTRITIONS

- Calories: 337
- Carbohydrates: 43 g
- Fat: 13 g

- Protein: 13 g

8. Feta Frittata

PREPARATION TIME

15 MIN

COOKING TIME

25 MIN

SERVINGS

2

INGREDIENTS

- 1 small clove Garlic
- 1 green onion
- 2 large eggs
- 1/2 cup egg substitute
- 4 tbsp. Crumbled feta cheese, divided
- 1/3 cup plum tomato
- 4 thin avocado slices
- 2 tbsp. reduced-fat sour cream
- Also needed: 6-inch skillet

DIRECTIONS

1. Thinly slice/mince the onion, garlic, and tomato. Peel the avocado before slicing. Heat the pan using the medium temperature setting and spritz it with cooking oil.
2. Whisk the egg substitute, eggs, and the feta cheese. Add the egg mixture into the pan. Cover and simmer for four to six minutes.
3. Sprinkle it using the rest of the feta cheese and tomato. Cover and continue cooking until the eggs are set or about two to three more minutes.
4. Wait for about five minutes before cutting it into halves. Serve with avocado and sour cream.

NUTRITIONS

- Calories: 460
- Carbohydrates: 8 g
- Fat: 37 g

- Protein: 24 g

9. Smoked Salmon and Poached Eggs on Toast

10 MIN

4 MIN

4

INGREDIENTS

- 2 oz. avocado smashed
- 2 slices of bread toasted
- A pinch of kosher salt and cracked black pepper
- 1/4 tsp freshly squeezed lemon juice
- 2 eggs, poached
- 3.5 oz. smoked salmon
- 1 tbsp. Thinly sliced scallions
- Splash of Kikkoman soy sauce optional
- Microgreens are optional

DIRECTIONS

1. Take a small bowl and then smash the avocado into it. Then, add the lemon juice and also a pinch of salt into the mixture. Then, mix it well and set it aside.
2. After that, poach the eggs and toast the bread for some time. Once the bread is toasted, you will have to spread the avocado on both slices and after that, add the smoked salmon to each slice.
3. Thereafter, carefully transfer the poached eggs to the respective toasts. Add a splash of Kikkoman soy sauce and some cracked pepper; then, just garnish with scallions and microgreens.

NUTRITIONS

- Calories: 459
- Carbohydrates: 33 g
- Fat: 22 g

- Protein: 31 g

10. Honey Almond Ricotta Spread With Peaches

5 MIN

8 MIN

4

INGREDIENTS

- 1/2 cup Fisher Sliced Almonds
- 1 cup whole milk ricotta
- 1/4 tsp. almond extract
- Zest from an orange, optional
- 1 tsp. honey
- Hearty whole-grain toast
- English muffin or bagel
- Extra fisher sliced almonds
- Sliced peaches
- Extra honey for drizzling
- 2 tbsp. Olive oil
- ½ cup Crushed amaretti cookies
- 2 tbsp. Mint leaves

DIRECTIONS

1. Cut peaches into a proper shape and then brush them with olive oil. After that, set it aside. Take a bowl; combine the ingredients for the filling. Set aside.
2. Then just pre-heat the grill to medium. Place peaches cut side down onto the greased grill. Close lid cover and then just grill until the peaches have softened, approximately 6 to10 minutes, depending on the size of the peaches.
3. Then you will have to place peach halves onto a serving plate. Put 1 tbsp. ricotta mixture into the cavity (you are also allowed to use a small scooper).
4. Sprinkle it with slivered almonds, crushed amaretti cookies, and honey. Decorate with the mint leaves.

NUTRITIONS

- Calories: 187
- Carbohydrates: 18 g
- Fat: 9 g

- Protein: 7 g

11. Low-Carb Baked Eggs With Avocado and Feta

PREPARATION TIME

10 MIN

COOKING TIME

15 MIN

SERVINGS

2

INGREDIENTS

- 1 avocado
- 4 eggs
- 2–3 tbsp. Crumbled feta cheese
- Nonstick cooking spray
- Pepper and salt to taste

DIRECTIONS

1. First, you will have to preheat the oven to 400°F. After that, when the oven is at the proper temperature, you will have to put the gratin dishes right on the baking sheet.
2. Then, leave the dishes to heat in the oven for almost 10 minutes after that process, you need to break the eggs into individual ramekins.
3. Then, let the avocado and eggs come to room temperature for at least 10 minutes. Then, peel the avocado properly and cut it each half into 6–8 slices.
4. You will have to remove the dishes from the oven and spray them with the non-stick spray. Then, you will have to arrange all the sliced avocados in the dishes and tip two eggs into each dish. Sprinkle with feta, add pepper and salt to taste, serve.

NUTRITIONS

- Calories: 280
- Carbohydrates: 10 g
- Fat: 23 g
- Protein: 11 g

12 Strawberry, Orange, and Beet Smoothie

PREPARATION TIME

5 MIN

COOKING TIME

0 MIN

SERVINGS

2

INGREDIENTS

- 1 cup nonfat milk
- 1 cup of frozen strawberries
- 1 medium beet, cooked, peeled, and cubed
- 1 orange, peeled and quartered
- 1 frozen banana, peeled and chopped
- 1 cup nonfat vanilla Greek yogurt
- 1 cup ice

DIRECTIONS

1. In a blender, combine all of the ingredients, and blend until smooth. Serve immediately.

NUTRITIONS

- Calories: 266
- Carbohydrates: 51 g
- Fat: 0 g
- Cholesterol: 7 mg
- Sodium: 104 mg
- Fiber: 6 g
- Sugars: 34 g
- Protein: 15 g

13. Blueberry-Vanilla Yogurt Smoothie

5 MIN

COOKING TIME

0 MIN

SERVINGS

2

INGREDIENTS

- 11/2 cups frozen blueberries
- 1 cup nonfat vanilla Greek yogurt
- 1 frozen banana, peeled and sliced
- 1/2 cup nonfat or low-fat milk
- 1 cup ice

DIRECTIONS

1. In a blender, combine all of the ingredients listed, and blend until smooth and creamy. Serve immediately.

NUTRITIONS

- Calories: 228
- Carbohydrates: 45 g
- Fat: 1 g

- Sodium: 63 mg
- Potassium: 470 mg
- Fiber: 5 g

- Sugars: 34 g
- Protein: 12 g

14. Greek Yogurt Oat Pancakes

PREPARATION TIME

15 MIN

COOKING TIME

10 MIN

SERVINGS

2

INGREDIENTS

- 6 egg whites (or 3/4 cup liquid egg whites)
- 1 cup rolled oats
- 1 cup plain nonfat Greek yogurt
- 1 medium banana, peeled and sliced
- 1 tsp. ground cinnamon
- 1 tsp. baking powder
- Cooking spray

DIRECTIONS

1. Blend all of the listed ingredients using a blender. Warm a griddle over medium heat. Spray the skillet with nonstick cooking spray.
2. Put 1/3 cup of the mixture or batter onto the griddle. Allow to cook and flip when bubbles on the top burst, about 5 minutes. Cook again for a minute until golden brown. Repeat with the remaining batter. Divide between two serving plates and enjoy.

NUTRITIONS

- Calories: 318
- Carbohydrates: 47 g
- Fat: 4 g

- Sodium: 467 mg
- Potassium: 634 mg
- Fiber: 6 g

- Sugars: 13 g
- Protein: 28 g

15. Scrambled Egg and Veggie Breakfast Quesadillas

15 MIN

COOKING TIME

15 MIN

SERVINGS

2

INGREDIENTS

- 2 eggs
- 2 egg whites
- 2–4 tbsp. nonfat or low-fat milk
- 1/4 tsp. freshly ground black pepper
- 1 large tomato, chopped
- 2 tbsp. chopped cilantro
- 1/2 cup canned black beans, rinsed and drained
- 1 1/2 tbsp. olive oil, divided
- 4 corn tortillas
- 1/2 avocado, peeled, pitted, and thinly sliced

DIRECTIONS

1. Mix the eggs, egg whites, milk, and black pepper in a bowl. Using an electric mixer, beat until smooth. To the same bowl, add the tomato, cilantro, and black beans, and fold into the eggs with a spoon.
2. Warm up half of the olive oil in a medium pan over medium heat. Add the scrambled egg mixture and cook for a few minutes, stirring, until cooked through. Remove from the pan.
3. Divide the scrambled egg mixture between the tortillas, layering only on one half of the tortilla. Top with avocado slices and fold the tortillas in half.
4. Heat the remaining oil over medium heat, and add one of the folded tortillas to the pan. Cook for 1 to 2 minutes on each side or until browned. Repeat with remaining tortillas. Serve immediately.

NUTRITIONS

- Calories: 445
- Carbohydrates: 42 g
- Fat: 24 g
- Sodium: 228 mg
- Potassium: 614 mg
- Fiber: 11 g
- Sugars: 2 g
- Protein: 19 g

16. Stuffed Breakfast Peppers

PREPARATION TIME

15 MIN

COOKING TIME

45 MIN

SERVINGS

4

INGREDIENTS

- 4 bell peppers (any color)
- 1 (16 oz.) bag frozen spinach
- 4 eggs
- 1/4 cup shredded low-fat cheese (optional)
- Freshly ground black pepper

DIRECTIONS

1. Preheat the oven to 400°F. Line a baking dish with aluminum foil. Cut the tops off the pepper, then discard the seeds. Discard the tops and seeds. Put the peppers in the baking dish, and bake for about 15 minutes.
2. While the peppers bake, defrost the spinach and drain off the excess moisture. Remove the peppers, then stuff the bottoms evenly with the defrosted spinach.
3. Crack an egg over the spinach inside each pepper. Top each egg with a tbsp. of the cheese (if using) and season with black pepper to taste. Bake for 15 to 20 minutes, or until the egg whites are set and opaque.

NUTRITIONS

- Calories: 136
- Carbohydrates: 15 g
- Fat: 5 g
- Sodium: 131 mg
- Potassium: 576 mg
- Protein: 11 g

17. Sweet Potato Toast Three Ways

15 MIN

COOKING TIME

2-5 MIN

SERVINGS

1

INGREDIENTS

- 1 large sweet potato, unpeeled

Topping choice #1:
- 4 tbsp. peanut butter
- 1 ripe banana, sliced
- Dash ground cinnamon

Topping choice #2:
- 1/2 avocado, peeled, pitted, and mashed
- 2 eggs (1 per slice)

Topping choice #3:
- 4 tbsp. nonfat or low-fat ricotta cheese
- 1 tomato, sliced
- Dash black pepper

DIRECTIONS

1. Slice the sweet potato lengthwise into 1/4-inch thick slices. Place the sweet potato slices in a toaster on high for about 5 minutes or until cooked through.
2. Repeat multiple times, if necessary, depending on your toaster settings. Top with your desired topping choices and enjoy.

NUTRITIONS

- Calories: 137
- Carbohydrates: 32 g
- Fat: 0 g
- Sodium: 17 mg
- Potassium: 265 mg
- Fiber: 4 g
- Sugars: 0 g
- Protein: 2 g

18. Apple-Apricot Brown Rice Breakfast Porridge

PREPARATION TIME

15 MIN

COOKING TIME

8 MIN

SERVINGS

4

INGREDIENTS

- 3 cups cooked brown rice
- 1 3/4 cups nonfat or low-fat milk
- 2 tbsp. lightly packed brown sugar
- 4 dried apricots, chopped
- 1 medium apple, cored and diced
- 3/4 tsp. ground cinnamon
- 3/4 tsp. vanilla extract

DIRECTIONS

1. Combine the rice, milk, sugar, apricots, apple, and cinnamon in a medium saucepan. Boil it on medium heat, lower the heat down slightly and cook for 2 to 3 minutes. Turn it off, then stir in the vanilla extract. Serve warm.

NUTRITIONS

- Calories: 260
- Carbohydrates: 57 g
- Fat: 2 g
- Sodium: 50 mg
- Potassium: 421 mg
- Carbohydrates: 57 g
- Fiber: 4 g
- Sugars: 22 g
- Protein: 7 g

19. Carrot Cake Overnight Oats

OVERNIGHT

2 MIN

1

- 1/2 cup rolled oats
- 1/2 cup plain nonfat or low-fat Greek yogurt
- 1/2 cup nonfat or low-fat milk
- 1/4 cup shredded carrot
- 2 tbsp. raisins
- 1/2 tsp. ground cinnamon
- 1–2 tbsp. chopped walnuts (optional)

1. Mix all of the ingredients in a lidded jar, shake well, and refrigerate overnight. Serve.

- Calories: 331
- Carbohydrates: 59 g
- Fat: 3 g
- Sodium: 141 mg
- Fiber: 8 g
- Sugars: 26 g
- Protein: 22 g

20. Steel-Cut Oatmeal With Plums and Pear

15 MIN

25 MIN

4

- 2 cups of water
- 1 cup nonfat or low-fat milk
- 1 cup steel-cut oats
- 1 cup dried plums, chopped
- 1 medium pear, cored, and skin removed, diced
- 4 tbsp. almonds, roughly chopped

1. Mix the water, milk, plus oats in a medium pot and bring to a boil over high heat. Reduce the heat and cover. Simmer for about 10 minutes, stirring occasionally.
2. Add the plums and pear, and cover. Simmer for another 10 minutes. Turn off the heat and let stand for 5 minutes until all of the liquid is absorbed. To serve, top each portion with a sprinkling of almonds.

- Calories: 307
- Carbohydrates: 58 g
- Fat: 6 g
- Sodium: 132 mg
- Potassium: 640 mg
- Fiber: 9 g
- Sugars: 24 g
- Protein: 9 g

21. French Toast With Applesauce

5 MIN

COOKING TIME

5 MIN

SERVINGS

6

INGREDIENTS

- 1/4 cup unsweetened applesauce
- 1/2 cup skim milk
- 2 packets Stevia
- 2 eggs
- 6 slices whole-wheat bread
- 1 tsp. ground cinnamon

DIRECTIONS

1. Mix well applesauce, sugar, cinnamon, milk, and eggs in a mixing bowl. Soak the bread into the applesauce mixture until wet. On medium fire, heat a large nonstick skillet.
2. Add soaked bread on one side and another on the other side. Cook in a single layer for 2 to 3 minutes per side on medium-low fire or until lightly browned. Serve and enjoy.

NUTRITIONS

- Calories: 122.6
- Carbohydrates:18.3 g
- Fat: 2.6 g

- Sugars:14.8 g
- Sodium: 11 mg
- Protein: 6.5 g

22. Banana-Peanut Butter and Greens Smoothie

PREPARATION TIME

5 MIN

COOKING TIME

0 MIN

SERVINGS

1

INGREDIENTS

- 1 cup chopped and packed Romaine lettuce
- 1 frozen medium banana
- 1 tbsp. all-natural peanut butter
- 1 cup cold almond milk

DIRECTIONS

1. In a heavy-duty blender, add all ingredients. Puree until smooth and creamy. Serve and enjoy.

NUTRITIONS

- Calories: 349.3
- Carbohydrates:57.4 g
- Fat:9.7 g

- Sugars:4.3 g
- Sodium:18 mg
- Protein:8.1 g

23. Baking Powder Biscuits

PREPARATION TIME

5 MIN

COOKING TIME

5 MIN

SERVINGS

1

INGREDIENTS

- 1 egg white
- 1 cup white whole-wheat flour
- 4 tbsp. Non-hydrogenated vegetable shortening
- 1 tbsp. sugar
- 2/3 cups low-Fat milk
- 1 cup unbleached all-purpose flour
- 4 tsp. sodium-free baking powder

DIRECTIONS

1. Warm oven to 450°F. Put the flours, sugar, plus baking powder into a mixing bowl and mix. Split the shortening into the batter using your fingers until it resembles coarse crumbs. Put the egg white plus milk and stir to combine.
2. Put the dough out onto a lightly floured surface and knead for 1 minute. Roll dough to 3/4 inch thickness and cut into 12 rounds. Place rounds on the baking sheet. Bake 10 minutes, then remove the baking sheet and place biscuits on a wire rack to cool.

NUTRITIONS

- Calories: 118
- Carbohydrates:16 g
- Fat:4 g

- Sugars:0.2 g
- Sodium: 6 mg
- Protein:3 g

24. Oatmeal Banana Pancakes With Walnuts

PREPARATION TIME

15 MIN

COOKING TIME

5 MIN

SERVINGS

8

INGREDIENTS

- 1 finely diced firm banana
- 1 cup whole wheat pancake mix
- 1/8 cup chopped walnuts
- 1/4 cup old-fashioned oats
- Cooking spray

DIRECTIONS

1. Make the pancake mix, as stated in the directions on the package. Add walnuts, oats, and chopped banana. Coat a griddle with cooking spray. Add about 1/4 cup of the pancake batter onto the griddle when hot.
2. Turn pancake over when bubbles form on top. Cook until golden brown. Serve immediately.

NUTRITIONS

- Calories: 155
- Carbohydrates:28 g
- Fat:4 g

- Sugars:2.2 g
- Sodium:16 mg
- Protein:7 g

25. Creamy Oats, Greens & Blueberry Smoothie

4 MIN

COOKING TIME

0 MIN

SERVINGS

1

INGREDIENTS

- 1 cup water cold
- Fat-free milk
- 1 cup salad greens
- 1/2 cup fresh frozen blueberries
- 1/2 cup frozen cooked oatmeal
- 1 tbsp. sunflower seeds

DIRECTIONS

1. Blend all ingredients using a powerful blender until smooth and creamy. Serve and enjoy.

NUTRITIONS

- Calories: 280
- Carbohydrates:44.0 g
- Fat:6.8 g

- Sugars:32 g
- Sodium:141 mg
- Protein:14.0 g

26. Banana & Cinnamon Oatmeal

PREPARATION TIME

5 MIN

COOKING TIME

0 MIN

SERVINGS

6

INGREDIENTS

- 2 cups quick-cooking oats
- 4 cups Fat-free milk
- 1 tsp. ground cinnamon
- 2 chopped large ripe banana
- 4 tsp. Brown sugar
- Extra ground cinnamon

DIRECTIONS

1. Place milk in a skillet and bring to boil. Add oats and cook over medium heat until thickened, for 2 to 4 minutes.
2. Stir intermittently. Add cinnamon, brown sugar, and banana and stir to combine. If you want, serve with the extra cinnamon. Enjoy!

NUTRITIONS

- Calories: 215
- Carbohydrates:42 g
- Fat:2 g

- Sugars:1 g
- Sodium:40 mg
- Protein:10 g

27. Bagels Made Healthy

5 MIN

COOKING TIME

40 MIN

SERVINGS

8

INGREDIENTS

- 1 1/2 cup warm water
- 1 1/4 cup bread flour
- 2 tbsps. honey
- 2 cups whole wheat flour
- 2 tsp. yeast
- 1 1/2 tbsp. olive oil
- 1 tbsp. vinegar

DIRECTIONS

1. In a bread machine, mix all ingredients, and then process on dough cycle. Once done, create 8 pieces shaped like a flattened ball. Create a donut shape using your thumb to make a hole at the center of each ball.
2. Place donut-shaped dough on a greased baking sheet then covers and let it rise for about 1/2 hour. Prepare about 2 inches of water to boil in a large pan.
3. In boiling water, drop one at a time the bagels and boil for 1 minute, then turn them once. Remove them and return them to the baking sheet and bake at 350oF for about 20 to 25 minutes until golden brown.

NUTRITIONS

- Calories: 228
- Carbohydrates:41.8 g
- Fat:3.7 g

- Sugars:0 g
- Sodium:15 mg
- Protein:6.9 g

28. Cereal With Cranberry-Orange Twist

PREPARATION TIME

5 MIN

COOKING TIME

0 MIN

SERVINGS

1

INGREDIENTS

- 1/2 cup water
- 1/2 cup orange juice
- 1/3 cup oat bran
- 1/4 cup dried cranberries
- 1 tbsp. Sugar
- ½ cup Milk

DIRECTIONS

1. In a bowl, combine all ingredients. For about 2 minutes, microwave the bowl, then serve with sugar and milk. Enjoy!

NUTRITIONS

- Calories: 220
- Carbohydrates:43.5 g
- Fat:2.4 g

- Sugars:8 g
- Sodium:1 mg
- Protein:6.2 g

29. No-Cook Overnight Oats

5 MIN

COOKING TIME

0 MIN

SERVINGS

1

INGREDIENTS

- 1 1/2 cup low-fat milk
- 5 whole almond pieces
- 1 tsp. chia seeds
- 2 tbsp. oats
- 1 tsp. sunflower seeds
- 1 tbsp. Craisins

DIRECTIONS

1. In a jar or mason bottle with a cap, mix all ingredients. Refrigerate overnight. Enjoy breakfast.

NUTRITIONS

- Calories: 271
- Carbohydrates:35.4 g
- Fat:9.8 g

- Sugars:9
- Sodium:103 mg
- Protein:16.7 g

30. Avocado Cup With Egg

PREPARATION TIME

5 MIN

COOKING TIME

0 MIN

SERVINGS

4

INGREDIENTS

- 4 tsp. parmesan cheese
- 1 chopped stalk scallion
- 4 dashes pepper
- 4 dashes paprika
- 2 ripe avocados
- 4 medium eggs

DIRECTIONS

1. Preheat oven to 375°F. Slice avocadoes in half and discard the seed. Slice the rounded portions of the avocado to make it level and sit well on a baking sheet.
2. Place avocadoes on a baking sheet and crack one egg in each hole of the avocado. Season each egg evenly with pepper, stalk scallion, and paprika. Bake for 25 minutes or until eggs are cooked to your liking. Serve with a sprinkle of parmesan.

NUTRITIONS

- Calories: 206
- Carbohydrates:11.3 g
- Fat:15.4 g

- Sugars:0.4 g
- Sodium:21 mg
- Protein:8.5 g

31. Instant Banana Oatmeal

1 MIN

COOKING TIME

2 MIN

SERVINGS

1

INGREDIENTS

- 1 mashed ripe banana
- 1/2 cup water
- 1/2 cup quick oats

DIRECTIONS

1. Measure the oats and water into a microwave-safe bowl and stir to combine. Place bowl in microwave and heat on high for 2 minutes. Remove the bowl, then stir in the mashed banana and serve.

NUTRITIONS

- Calories: 243
- Carbohydrates:50 g
- Fat:3 g

- Sugars:20 g
- Sodium:30 mg
- Protein:6 g

32. Almond Butter-Banana Smoothie

PREPARATION TIME

5 MIN

COOKING TIME

0 MIN

SERVINGS

1

INGREDIENTS

- 1 tbsp. Almond butter
- 1/2 cup ice cubes
- 1/2 cup packed spinach
- 1 peeled and a frozen medium banana
- 1 cup fat-free milk

DIRECTIONS

1. Blend all the listed ingredients above in a powerful blender until smooth and creamy. Serve and enjoy.

NUTRITIONS

- Calories: 293
- Carbohydrates:42.5 g
- Fat:9.8 g

- Sugars:12 g
- Sodium:40 mg
- Protein:13.5 g

33. Brown Sugar Cinnamon Oatmeal

1 MIN

COOKING TIME

3 MIN

SERVINGS

4

INGREDIENTS

- 1/2 tsp. ground cinnamon
- 1 1/2 tsp pure vanilla extract
- 1/4 cup light brown sugar
- 2 cups low-fat milk
- 1 1/3 cup quick oats

DIRECTIONS

1. Put the milk plus vanilla into a medium saucepan and boil over medium-high heat.
2. Lower the heat to medium once it boils. Mix in oats, brown sugar, plus cinnamon, and cook, stirring2 to 3 minutes. Serve immediately.

NUTRITIONS

- Calories: 208
- Carbohydrates: 38 g
- Fat: 3 g

- Sugars: 15 g
- Sodium: 33 mg
- Protein: 8 g

34. Buckwheat Pancakes With Vanilla Almond Milk

PREPARATION TIME

10 MIN

COOKING TIME

10 MIN

SERVINGS

1

INGREDIENTS

- 1/2 cup unsweetened vanilla almond milk
- 2–4 packets of natural sweetener
- 1/8 tsp. salt
- 1/2 cup buckwheat flour
- 1/2 tsp. double-acting baking powder
- Cooking spray

DIRECTIONS

1. Prepare a nonstick pancake griddle and spray with the cooking spray, place over medium heat. Whisk the buckwheat flour, salt, baking powder, and stevia in a small bowl and stir in the almond milk after.
2. Onto the pan, scoop a large spoonful of batter, cook until bubbles no longer pop on the surface and the entire surface looks dry and (2 to 4 minutes). Flip and cook for another 2 to 4 minutes. Repeat with all the remaining batter.

NUTRITIONS

- Calories: 240
- Carbohydrates: 2 g
- Fat: 4.5 g

- Sugars:17 g
- Sodium:38 mg
- Protein:11 g

35. Salmon and Egg Scramble

15 MIN

COOKING TIME

4 MIN

SERVINGS

4

INGREDIENTS

- 1 tsp. olive oil
- 3 organic whole eggs
- 3 tbsp. water
- 1 minced garlic
- 6 oz. Smoked salmon, sliced
- 2 avocados, sliced
- Black pepper to taste
- 1 green onion, chopped

DIRECTIONS

1. Warm-up olive oil in a large skillet and sauté onion in it. Take a medium bowl and whisk eggs in it, add water and make a scramble with the help of a fork. Add to the skillet the smoked salmon along with garlic and black pepper.
2. Stir for about 4 minutes until all ingredients get fluffy. At this stage, add the egg mixture. Once the eggs get firm, serve on a plate with a garnish of avocados.

NUTRITIONS

- Calories: 120
- Carbohydrates: 3 g
- Fat: 4 g

- Sodium: 898 mg
- Potassium: 129 mg
- Protein: 19 g

36. Pumpkin Muffins

PREPARATION TIME

15 MIN

COOKING TIME

20 MIN

SERVINGS

4

INGREDIENTS

- 4 cups of almond flour
- 2 cups of pumpkin, cooked and pureed
- 2 large whole organic eggs
- 3 tsp. baking powder
- 2 tsp. ground cinnamon
- 1/2 cup raw honey
- 4 tsp. almond butter

DIRECTIONS

1. Preheat the oven to 400°F. Line the muffin paper on the muffin tray. Mix almond flour, pumpkin puree, eggs, baking powder, cinnamon, almond butter, and honey in a large bowl.
2. Put the prepared batter into a muffin tray and Bake for 20 minutes. Once golden-brown, serve and enjoy.

NUTRITIONS

- Calories: 136
- Carbohydrates: 22 g
- Fat: 5 g

- Sodium: 11 mg
- Potassium: 699 mg
- Protein: 2 g

37. Sweet Berries Pancake

15 MIN

COOKING TIME

15 MIN

SERVINGS

4

INGREDIENTS

- 4 cups of almond flour
- A pinch of sea salt
- 2 organic eggs
- 4 tsp. walnut oil
- 1 cup of strawberries, mashed
- 1 cup of blueberries, mashed
- 1 tsp. baking powder
- Honey for topping, optional

DIRECTIONS

1. Take a bowl and add almond flour, baking powder, and sea salt. Take another bowl and add eggs, walnut oil, strawberries, and blueberries mash. Combine ingredients of both bowls.
2. Heat a bit of walnut oil in a cooking pan and pour the spoonful mixture to make pancakes. Once the bubble comes on the top, flip the pancake to cook from the other side. Once done, serve with the glaze of honey on top.

NUTRITIONS

- Calories: 161
- Carbohydrates: 23 g
- Fat: 6 g

- Cholesterol: 82 mg
- Sodium: 91 mg
- Potassium: 252 mg

- Protein: 3 g

38. Zucchini Pancakes

PREPARATION TIME

15 MIN

COOKING TIME

10 MIN

SERVINGS

4

INGREDIENTS

- 4 large zucchinis
- 4 green onions, diced
- 1/3 cup of milk
- 1 organic egg
- Sea salt, just a pinch
- Black pepper, grated
- 2 tbsp. olive oil

DIRECTIONS

1. First, wash the zucchinis and grate them with a cheese grater. Mix the egg and add in the grated zucchinis and milk in a large bowl. Warm oil in a skillet and sauté onions in it.
2. Put the egg batter into the skillet and make pancakes. Once cooked from both sides. Serve by sprinkling salt and pepper on top.

NUTRITIONS

- Calories: 70
- Carbohydrates: 8 g
- Fat: 3 g

- Protein: 2 g
- Cholesterol: 43 mg
- Sodium: 60 mg

- Potassium: 914 mg

39. Breakfast Banana Split

15 MIN

COOKING TIME

0 MIN

SERVINGS

3

INGREDIENTS

- 2 bananas, peeled
- 1 cup oats, cooked
- 1/2 cup low-fat strawberry yogurt
- 1/3 tsp. honey, optional
- 1/2 cup pineapple, chunks

DIRECTIONS

1. Peel the bananas and cut lengthwise. Place half of the banana in each separate bowl. Spoon strawberry yogurt on top and pour cooked oats with pineapple chunks on each banana. Serve immediately with a glaze of honey of liked.

NUTRITIONS

- Calories: 145
- Carbohydrates: 18 g
- Fat: 7 g

- Protein: 3 g
- Sodium: 2 mg
- Potassium: 380 mg

40. Easy Veggie Muffins

PREPARATION TIME

10 MIN

COOKING TIME

40 MIN

SERVINGS

4

INGREDIENTS

- 3/4 cup cheddar cheese, shredded
- 1 cup green onion, chopped
- 1 cup tomatoes, chopped
- 1 cup broccoli, chopped
- 2 cups non-fat milk
- 1 cup biscuit mix
- 4 eggs
- Cooking spray
- 1 tsp. Italian seasoning
- A pinch of black pepper

DIRECTIONS

1. Grease a muffin tray with cooking spray and divide broccoli, tomatoes, cheese, and onions in each muffin cup.
2. In a bowl, combine green onions with milk, biscuit mix, eggs, pepper, and Italian seasoning, whisk well and pour into the muffin tray as well.
3. Cook the muffins in the oven at 375°F for 40 minutes, divide them between plates, and serve.

NUTRITIONS

- Calories: 80
- Carbohydrates: 3 g
- Fat: 5 g

- Protein: 7 g
- Sodium: 25 mg

41. Artichoke Frittata

PREPARATION TIME

5 MIN

COOKING TIME

10 MIN

SERVINGS

4

INGREDIENTS

- 8 large eggs
- 1/4 cup Asiago cheese, grated
- 1 tbsp. fresh basil, chopped
- 1 tsp. fresh oregano, chopped
- A pinch of salt
- 1 tsp. extra virgin olive oil
- 1 tsp. garlic, minced
- 1 cup canned artichokes, drained
- 1 tomato, chopped
- Pepper to taste

DIRECTIONS

1. Preheat your oven to broil. Take a medium bowl and whisk in eggs, Asiago cheese, oregano, basil, sea salt, and pepper. Blend in a bowl.
2. Place a large ovenproof skillet over medium-high heat and add olive oil. Add garlic and sauté for 1 minute. Remove the skillet from heat and pour in the egg mix.
3. Return skillet to heat and sprinkle artichoke hearts and tomato over eggs. Cook frittata without stirring for 8 minutes.
4. Place skillet under the broiler for 1 minute until the top is lightly browned. Cut frittata into 4 pieces and serve. Enjoy!

NUTRITIONS

- Calories: 199
- Carbohydrates: 5 g
- Fat: 13 g

- Protein: 16 g

42. Full Eggs in a Squash

PREPARATION TIME

15 MIN

COOKING TIME

20 MIN

SERVINGS

5

INGREDIENTS

- 2 acorn squash
- 6 whole eggs
- 2 tbsp. extra-virgin olive oil
- Salt and pepper as needed
- 5–6 pitted dates
- 8 walnut halves
- A fresh bunch of parsley
- Maple syrup

DIRECTIONS

1. Preheat your oven to 375°F. Slice squash crosswise and prepare 3 slices with holes. While slicing the squash, make sure that each slice has a measurement of 3/4 inch thickness.
2. Remove the seeds from the slices. Take a baking sheet and line it with parchment paper. Transfer the slices to your baking sheet and season them with salt and pepper.
3. Bake in your oven for 20 minutes. Chop the walnuts and dates on your cutting board. Take the baking dish out of the oven and drizzle slices with olive oil.
4. Crack an egg into each of the holes in the slices and season with pepper and salt. Sprinkle the chopped walnuts on top. Bake for 10 minutes more. Garnish with parsley and add maple syrup.

NUTRITIONS

- Calories: 198
- Carbohydrates: 17 g
- Fat: 12 g

- Protein: 8 g

43. Barley Porridge

5 MIN

COOKING TIME

25 MIN

SERVINGS

4

INGREDIENTS

- 1 cup barley
- 1 cup wheat berries
- 2 cups unsweetened almond milk
- 2 cups water
- 1/2 cup blueberries
- 1/2 cup pomegranate seeds
- 1/2 cup hazelnuts, toasted and chopped
- 1/4 cup honey

DIRECTIONS

1. Take a medium saucepan and place it over medium-high heat. Place barley, almond milk, wheat berries, water and bring to a boil. Reduce the heat to low and simmer for 25 minutes.
2. Divide amongst serving bowls and top each serving with 2 tbsp. blueberries, 2 tbsp. pomegranate seeds, 2 tbsp. hazelnuts, 1 tbsp. honey. Serve and enjoy!

NUTRITIONS

- Calories: 295
- Carbohydrates: 56 g
- Fat: 8 g

- Protein: 6 g

44. Tomato and Dill Frittata

PREPARATION TIME

5 MIN

COOKING TIME

10 MIN

SERVINGS

4

INGREDIENTS

- 2 tbsp. olive oil
- 1 medium onion, chopped
- 1 tsp. garlic, minced
- 2 medium tomatoes, chopped
- 6 large eggs
- 1/2 cup half and half
- 1/2 cup feta cheese, crumbled
- 1/4 cup dill weed
- Salt as needed
- Ground black pepper as needed

DIRECTIONS

1. Preheat your oven to a temperature of 400°F. Take a large-sized ovenproof pan and heat up your olive oil over medium-high heat. Toss in the onion, garlic, tomatoes and stir fry them for 4 minutes.
2. While they are being cooked, take a bowl and beat together your eggs, half and half cream, and season the mix with some pepper and salt.
3. Pour the mixture into the pan with your vegetables and top it with crumbled feta cheese and dill weed. Cover it with the lid and let it cook for 3 minutes.
4. Place the pan inside your oven and let it bake for 10 minutes. Serve hot.

NUTRITIONS

- Calories: 191
- Carbohydrates: 6 g
- Fat: 15 g

- Protein: 9 g

45. Strawberry and Rhubarb Smoothie

5 MIN

COOKING TIME

3 MIN

SERVINGS

3

INGREDIENTS

- 1 rhubarb stalk, chopped
- 1 cup fresh strawberries, sliced
- 1/2 cup plain Greek strawberries
- A pinch of ground cinnamon
- 3 ice cubes
- 2 tbs Honey
- ½ cup Yogurt

DIRECTIONS

1. Take a small saucepan and fill it with water over high heat. Bring to boil and add rhubarb, boil for 3 minutes. Drain and transfer to the blender.
2. Add strawberries, honey, yogurt, cinnamon, and pulse mixture until smooth. Add ice cubes and blend until thick with no lumps. Pour into glass and enjoy chilled.

NUTRITIONS

- Calories: 295
- Carbohydrates: 56 g
- Fat: 8 g

- Protein: 6 g

46. Bacon and Brie Omelet Wedges

PREPARATION TIME

10 MIN

COOKING TIME

10 MIN

SERVINGS

6

INGREDIENTS

- 2 tbsp. olive oil
- 7 oz. smoked bacon
- 6 beaten eggs
- Small bunch chives, snipped
- 3 1/2 oz. brie, sliced
- 1 tsp. red wine vinegar
- 1 tsp. Dijon mustard
- 1 cucumber, halved, deseeded and sliced diagonally
- 7 oz. radish, quartered
- Ground pepper

DIRECTIONS

1. Turn your grill on and set it to high. Take a small-sized pan and add 1 tsp. oil, allow the oil to heat up. Add lardons and fry until crisp. Drain the lardon on kitchen paper.
2. Take another non-stick cast iron frying pan and place it over the grill, heat 2 tsp. of oil. Add lardons, eggs, chives, ground pepper to the frying pan. Cook on low until they are semi-set.
3. Carefully lay brie on top and grill until the Brie sets and is a golden texture. Remove it from the pan and cut it up into wedges.
4. Take a small bowl and create dressing by mixing olive oil, mustard, vinegar, radish, and seasoning. Add cucumber to the bowl and mix, serve alongside the omelet wedges.

NUTRITIONS

- Calories: 35
- Carbohydrates: 3 g
- Fat: 31 g

- Protein: 25 g

47. Pearl Couscous Salad

15 MIN

COOKING TIME

0 MIN

SERVINGS

6

INGREDIENTS

- 1 cup all-purpose flour
- 1 cup whole-wheat flour
- 1/4 tsp. salt
- 4 tsp. baking powder
- 1 tbsp. sugar
- 1 1/2 cups unsweetened almond milk
- 2 tsp. vanilla extract
- 2 large eggs
- 1/2 cup plain 2% Greek yogurt
- Fruit, for serving
- Maple syrup, for serving

DIRECTIONS

1. First, you will have to pour the curds into the bowl and mix them well until creamy. After that, you will have to add egg whites and mix them well until combined.
2. Then take a separate bowl, pour the wet mixture into the dry mixture. Stir to combine. The batter will be extremely thick.
3. Then, simply spoon the batter onto the sprayed pan heated too medium-high. The batter must make 4 large pancakes.
4. Then, you will have to flip the pancakes once when they start to bubble a bit on the surface. Cook until golden brown on both sides.

NUTRITIONS

- Calories: 166
- Carbohydrates: 52 g
- Fat: 5 g

- Protein: 14 g

48. Coconut Porridge

PREPARATION TIME

15 MIN

COOKING TIME

0 MIN

SERVINGS

6

INGREDIENTS

- Powdered erythritol as needed
- 1 1/2 cups almond milk, unsweetened
- 2 tbsp. vanilla protein powder
- 3 tbsp. Golden Flaxseed meal
- 2 tbsp. coconut flour

DIRECTIONS

1. Take a bowl and mix in a flaxseed meal, protein powder, coconut flour, and mix well. Add mix to the saucepan (placed over medium heat).
2. Add almond milk and stir, let the mixture thicken. Add your desired amount of sweetener and serve. Enjoy!

NUTRITIONS

- Calories: 259
- Carbohydrates: 5 g
- Fat: 13 g

- Protein: 16 g

49. Crumbled Feta and Scallions

5 MIN

COOKING TIME

15 MIN

SERVINGS

12

INGREDIENTS

- 2 tbsp. unsalted butter (replace with canola oil for full effect)
- 1/2 cup of chopped up scallions
- 1 cup of crumbled feta cheese
- 8 large-sized eggs
- 2/3 cup of milk
- 1/2 tsp. dried Italian seasoning
- Salt as needed
- Freshly ground black pepper as needed
- Cooking oil spray

DIRECTIONS

1. Preheat your oven to 400 degrees Fahrenheit. Take a 3–4 oz. muffin pan and grease with cooking oil. Take a non-stick pan and place it over medium heat.
2. Add butter and allow the butter to melt. Add half of the scallions and stir fry. Keep them to the side. Take a medium-sized bowl and add eggs, Italian seasoning, and milk and whisk well.
3. Add the stir-fried scallions and feta cheese and mix. Season with pepper and salt. Pour the mix into the muffin tin. Transfer the muffin tin to your oven and bake for 15 minutes. Serve with a sprinkle of scallions.

NUTRITIONS

- Calories: 106
- Carbohydrates: 2 g
- Fat: 8 g

- Protein: 7 g

50. Gnocchi Ham Olives

PREPARATION TIME

5 MIN

COOKING TIME

15 MIN

SERVINGS

4

INGREDIENTS

- 2 tbsp. olive oil
- 1 medium-sized onion chopped up
- 3 minced garlic cloves
- 1 medium-sized red pepper completely deseeded and finely chopped
- 1 cup of tomato puree
- 2 tbsp. tomato paste
- 1 lb. gnocchi
- 1 cup of coarsely chopped turkey ham
- 1/2 cup of sliced pitted olives
- 1 tsp. Italian seasoning
- Salt as needed
- Freshly ground black pepper
- Bunch of fresh basil leaves

DIRECTIONS

1. Take a medium-sized saucepan and place over medium-high heat. Pour some olive oil and heat it up. Toss in the bell pepper, onion, and garlic and sauté for 2 minutes.
2. Pour in the tomato puree, gnocchi, tomato paste, and add the turkey ham, Italian seasoning, and olives. Simmer the whole mix for 15 minutes, making sure to stir from time to time.
3. Season the mix with some pepper and salt. Once done, transfer the mix to a dish and garnish it with some basil leaves. Serve hot and have fun.

NUTRITIONS

- Calories: 335
- Carbohydrates: 45 g
- Fat: 12 g

- Protein: 15 g

51. Spicy Early Morning Seafood Risotto

5 MIN

15 MIN

4

INGREDIENTS

- 3 cups of clam juice
- 2 cups of water
- 2 tbsp. olive oil
- 1 medium-sized chopped up onion
- 2 minced garlic cloves
- 1 1/2 cups of Arborio Rice
- 1/2 cup of dry white wine
- 1 tsp. Saffron
- 1/2 tsp. ground cumin
- 1/2 tsp. paprika
- 1 lb. marinara seafood mix
- Salt as needed
- Ground pepper as needed

DIRECTIONS

1. Place a saucepan over high heat and pour in your clam juice with water and bring the mixture to a boil. Remove the heat.
2. Take a heavy-bottomed saucepan and stir fry your garlic and onion in oil over medium heat until a nice fragrance comes off.
3. Add in the rice and keep stirring for 2–3 minutes until the rice has been fully covered with the oil. Pour the wine and then add the saffron.
4. Keep stirring constantly until it is fully absorbed. Add in the cumin, clam juice, paprika mixture 1 cup at a time, making sure to keep stirring it from time to time.
5. Cook the rice for 20 minutes until perfect. Finally, add the seafood marinara mix and cook for another 5–7 minutes.
6. Season with some pepper and salt. Transfer the meat to a serving dish. Serve hot.

NUTRITIONS

- Calories: 386
- Carbohydrates: 55 g
- Fat: 7 g
- Protein: 21 g

Chapter 4
Lunch Recipes

52. Creamy Chicken Breast

10 MIN

COOKING TIME

20 MIN

SERVINGS

4

INGREDIENTS

- 1 tbsp. olive oil
- A pinch of black pepper
- 2 lb. chicken breasts, skinless, boneless, and cubed
- 4 garlic cloves, minced
- 2 1/2 cups low-sodium chicken stock
- 2 cups coconut cream
- 1/2 cup low-fat parmesan, grated
- 1 tbsp. basil, chopped

DIRECTIONS

1. Heat up a pan with the oil over medium-high heat, add chicken cubes, and brown them for 3 minutes on each side. Add garlic, black pepper, stock, and cream, toss, cover the pan and cook everything for 10 minutes more. Add cheese and basil, toss, divide between plates and serve for lunch. Enjoy!

NUTRITIONS

- Calories: 221
- Carbohydrates: 14 g
- Fat: 6 g
- Fiber: 9 g
- Protein: 7 g
- Sodium: 197 mg

53. Indian Chicken Stew

PREPARATION TIME

1 HOUR

COOKING TIME

20 MIN

SERVINGS

4

INGREDIENTS

- 1 lb. chicken breasts, skinless, boneless, and cubed
- 1 tbsp. garam masala
- 1 cup fat-free yogurt
- 1 tbsp. lemon juice
- A pinch of black pepper
- 1/4 tsp. ginger, ground
- 15 oz. tomato sauce, no-salt-added
- 5 garlic cloves, minced
- 1/2 tsp. sweet paprika

DIRECTIONS

1. In a bowl, mix the chicken with garam masala, yogurt, lemon juice, black pepper, ginger, and fridge for 1 hour. Heat up a pan over medium heat, add chicken mix, toss and cook for 5–6 minutes.
2. Add tomato sauce, garlic and paprika, toss, cook for 15 minutes, divide between plates and serve for lunch. Enjoy!

NUTRITIONS

- Calories: 221
- Carbohydrates: 14 g
- Fat: 6 g
- Fiber: 9 g
- Protein: 16 g
- Sodium: 4 mg

54. Chicken, Bamboo, and Chestnuts Mix

10 MIN

20 MIN

4

- 1 lb. chicken thighs, boneless, skinless, and cut into medium chunks
- 1 cup low-sodium chicken stock
- 1 tbsp. olive oil
- 2 tbsp. coconut aminos
- 1-inch ginger, grated
- 1 carrot, sliced
- 2 garlic cloves, minced
- 8 oz. canned bamboo shoots, no-salt-added and drained
- 8 oz. water chestnuts

1. Heat up a pan with the oil over medium-high heat, add chicken, stir, and brown for 4 minutes on each side. Add the stock, aminos, ginger, carrot, garlic, bamboo, and chestnuts, toss, cover the pan, and cook everything over medium heat for 12 minutes. Divide everything between plates and serve. Enjoy!

- Calories: 281
- Carbohydrates: 14 g
- Fat: 7 g
- Fiber: 9 g
- Protein: 14 g
- Sodium: 125 mg

55. Salsa Chicken

10 MIN

25 MIN

4

- 1 cup mild salsa, no-salt-added
- 1/2 tsp. cumin, ground
- Black pepper to the taste
- 1 tbsp. chipotle paste
- 1 lb. chicken thighs, skinless and boneless
- 2 cups corn
- Juice of 1 lime
- 1/2 tbsp. olive oil
- 2 tbsp. cilantro, chopped
- 1 cup cherry tomatoes, halved
- 1 small avocado, pitted, peeled, and cubed

1. In a pot, combine the salsa with cumin, black pepper, chipotle paste, chicken thighs, and corn, toss, bring to a simmer and cook over medium heat for 25 minutes. Add lime juice, oil, cherry tomatoes, and avocado, toss, divide into bowls and serve for lunch. Enjoy!

- Calories: 269
- Carbohydrates: 18 g
- Fat: 6 g
- Fiber: 9 g
- Protein: 7 g
- Sodium: 500 mg

56. Quinoa Chicken Salad

15 MIN

COOKING TIME

20 MIN

SERVINGS

8

INGREDIENTS

- 2 cups of water
- 2 cubes of chicken bouillon
- 1 smashed garlic clove
- 1 cup of uncooked quinoa
- 2 large-sized chicken breasts cut up into bite-sized portions and cooked
- 1 large-sized diced red onion
- 1 large-sized green bell pepper
- 1/2 cup of Kalamata olives
- 1/2 cup of crumbled feta cheese
- 1/4 cup of chopped up parsley
- 1/4 cup of chopped up fresh chives
- 1/2 tsp. salt
- 1 tbsp. balsamic vinegar
- 1/4 cup of olive oil
- Lemon juice

DIRECTIONS

1. Take a saucepan and bring your water, garlic, and bouillon cubes to a boil. Stir in quinoa and reduce the heat to medium-low.
2. Simmer for about 15–20 minutes until the quinoa has absorbed all the water and is tender. Discard your garlic cloves and scrape the quinoa into a large-sized bowl.
3. Gently stir in the cooked chicken breast, bell pepper, onion, feta cheese, chive, Kalamata olives, salt, and parsley into your quinoa.
4. Drizzle some lemon juice, olive oil, and balsamic vinegar. Stir everything until mixed well. Serve warm and enjoy!

NUTRITIONS

- Calories: 99
- Carbohydrates: 7 g
- Fat: 7 g

- Protein: 3.4 g

57. Rice With Chicken

PREPARATION TIME

10 MIN

COOKING TIME

30 MIN

SERVINGS

4

INGREDIENTS

- 1/2 cup coconut aminos
- 1/3 cup rice wine vinegar
- 2 tbsp. olive oil
- 1 chicken breast, skinless, boneless, and cubed
- 1/2 cup red bell pepper, chopped
- A pinch of black pepper
- 2 garlic cloves, minced
- 1/2 tsp. ginger, grated
- 1/2 cup carrots, grated
- 1 cup white rice
- 2 cups of water

DIRECTIONS

1. Heat up a pan with the oil over medium-high heat, add the chicken, stir and brown for 4 minutes on each side. Add aminos, vinegar, bell pepper, black pepper, garlic, ginger, carrots, rice, and stock, stock, cover the pan and cook over medium heat for 20 minutes. Divide everything into bowls and serve for lunch. Enjoy!

NUTRITIONS

- Calories: 70
- Carbohydrates: 13g
- Fat: 2g

- Sodium: 5 mg
- Protein: 2g

58. Tomato Soup

10 MIN

COOKING TIME

20 MIN

SERVINGS

4

INGREDIENTS

- 3 garlic cloves, minced
- 1 yellow onion, chopped
- 3 carrots, chopped
- 15 oz. tomato sauce, no-salt-added
- 1 tbsp. olive oil
- 15 oz. roasted tomatoes, no-salt-added
- 1 cup low-sodium veggie stock
- 1 tbsp. tomato paste, no-salt-added
- 1 tbsp. basil, dried
- 1/4 tsp. oregano, dried
- 3 oz. coconut cream
- A pinch of black pepper

DIRECTIONS

1. Heat up a pot with the oil over medium heat, add garlic and onion, stir and cook for 5 minutes. Add carrots, tomato sauce, tomatoes, stock, tomato paste, basil, oregano, and black pepper, stir, bring to a simmer, cook for 15 minutes, add cream, blend the soup using an immersion blender, divide into bowls and serve for lunch. Enjoy!

NUTRITIONS

- Calories: 90
- Carbohydrates: 20 g
- Fat: 0 g

- Sodium: 480 mg
- Protein: 2 g

59. Cod Soup

PREPARATION TIME

10 MIN

COOKING TIME

25 MIN

SERVINGS

4

INGREDIENTS

- 1 yellow onion, chopped
- 12 cups low-sodium fish stock
- 1 lb. carrots, sliced
- 1 tbsp. olive oil
- Black pepper to the taste
- 2 tbsp. ginger, minced
- 1 cup of water
- 1 lb. cod, skinless, boneless, and cut into medium chunks

DIRECTIONS

1. Heat up a pot with the oil over medium-high heat, add onion, stir and cook for 4 minutes. Add water, stock, ginger, and carrots, stir and cook for 10 minutes more.
2. Blend soup using an immersion blender, add the fish and pepper, stir, cook for 10 minutes more, ladle into bowls and serve. Enjoy!

NUTRITIONS

- Calories: 344
- Carbohydrates: 35 g
- Fat: 4 g

- Sodium: 334 mg
- Protein: 46 g

60. Sweet Potato Soup

10 MIN

COOKING TIME

1H 40 MIN

SERVINGS

6

INGREDIENTS

- 4 big sweet potatoes
- 28 oz. veggie stock
- A pinch of black pepper
- 1/4 tsp. nutmeg, ground
- 1/3 cup low-sodium heavy cream

DIRECTIONS

1. Put the sweet potatoes on a lined baking sheet, bake them at 350°F for 1 hour and 30 minutes, cool them down, peel, roughly chop them, and put them in a pot.
2. Add stock, nutmeg, cream, and pepper pulse well using an immersion blender, heat the soup over medium heat, cook for 10 minutes, ladle into bowls and serve. Enjoy!

NUTRITIONS

- Calories: 110
- Carbohydrates: 23 g
- Fat: 1 g
- Sodium: 140 mg
- Protein: 2 g

61. Sweet Potatoes and Zucchini Soup

PREPARATION TIME

10 MIN

COOKING TIME

20 MIN

SERVINGS

8

INGREDIENTS

- 4 cups veggie stock
- 2 tbsp. olive oil
- 2 sweet potatoes, peeled and cubed
- 8 zucchinis, chopped
- 2 yellow onions, chopped
- 1 cup of coconut milk
- A pinch of black pepper
- 1 tbsp. coconut aminos
- 4 tbsp. dill, chopped
- 1/2 tsp. basil, chopped

DIRECTIONS

1. Heat up a pot with the oil over medium heat, add onion, stir and cook for 5 minutes. Add zucchinis, stock, basil, potato, and pepper, stir and cook for 15 minutes more. Add milk, aminos, and dill, pulse using an immersion blender, ladle into bowls and serve for lunch.

NUTRITIONS

- Calories: 270
- Carbohydrates: 50 g
- Fat: 4 g
- Sodium: 416 mg
- Protein: 11 g

62. Lemongrass and Chicken Soup

10 MIN

COOKING TIME

25 MIN

SERVINGS

4

INGREDIENTS

- 4 lime leaves, torn
- 4 cups veggie stock, low-sodium
- 1 lemongrass stalk, chopped
- 1 tbsp. ginger, grated
- 1 lb. chicken breast, skinless, boneless, and cubed
- 8 oz. mushrooms, chopped
- 4 Thai chilies, chopped
- 13 oz. of coconut milk
- 1/4 cup lime juice
- 1/4 cup cilantro, chopped
- A pinch of black pepper

DIRECTIONS

1. Put the stock into a pot, bring to a simmer over medium heat, add lemongrass, ginger, and lime leaves, stir, cook for 10 minutes, strain into another pot, and heat up over medium heat again.
2. Add chicken, mushrooms, milk, cilantro, black pepper, chilies, and lime juice, stir, simmer for 15 minutes, ladle into bowls and serve.

NUTRITIONS

- Calories: 105
- Carbohydrates: 1 g
- Fat: 2 g
- Sodium: 200 mg
- Protein: 15 g

63. Easy Lunch Salmon Steaks

PREPARATION TIME

10 MIN

COOKING TIME

20 MIN

SERVINGS

4

INGREDIENTS

- 1 big salmon fillet, cut into 4 steaks
- 3 garlic cloves, minced
- 1 yellow onion, chopped
- Black pepper to the taste
- 2 tbsp. olive oil
- 1/4 cup parsley, chopped
- Juice of 1 lemon
- 1 tbsp. thyme, chopped
- 4 cups of water

DIRECTIONS

1. Heat a pan with the oil on medium-high heat, cook onion and garlic for 3 minutes.
2. Add black pepper, parsley, thyme, water, and lemon juice, stir, bring to a gentle boil, add salmon steaks, cook them for 15 minutes, drain, divide between plates and serve with a side salad for lunch.

NUTRITIONS

- Calories: 110
- Carbohydrates: 3 g
- Fat: 4 g
- Sodium: 330 mg
- Protein: 15 g

64. Light Balsamic Salad

10 MIN

COOKING TIME

0 MIN

SERVINGS

3

INGREDIENTS

- 1 orange, cut into segments
- 2 green onions, chopped
- 1 romaine lettuce head, torn
- 1 avocado, pitted, peeled, and cubed
- 1/4 cup almonds, sliced

For the salad dressing:
- 1 tsp. mustard
- 1/4 cup olive oil
- 2 tbsp. balsamic vinegar
- Juice of 1/2 orange
- Salt and black pepper

DIRECTIONS

1. In a salad bowl, mix oranges with avocado, lettuce, almonds, and green onions. In another bowl, mix olive oil with vinegar, mustard, orange juice, salt, and pepper, whisk well, add this to your salad, toss and serve.

NUTRITIONS

- Calories: 35
- Carbohydrates: 5 g
- Fat: 2 g

- Protein: 0 g
- Sodium: 400 mg

65. Purple Potato Soup

PREPARATION TIME

10 MIN

COOKING TIME

1H 15 MIN

SERVINGS

6

INGREDIENTS

- 6 purple potatoes, chopped
- 1 cauliflower head, florets separated
- Black pepper to the taste
- 4 garlic cloves, minced
- 1 yellow onion, chopped
- 3 tbsp. olive oil 1 tbsp. thyme, chopped
- 1 leek, chopped
- 2 shallots, chopped
- 4 cups chicken stock, low-sodium

DIRECTIONS

1. In a baking dish, mix potatoes with onion, cauliflower, garlic, pepper, thyme, and half of the oil, toss to coat, introduce in the oven and bake for 45 minutes at 400°F.
2. Heat a pot with the rest of the oil over medium-high heat, add leeks and shallots, stir and cook for 10 minutes.
3. Add roasted veggies and stock, stir, bring to a boil, cook for 20 minutes, transfer soup to your food processor, blend well, divide into bowls, and serve.

NUTRITIONS

- Calories: 70
- Carbohydrates: 15 g
- Fat: 0 g

- Protein: 2 g
- Sodium: 6 mg

66. Leeks Soup

10 MIN

COOKING TIME

1H 15 MIN

SERVINGS

6

INGREDIENTS

- 2 gold potatoes, chopped
- 1 cup cauliflower florets
- Black pepper to the taste
- 5 leeks, chopped
- 4 garlic cloves, minced
- 1 yellow onion, chopped
- 3 tbsp. olive oil
- Handful parsley, chopped
- 4 cups low-sodium chicken stock

DIRECTIONS

1. Heat up a pot with the oil over medium-high heat, add onion and garlic, stir and cook for 5 minutes.
2. Add potatoes, cauliflower, black pepper, leeks, and stock, stir, bring to a simmer, cook over medium heat for 30 minutes, blend using an immersion blender, add parsley, stir, ladle into bowls and serve.

NUTRITIONS

- Calories: 125
- Carbohydrates: 29 g
- Fat: 1 g

- Protein: 4 g
- Sodium: 52 mg

67. Cauliflower Lunch Salad

PREPARATION TIME

2 HOURS

COOKING TIME

10 MIN

SERVINGS

4

INGREDIENTS

- 1/3 cup low-sodium veggie stock
- 2 tbsp. olive oil
- 6 cups cauliflower florets, grated
- Black pepper to the taste
- 1/4 cup red onion, chopped
- 1 red bell pepper, chopped
- Juice of 1/2 lemon
- 1/2 cup kalamata olives halved
- 1 tsp. mint, chopped
- 1 tbsp. cilantro, chopped

DIRECTIONS

1. Heat up a pan with the oil over medium-high heat, add cauliflower, pepper, and stock, stir, cook for 10 minutes, transfer to a bowl, and keep in the fridge for 2 hours. Mix cauliflower with olives, onion, bell pepper, black pepper, mint, cilantro, and lemon juice, toss to coat, and serve.

NUTRITIONS

- Calories: 102
- Carbohydrates: 3 g
- Fat: 10 g

- Protein: 0 g
- Sodium: 97 mg

68. Shrimp Cocktail

10 MIN

COOKING TIME

5 MIN

SERVINGS

8

INGREDIENTS

- 2 lb. big shrimp, deveined
- 4 cups of water
- 2 bay leaves
- 1 small lemon, halved
- Ice for cooling the shrimp
- Ice for serving
- 1 medium lemon sliced for serving
- 3/4 cup tomato passata
- 2 1/2 tbsp. horseradish, prepared
- 1/4 tsp. chili powder
- 2 tbsp. lemon juice

DIRECTIONS

1. Pour the 4 cups water into a large pot, add lemon and bay leaves. Boil over medium-high heat, reduce temperature, and boil for 10 minutes. Put shrimp, stir and cook for 2 minutes. Move the shrimp to a bowl filled with ice and leave aside for 5 minutes.
2. In a bowl, mix tomato passata with horseradish, chili powder, and lemon juice and stir well. Place shrimp in a serving bowl filled with ice, with lemon slices, and serve with the cocktail sauce you've prepared.

NUTRITIONS

- Calories: 276
- Carbohydrates: 0 g
- Fat: 8 g

- Protein: 25 g
- Sodium:: 182 mg

69. Quinoa and Scallops Salad

PREPARATION TIME

10 MIN

COOKING TIME

35 MIN

SERVINGS

6

INGREDIENTS

- 12 oz. dry sea scallops
- 4 tbsp. canola oil
- 2 tsp. canola oil
- 4 tsp. low sodium soy sauce
- 1 1/2 cup quinoa, rinsed
- 2 tsp. garlic, minced
- 3 cups of water
- 1 cup snow peas, sliced diagonally
- 1 tsp. sesame oil
- 1/3 cup rice vinegar
- 1 cup scallions, sliced
- 1/3 cup red bell pepper, chopped
- 1/4 cup cilantro, chopped

DIRECTIONS

1. In a bowl, mix scallops with 2 tsp. soy sauce, stir gently, and leave aside for now. Heat a pan with 1 tbsp. canola oil over medium-high heat, add the quinoa, stir and cook for 8 minutes. Put garlic, stir and cook for 1 more minute.
2. Put the water, boil over medium heat, stir, cover, and cook for 15 minutes. Remove from heat and leave aside covered for 5 minutes. Add snow peas, cover again and leave for 5 more minutes.
3. Meanwhile, in a bowl, mix 3 tbsp. canola oil with 2 tsp. soy sauce, vinegar, and sesame oil and stir well. Add quinoa and snow peas to this mixture and stir again. Add scallions, bell pepper, and stir again.
4. Pat dry the scallops and discard the marinade. Heat another pan with 2 tsp. canola oil over high heat, add scallops and cook for 1 minute on each side. Add them to the quinoa salad, stir gently, and serve with chopped cilantro.

NUTRITIONS

- Calories: 181
- Carbohydrates: 12 g
- Fat: 6 g

- Protein: 13 g
- Sodium: 153 mg

70. Squid and Shrimp Salad

PREPARATION TIME

10 MIN

COOKING TIME

15 MIN

SERVINGS

4

NUTRITIONS

- Calories: 235
- Carbohydrates: 9 g
- Fat: 8 g

INGREDIENTS

- 8 oz. squid, cut into medium pieces
- 8 oz. shrimp, peeled and deveined
- 1 red onion, sliced
- 1 cucumber, chopped
- 2 tomatoes, cut into medium wedges
- 2 tbsp. cilantro, chopped
- 1 hot jalapeno pepper, cut in rounds
- 3 tbsp. rice vinegar
- 3 tbsp. dark sesame oil
- Black pepper to the taste

DIRECTIONS

1. In a bowl, mix the onion with cucumber, tomatoes, pepper, cilantro, shrimp, and squid and stir well. Cut a big parchment paper in half, fold it in half heart shape and open. Place the seafood mixture in this parchment piece, fold over, seal edges, place on a baking sheet, and introduce in the oven at 400°F for 15 minutes.
2. Meanwhile, in a small bowl, mix sesame oil with rice vinegar and black pepper and stir very well. Take the salad out of the oven, leave to cool down for a few minutes, and transfer to a serving plate. Put the dressing over the salad and serve right away.

- Protein: 30 g
- Sodium:: 165 mg

71. Parsley Seafood Cocktail

PREPARATION TIME

2H 10 MIN

COOKING TIME

1H 30 MIN

SERVINGS

4

INGREDIENTS

- 1 big octopus, cleaned
- 1 lb. mussels
- 2 lb. clams
- 1 big squid cut in rings
- 3 garlic cloves, chopped
- 1 celery rib, cut crosswise into thirds
- 1/2 cup celery rib, sliced
- 1 carrot, cut crosswise into 3 pieces
- 1 small white onion, chopped
- 1 bay leaf
- 3/4 cup white wine
- 2 cups radicchio, sliced
- 1 red onion, sliced
- 1 cup parsley, chopped
- 1 cup olive oil
- 1 cup red wine vinegar
- Black pepper to the taste
- Water
- Salt to taste

DIRECTIONS

1. Put the octopus in a pot with celery rib cut in thirds, garlic, carrot, bay leaf, white onion, and white wine. Add water to cover the octopus, cover with a lid, bring to a boil over high heat, reduce to low, and simmer for 1 and 1/2 hours.
2. Drain octopus, reserve boiling liquid, and leave aside to cool down. Put 1/4 cup octopus cooking liquid in another pot, add mussels, heat up over medium-high heat, cook until they open, transfer to a bowl, and leave aside.
3. Add clams to the pan, cover, cook over medium-high heat until they open, transfer to the bowl with mussels, and leave aside. Add squid to the pan, cover and cook over medium-high heat for 3 minutes, transfer to the bowl with mussels and clams.
4. Meanwhile, slice octopus into small pieces and mix with the rest of the seafood. Add sliced celery, radicchio, red onion, vinegar, olive oil, parsley, salt, and pepper, stir gently and leave aside in the fridge for 2 hours before serving.

NUTRITIONS

- Calories: 102
- Carbohydrates: 7 g
- Fat: 1 g

- Protein: 16 g
- Sodium: 0 mg

72. Shrimp and Onion Ginger Dressing

PREPARATION TIME

10 MIN

COOKING TIME

5 MIN

SERVINGS

2

INGREDIENTS

- 8 medium shrimp, peeled and deveined
- 12 oz. package mixed salad leaves
- 10 cherry tomatoes, halved
- 2 green onions, sliced
- 2 medium mushrooms, sliced
- 1/3 cup rice vinegar
- 1/4 cup sesame seeds, toasted
- 1 tbsp. low-sodium soy sauce
- 2 tsp. ginger, grated
- 2 tsp. garlic, minced
- 2/3 cup canola oil
- 1/3 cup sesame oil

DIRECTIONS

1. In a bowl, mix rice vinegar with sesame seeds, soy sauce, garlic, ginger, and stir well. Pour this into your kitchen blender, add canola oil and sesame oil, pulse very well, and leave aside. Brush shrimp with 3 tbsp. the ginger dressing you've prepared.
2. Heat your kitchen grill over high heat, add shrimp and cook for 3 minutes, flipping once. In a salad bowl, mix salad leaves with grilled shrimp, mushrooms, green onions, and tomatoes. Drizzle ginger dressing on top and serve right away!

NUTRITIONS

- Calories: 360
- Carbohydrates: 14 g
- Fat: 11 g

- Protein: 49 g
- Sodium: 469 mg

73. Fruit Shrimp Soup

PREPARATION TIME

10 MIN

COOKING TIME

25 MIN

SERVINGS

6

INGREDIENTS

- 8 oz. shrimp, peeled and deveined
- 1 stalk lemongrass, smashed
- 2 small ginger pieces, grated
- 6 cup chicken stock
- 2 jalapenos, chopped
- 4 lime leaves
- 1 1/2 cups pineapple, chopped
- 1 cup shiitake mushroom caps, chopped
- 1 tomato, chopped
- 1/2 bell pepper, cubed
- 2 tbsp. fish sauce
- 1 tsp. sugar
- 1/4 cup lime juice
- 1/3 cup cilantro, chopped
- 2 scallions, sliced

DIRECTIONS

1. In a pot, mix ginger with lemongrass, stock, jalapenos, and lime leaves, stir, boil over medium heat, cook for 15 minutes. Strain liquid in a bowl and discard solids.
2. Return soup to the pot again, add pineapple, tomato, mushrooms, bell pepper, sugar, and fish sauce, stir, boil over medium heat, cook for 5 minutes, add shrimp and cook for 3 more minutes. Remove from heat, add lime juice, cilantro, and scallions, stir, ladle into soup bowls and serve.

NUTRITIONS

- Calories: 290
- Carbohydrates: 39 g
- Fat: 12 g

- Protein: 7 g
- Sodium: 21 mg

74. Mussels and Chickpea Soup

10 MIN

COOKING TIME

10 MIN

SERVINGS

6

INGREDIENTS

- 3 garlic cloves, minced
- 2 tbsp. olive oil
- A pinch of chili flakes
- 1 1/2 tbsp. fresh mussels, scrubbed
- 1 cup white wine
- 1 cup chickpeas, rinsed
- 1 small fennel bulb, sliced
- Black pepper to the taste
- Juice of 1 lemon
- 3 tbsp. parsley, chopped

DIRECTIONS

1. Heat a big saucepan with the olive oil over medium-high heat, add garlic and chili flakes, stir and cook for a couple of minutes. Add white wine and mussels, stir, cover, and cook for 3 to 4 minutes until mussels open.
2. Transfer mussels to a baking dish, add some of the cooking liquid over them, and fridge until they are cold enough. Take mussels out of the fridge and discard shells.
3. Heat another pan over medium-high heat, add mussels, reserved cooking liquid, chickpeas, and fennel, stir well, and heat them. Add black pepper to the taste, lemon juice, and parsley, stir again, divide between plates and serve.

NUTRITIONS

- Calories: 286
- Carbohydrates: 49 g
- Fat: 4 g

- Protein: 14 g
- Sodium: 145 mg

75. Fish Stew

PREPARATION TIME

10 MIN

COOKING TIME

30 MIN

SERVINGS

4

INGREDIENTS

- 1 red onion, sliced
- 2 tbsp. olive oil
- 1 lb. white fish fillets, boneless, skinless, and cubed
- 1 avocado, pitted and chopped
- 1 tbsp. oregano, chopped
- 1 cup chicken stock
- 2 tomatoes, cubed
- 1 tsp. sweet paprika
- A pinch of salt and black pepper
- 1 tbsp. parsley, chopped
- Juice of 1 lime

DIRECTIONS

1. Warm up oil in a pot over medium heat, add the onion and sauté for 5 minutes. Add the fish, the avocado, and the other ingredients, toss, cook over medium heat for 25 minutes more, divide into bowls and serve for lunch.

NUTRITIONS

- Calories: 78
- Carbohydrates: 8 g
- Fat: 1 g

- Protein: 11 g
- Sodium: 151 mg

76. Shrimp and Broccoli Soup

5 MIN

COOKING TIME

25 MIN

SERVINGS

4

INGREDIENTS

- 2 tbsp. olive oil
- 1 yellow onion, chopped
- 4 cups chicken stock
- Juice of 1 lime
- 1 lb. shrimp, peeled and deveined
- 1/2 cup coconut cream
- 1/2 lb. broccoli florets
- 1 tbsp. parsley, chopped

DIRECTIONS

1. Heat a pot with the oil over medium heat, add the onion and sauté for 5 minutes. Add the shrimp and the other ingredients, simmer over medium heat for 20 minutes more. Ladle the soup into bowls and serve.

NUTRITIONS

- Calories: 220
- Carbohydrates: 12 g
- Fat: 7 g

- Protein: 26 g
- Sodium: 577 mg

77. Coconut Turkey Mix

PREPARATION TIME

10 MIN

COOKING TIME

30 MIN

SERVINGS

4

INGREDIENTS

- 1 yellow onion, chopped
- 1 lb. turkey breast, skinless, boneless, and cubed
- 2 tbsp. olive oil
- 2 garlic cloves, minced
- 1 zucchini, sliced
- 1 cup coconut cream
- A pinch of sea salt
- Black pepper

DIRECTIONS

1. Bring the pan to medium heat, add the onion and the garlic and sauté for 5 minutes. Put the meat and brown for 5 minutes more. Add the rest of the ingredients, toss, bring to a simmer and cook over medium heat for 20 minutes more. Serve for lunch.

NUTRITIONS

- Calories: 200
- Carbohydrates: 14 g
- Fat: 4 g

- Fiber: 2 g
- Protein: 7 g
- Sodium: 111 mg

78. Lime Shrimp and Kale

10 MIN

COOKING TIME

20 MIN

SERVINGS

4

INGREDIENTS

- 1 lb. shrimp, peeled and deveined
- 4 scallions, chopped
- 1 tsp. sweet paprika
- 1 tbsp. olive oil
- Juice of 1 lime
- Zest of 1 lime, grated
- A pinch of salt and black pepper
- 2 tbsp. parsley, chopped
- 1 cup Kale

DIRECTIONS

1. Bring the pan to medium heat, add the scallions and sauté for 5 minutes. Add the shrimp and the other ingredients, toss, cook over medium heat for 15 minutes more, divide into bowls and serve.

NUTRITIONS

- Calories: 149
- Carbohydrates: 12 g
- Fat: 4 g

- Protein: 21 g
- Sodium: 250 mg

79. Parsley Cod Mix

PREPARATION TIME

10 MIN

COOKING TIME

20 MIN

SERVINGS

4

INGREDIENTS

- 1 tbsp. olive oil
- 2 shallots, chopped
- 4 cod fillets, boneless and skinless
- 2 garlic cloves, minced
- 2 tbsp. lemon juice
- 1 cup chicken stock
- A pinch of salt and black pepper
- ½ cup Parsley

DIRECTIONS

1. Bring the pan to medium heat -high heat, add the shallots and the garlic and sauté for 5 minutes. Add the cod and the other ingredients, cook everything for 15 minutes more, divide between plates and serve for lunch.

NUTRITIONS

- Calories: 216
- Carbohydrates: 7 g
- Fat: 5 g

- Protein: 34 g
- Sodium: 380 mg

80. Salmon and Cabbage Mix

5 MIN

COOKING TIME

25 MIN

SERVINGS

4

INGREDIENTS

- 4 salmon fillets, boneless
- 1 yellow onion, chopped
- 2 tbsp. olive oil
- 1 cup red cabbage, shredded
- 1 red bell pepper, chopped
- 1 tbsp. rosemary, chopped
- 1 tbsp. coriander, ground
- 1 cup tomato sauce
- A pinch of sea salt
- Black pepper

DIRECTIONS

1. Bring the pan to medium heat, add the onion and sauté for 5 minutes. Put the fish and sear it for 2 minutes on each side. Add the cabbage and the remaining ingredients, toss, cook over medium heat for 20 minutes more, divide between plates and serve.

NUTRITIONS

- Calories: 130
- Carbohydrates: 8 g
- Fat: 6 g

- Protein: 12 g
- Sodium: 345 mg

81. Tofu & Green Bean Stir-Fry

PREPARATION TIME

15 MIN

COOKING TIME

20 MIN

SERVINGS

4

INGREDIENTS

- 1 (14 oz.) package extra-firm tofu
- 2 tbsp. canola oil
- 1 lb. green beans, chopped
- 2 carrots, peeled and thinly sliced
- 1/2 cup Stir-Fry Sauce or store-bought lower-sodium stir-fry sauce
- 2 cups Fluffy Brown Rice
- 2 scallions, thinly sliced
- 2 tbsp. sesame seeds

DIRECTIONS

1. Put the tofu on your plate lined with a kitchen towel, put a separate kitchen towel over the tofu, and place a heavy pot on top, changing towels every time they become soaked. Let sit for 15 minutes to remove the moisture. Cut the tofu into 1-inch cubes.
2. Heat the canola oil in a large wok or skillet to medium-high heat. Add the tofu cubes and cook, flipping every 1 to 2 minutes, so all sides become browned. Remove from the skillet and place the green beans and carrots in the hot oil. Stir-fry for 4 to 5 minutes, occasionally tossing, until crisp and slightly tender.
3. While the vegetables are cooking, prepare the Stir-Fry Sauce (if using homemade). Place the tofu back in the skillet. Put the sauce over the tofu and vegetables and let simmer for 2 to 3 minutes. Serve over rice, then top with scallions and sesame seeds.

NUTRITIONS

- Calories: 380
- Carbohydrate: 45 g
- Fat: 15 g

- Sodium: 440 mg
- Potassium: 454 mg
- Protein: 16 g

82. Peanut Vegetable Pad Thai

15 MIN

COOKING TIME

20 MIN

SERVINGS

6

INGREDIENTS

- 8 oz. brown rice noodles
- 1/3 cup natural peanut butter
- 3 tbsp. unsalted vegetable broth
- 1 tbsp. low-sodium soy sauce
- 2 tbsp. rice wine vinegar
- 1 tbsp. honey
- 2 tsp. sesame oil
- 1 tsp. sriracha (optional)
- 1 tbsp. canola oil
- 1 red bell pepper, thinly sliced
- 1 zucchini, cut into matchsticks
- 2 large carrots, cut into matchsticks
- 3 large eggs, beaten
- 3/4 tsp. kosher or sea salt
- 1/2 cup unsalted peanuts, chopped
- 1/2 cup cilantro leaves, chopped

DIRECTIONS

1. Boil a large pot of water. Cook the rice noodles as stated in package directions. Mix the peanut butter, vegetable broth, soy sauce, rice wine vinegar, honey, sesame oil, and sriracha in a bowl. Set aside.
2. Warm-up canola oil over medium heat in a large nonstick skillet. Add the red bell pepper, zucchini, and carrots, and sauté for 2 to 3 minutes, until slightly soft. Stir in the eggs and fold with a spatula until scrambled. Add the cooked rice noodles, sauce, and salt. Toss to combine. Spoon into bowls and evenly top with the peanuts and cilantro.

NUTRITIONS

- Calories: 393
- Carbohydrate: 45 g
- Fat: 19 g

- Protein: 13 g
- Sodium: 561 mg

83. Spicy Tofu Burrito Bowls With Cilantro Avocado Sauce

PREPARATION TIME

15 MIN

COOKING TIME

15 MIN

SERVINGS

4

INGREDIENTS

- For the sauce:
- 1/4 cup plain nonfat Greek yogurt
- 1/2 cup fresh cilantro leaves
- 1/2 ripe avocado, peeled
- Zest and juice of 1 lime
- 2 garlic cloves, peeled
- 1/4 tsp. kosher or sea salt
- 2 tbsp. water
- For the burrito bowls:
- 1 (14 oz.) package extra-firm tofu
- 1 tbsp. canola oil
- 1 yellow or orange bell pepper, diced
- 2 tbsp. Taco Seasoning
- 1/4 tsp. kosher or sea salt
- 2 cups Fluffy Brown Rice
- 1 (15 oz.) can black beans, drained
- 1/4 cup of water

DIRECTIONS

1. Place all the sauce ingredients in the bowl of a food processor or blender and purée until smooth. Taste and adjust the seasoning, if necessary. Refrigerate until ready for use.
2. Put the tofu on your plate lined with a kitchen towel. Put another kitchen towel over the tofu and place a heavy pot on top, changing towels if they become soaked. Let it stand for 15 minutes to remove the moisture. Cut the tofu into 1-inch cubes.
3. Warm-up canola oil in a large skillet over medium heat. Add the tofu and bell pepper and sauté, breaking up the tofu into smaller pieces for 4 to 5 minutes. Stir in the taco seasoning, salt, and 1/4 cup of water. Evenly divide the rice and black beans among 4 bowls. Top with the tofu/bell pepper mixture and top with the cilantro avocado sauce.

NUTRITIONS

- Calories: 383
- Carbohydrate: 48 g
- Fat: 13 g

- Sodium: 438 mg
- Protein: 21 g

84. Sweet Potato Cakes With Classic Guacamole

PREPARATION TIME

15 MIN

COOKING TIME

20 MIN

SERVINGS

4

NUTRITIONS

- Calories: 369
- Carbohydrate: 38 g
- Fat: 22 g

INGREDIENTS

- For the guacamole:
- 2 ripe avocados, peeled and pitted
- 1/2 jalapeño, seeded and finely minced
- 1/4 red onion, peeled and finely diced
- 1/4 cup fresh cilantro leaves, chopped
- Zest and juice of 1 lime
- 1/4 tsp. kosher or sea salt
- For the cakes:
- 3 sweet potatoes, cooked and peeled
- 1/2 cup cooked black beans
- 1 large egg
- 1/2 cup panko bread crumbs
- 1 tsp. ground cumin
- 1 tsp. chili powder
- 1/2 tsp. kosher or sea salt
- 1/4 tsp. ground black pepper
- 2 tbsp. canola oil

DIRECTIONS

1. Mash the avocado, then stir in the jalapeño, red onion, cilantro, lime zest and juice, and salt in a bowl. Taste and adjust the seasoning, if necessary.
2. Put the cooked sweet potatoes plus black beans in a bowl and mash until a paste forms. Stir in the egg, bread crumbs, cumin, chili powder, salt, and black pepper until combined.
3. Warm-up canola oil in a large skillet at medium heat. Form the sweet potato mixture into 4 patties, place them in the hot skillet, and cook for 3 to 4 minutes per side, until browned and crispy. Serve the sweet potato cakes with guacamole on top.

- Sodium: 521 mg
- Protein: 8 g

85. Chickpea Cauliflower Tikka Masala

PREPARATION TIME

15 MIN

COOKING TIME

40 MIN

SERVINGS

6

NUTRITIONS

- Calories: 323
- Carbohydrate: 44 g
- Fat: 12 g

INGREDIENTS

- 2 tbsp. olive oil
- 1 yellow onion, peeled and diced
- 4 garlic cloves, peeled and minced
- 1-inch piece fresh ginger, peeled and minced
- 2 tbsp. Garam Masala
- 1 tsp. kosher or sea salt
- 1/2 tsp. ground black pepper
- 1/4 tsp. ground cayenne pepper
- 1/2 small head cauliflower, small florets
- 2 (15 oz.) cans of no-salt-added chickpeas, rinsed and drained
- 1 (15 oz.) can no-salt-added petite diced tomatoes, drained
- 1 1/2 cups unsalted vegetable broth
- 1/2 (15 oz.) can coconut milk
- Zest and juice of 1 lime
- 1/2 cup fresh cilantro leaves, chopped, divided
- 1 1/2 cups cooked Fluffy Brown Rice, divided

DIRECTIONS

1. Warm up olive oil over medium heat, then put the onion and sauté for 4 to 5 minutes in a large Dutch oven or stockpot. Stir in the garlic, ginger, garam masala, salt, black pepper, and cayenne pepper and toast for 30 to 60 seconds, until fragrant.
2. Stir in the cauliflower florets, chickpeas, diced tomatoes, and vegetable broth and increase to medium-high. Simmer for 15 minutes, until the cauliflower is fork-tender.
3. Remove, then stir in the coconut milk, lime juice, lime zest, and half of the cilantro. Taste and adjust the seasoning, if necessary. Serve over the rice and the remaining chopped cilantro.

- Sodium: 444 mg
- Protein: 11 g

86. Eggplant Parmesan Stacks

PREPARATION TIME

15 MIN

COOKING TIME

20 MIN

SERVINGS

4

INGREDIENTS

- 1 large eggplant, cut into thick slices
- 2 tbsp. olive oil, divided
- 1/4 tsp. kosher or sea salt
- 1/4 tsp. ground black pepper
- 1 cup panko bread crumbs
- 1/4 cup freshly grated Parmesan cheese
- 5–6 garlic cloves, minced
- 1/2 lb. fresh mozzarella, sliced
- 1 1/2 cups lower-sodium marinara
- 1/2 cup fresh basil leaves, torn

DIRECTIONS

1. Preheat the oven to 425°F. Coat the eggplant slices in 1 tbsp. olive oil and sprinkle with salt and black pepper. Put on a large baking sheet, then roast for 10 to 12 minutes, until soft with crispy edges. Remove the eggplant and set the oven to a low boil.
2. In a bowl, stir the remaining tablespoons of olive oil, bread crumbs, Parmesan cheese, and garlic. Remove the cooled eggplant from the baking sheet and clean it.
3. Create layers on the same baking sheet by stacking a roasted eggplant slice with a slice of mozzarella, a tablespoon of marinara, a tablespoon of the bread, and fresh basil leaves crumb mixture, repeating with 2 layers of each ingredient. Cook under the broiler for 3 to 4 minutes until the cheese is melted and bubbly.

NUTRITIONS

- Calories: 377
- Carbohydrate: 29 g
- Fat: 22 g
- Sodium: 509 mg
- Protein: 16 g

87. Roasted Vegetable Enchiladas

PREPARATION TIME

15 MIN

COOKING TIME

45 MIN

SERVINGS

8

INGREDIENTS

- 2 zucchinis, diced
- 1 red bell pepper, seeded and sliced
- 1 red onion, peeled and sliced
- 2 ears corn
- 2 tbsp. canola oil
- 1 can no-salt-added black beans, drained
- 1 1/2 tbsp. chili powder
- 2 tsp. ground cumin
- 1/8 tsp. kosher or sea salt
- 1/2 tsp. ground black pepper
- 8 (8-inch) whole-wheat tortillas
- 1 cup Enchilada Sauce or store-bought enchilada sauce
- 1/2 cup shredded Mexican-style cheese
- 1/2 cup plain nonfat Greek yogurt
- 1/2 cup cilantro leaves, chopped
- Cooking spray

DIRECTIONS

1. Preheat oven to 400°F. Place the zucchini, red bell pepper, and red onion on a baking sheet. Place the ears of corn separately on the same baking sheet. Drizzle all with the canola oil and toss to coat. Roast for 10 to 12 minutes, until the vegetables are tender. Remove and reduce the temperature to 375°F.
2. Cut the corn from the cob. Transfer the corn kernels, zucchini, red bell pepper, and onion to a bowl and stir in the black beans, chili powder, cumin, salt, and black pepper until combined.
3. Oiled a 9-by-13-inch baking dish with cooking spray. Line up the tortillas in the greased baking dish. Evenly distribute the vegetable bean filling into each tortilla. Pour half of the enchilada sauce and sprinkle half of the shredded cheese on top of the filling.
4. Roll each tortilla into an enchilada shape and place them seam-side down. Pour the remaining enchilada sauce and sprinkle the remaining cheese over the enchiladas. Bake for 25 minutes until the cheese is melted and bubbly. Serve the enchiladas with Greek yogurt and chopped cilantro.

NUTRITIONS

- Calories: 335
- Carbohydrate: 42 g
- Fat: 15 g
- Sodium: 557 mg
- Protein: 13 g

88. Lentil Avocado Tacos

15 MIN

COOKING TIME

35 MIN

SERVINGS

6

INGREDIENTS

- 1 tbsp. canola oil
- 1/2 yellow onion, peeled and diced
- 2–3 garlic cloves, minced
- 1 1/2 cups dried lentils
- 1/2 tsp. kosher or sea salt
- 3–3 1/2 cups unsalted vegetable or chicken stock
- 2 1/2 tbsp. Taco Seasoning or store-bought low-sodium taco seasoning
- 16 (6-inch) corn tortillas, toasted
- 2 ripe avocados, peeled and sliced

DIRECTIONS

1. Heat up the canola oil in a large skillet or Dutch oven over medium heat. Cook the onion for 4 to 5 minutes, until soft. Mix in the garlic and cook for 30 seconds until fragrant. Then add the lentils, salt, and stock. Bring to a simmer for 25 to 35 minutes, adding additional stock if needed.
2. When there's only a small amount of liquid left in the pan, and the lentils are al dente, stir in the taco seasoning and let simmer for 1 to 2 minutes. Taste and adjust the seasoning, if necessary. Spoon the lentil mixture into tortillas and serve with the avocado slices.

NUTRITIONS

- Calories: 400
- Carbohydrate: 64 g
- Fat: 14 g

- Sodium: 336 mg
- Fiber: 15 g
- Protein: 16 g

89. Tomato & Olive Orecchiette With Basil Pesto

PREPARATION TIME

15 MIN

COOKING TIME

25 MIN

SERVINGS

6

INGREDIENTS

- 12 oz. orecchiette pasta
- 2 tbsp. olive oil
- 1-pint cherry tomatoes, quartered
- 1/2 cup Basil Pesto or store-bought pesto
- 1/4 cup kalamata olives, sliced
- 1 tbsp. dried oregano leaves
- 1/4 tsp. kosher or sea salt
- 1/2 tsp. freshly cracked black pepper
- 1/4 tsp. crushed red pepper flakes
- 2 tbsp. freshly grated Parmesan cheese

DIRECTIONS

1. Boil a large pot of water. Cook the orecchiette, drain and transfer the pasta to a large nonstick skillet.
2. Put the skillet over medium-low heat, then heat the olive oil. Stir in the cherry tomatoes, pesto, olives, oregano, salt, black pepper, and crushed red pepper flakes. Cook for 8 to 10 minutes, until heated throughout. Serve the pasta with freshly grated Parmesan cheese.

NUTRITIONS

- Calories: 332
- Carbohydrate: 44 g
- Fat: 13 g

- Sodium: 389 mg
- Protein: 9 g

90. Italian Stuffed Portobello Mushroom Burgers

PREPARATION TIME

15 MIN

COOKING TIME

25 MIN

SERVINGS

4

INGREDIENTS

- 1 tbsp. olive oil
- 4 large portobello mushrooms, washed and dried
- 1/2 yellow onion, peeled and diced
- 4 garlic cloves, peeled and minced
- 1 can cannellini beans, drained
- 1/2 cup fresh basil leaves, torn
- 1/2 cup panko bread crumbs
- 1/8 tsp. kosher or sea salt
- 1/4 tsp. ground black pepper
- 1 cup lower-sodium marinara, divided
- 1/2 cup shredded mozzarella cheese
- 4 whole-wheat buns, toasted
- 1 cup fresh arugula

DIRECTIONS

1. Heat up the olive oil in a large skillet to medium-high heat. Sear the mushrooms for 4 to 5 minutes per side, until slightly soft. Place on a baking sheet. Preheat the oven to a low boil.
2. Put the onion in the skillet and cook for 4 to 5 minutes, until slightly soft. Mix in the garlic then cook for 30 to 60 seconds. Move the onions plus garlic to a bowl. Add the cannellini beans and smash with the back of a fork to form a chunky paste. Stir in the basil, bread crumbs, salt, and black pepper, and half of the marinara. Cook for 5 minutes.
3. Remove the bean mixture from the stove and divide among the mushroom caps. Spoon the remaining marinara over the stuffed mushrooms and top each with the mozzarella cheese. Broil for 3 to 4 minutes, until the cheese is melted and bubbly. Transfer the burgers to the toasted whole-wheat buns and top with the arugula.

NUTRITIONS

- Calories: 407
- Carbohydrate: 63 g
- Fat: 9 g
- Sodium: 575 mg
- Protein: 25 g

91. Gnocchi With Tomato Basil Sauce

PREPARATION TIME

15 MIN

COOKING TIME

25 MIN

SERVINGS

6

INGREDIENTS

- 2 tbsp. olive oil
- 1/2 yellow onion, peeled and diced
- 3 cloves garlic, peeled and minced
- 1 (32 oz.) can no-salt-added crushed San Marzano tomatoes
- 1/4 cup fresh basil leaves
- 2 tsp. Italian seasoning
- 1/2 tsp. kosher or sea salt
- 1 tsp. granulated sugar
- 1/2 tsp. ground black pepper
- 1/8 tsp. crushed red pepper flakes
- 1 tbsp. heavy cream (optional)
- 12 oz. gnocchi
- 1/4 cup freshly grated Parmesan cheese

DIRECTIONS

1. Heat up the olive oil in a Dutch oven or stockpot over medium heat. Add the onion and sauté for 5 to 6 minutes, until soft. Stir in the garlic and stir until fragrant, 30 to 60 seconds. Then stir in the tomatoes, basil, Italian seasoning, salt, sugar, black pepper, and crushed red pepper flakes.
2. Bring to a simmer for 15 minutes. Stir in the heavy cream, if desired. For a smooth, puréed sauce, use an immersion blender or transfer sauce to a blender and purée until smooth. Taste and adjust the seasoning, if necessary.
3. While the sauce simmers, cook the gnocchi according to the package instructions, remove with a slotted spoon, and transfer to 6 bowls. Pour the sauce over the gnocchi and top with the Parmesan cheese.

NUTRITIONS

- Calories: 287
- Carbohydrate: 41 g
- Fat: 7 g
- Sodium: 527 mg
- Protein: 10 g

92. Creamy Pumpkin Pasta

PREPARATION TIME

15 MIN

COOKING TIME

30 MIN

SERVINGS

6

INGREDIENTS

- 1 lb. whole-grain linguine
- 1 tbsp. olive oil
- 3 garlic cloves, peeled and minced
- 2 tbsp. chopped fresh sage
- 1 1/2 cups pumpkin purée
- 1 cup unsalted vegetable stock
- 1/2 cup low-fat evaporated milk
- 3/4 tsp. kosher or sea salt
- 1/2 tsp. ground black pepper
- 1/2 tsp. ground nutmeg
- 1/4 tsp. ground cayenne pepper
- 1/2 cup freshly grated Parmesan cheese, divided
- Water

DIRECTIONS

1. Cook the whole-grain linguine in a large pot of boiled water. Reserve 1/2 cup of pasta water and drain the rest. Set the pasta aside.
2. Warm-up olive oil over medium heat in a large skillet. Add the garlic and sage and sauté for 1 to 2 minutes, until soft and fragrant. Whisk in the pumpkin purée, stock, milk, and reserved pasta water and simmer for 4 to 5 minutes, until thickened.
3. Whisk in the salt, black pepper, nutmeg, and cayenne pepper, and half of the Parmesan cheese. Stir in the cooked whole-grain linguine. Evenly divide the pasta among 6 bowls and top with the remaining Parmesan cheese.

NUTRITIONS

- Calories: 381
- Carbohydrate: 63 g
- Fat: 8 g
- Sodium: 175 mg
- Protein: 15 g

93. Mexican-Style Potato Casserole

PREPARATION TIME

15 MIN

COOKING TIME

60 MIN

SERVINGS

8

INGREDIENTS

- Cooking spray
- 2 tbsp. canola oil
- 1/2 yellow onion, peeled and diced
- 4 garlic cloves, peeled and minced
- 2 tbsp. all-purpose flour
- 1 1/4 cups milk
- 1 tbsp. chili powder
- 1/2 tbsp. ground cumin
- 1 tsp. kosher salt or sea salt
- 1/2 tsp. ground black pepper
- 1/4 tsp. ground cayenne pepper
- 1 1/2 cups shredded Mexican-style cheese, divided
- 1 (4 oz.) can green chilis, drained
- 1 1/2 lb. baby Yukon Gold or red potatoes, thinly sliced
- 1 red bell pepper, thinly sliced

DIRECTIONS

1. Preheat the oven to 400°F. Oiled a 9-by-13-inch baking dish with cooking spray. In a large saucepan, warm canola oil on medium heat. Add the onion and sauté for 4 to 5 minutes, until soft. Mix in the garlic, then cook until fragrant, 30 to 60 seconds.
2. Mix in the flour, then put in the milk while whisking. Slow simmer for about 5 minutes, until thickened. Whisk in the chili powder, cumin, salt, black pepper, and cayenne pepper.
3. Remove from the heat and whisk in half of the shredded cheese and the green chilis. Taste and adjust the seasoning, if necessary. Line up one-third of the sliced potatoes and sliced bell pepper in the baking dish and top with a quarter of the remaining shredded cheese.
4. Repeat with 2 more layers. Pour the cheese sauce over the top and sprinkle with the remaining shredded cheese. Cover it with aluminum foil and bake for 45 to 50 minutes, until the potatoes are tender.
5. Remove the foil and bake again for 5 to 10 minutes, until the topping is slightly browned. Let cool for 20 minutes before slicing into 8 pieces. Serve.

NUTRITIONS

- Calories: 195
- Carbohydrate: 19 g
- Fat: 10 g
- Sodium: 487 mg
- Protein: 8 g

94. Black Bean Stew With Cornbread

15 MIN

55 MIN

6

- Calories: 359
- Carbohydrate: 61 g
- Fat: 7 g

- For the black bean stew:
- 2 tbsp. canola oil
- 1 yellow onion, peeled and diced
- 4 garlic cloves, peeled and minced
- 1 tbsp. chili powder
- 1 tbsp. ground cumin
- 1/4 tsp. kosher or sea salt
- 1/2 tsp. ground black pepper
- 2 cans of no-salt-added black beans, drained
- 1 (10 oz.) can fire-roasted diced tomatoes
- 1/2 cup fresh cilantro leaves, chopped
- For the cornbread topping:
- 1 1/4 cups cornmeal
- 1/2 cup all-purpose flour
- 1/2 tsp. baking powder
- 1/4 tsp. baking soda
- 1/8 tsp. kosher or sea salt
- 1 cup low-fat buttermilk
- 2 tbsp. honey
- 1 large egg

1. Warm-up canola oil over medium heat in a large Dutch oven or stockpot. Add the onion and sauté for 4 to 6 minutes, until the onion is soft. Stir in the garlic, chili powder, cumin, salt, and black pepper.
2. Cook for 1 to 2 minutes, until fragrant. Add the black beans and diced tomatoes. Bring to a simmer and cook for 15 minutes. Remove, then stir in the fresh cilantro. Taste and adjust the seasoning, if necessary.
3. Preheat the oven to 375°F. While the stew simmers, prepare the cornbread topping. Mix the cornmeal, baking soda, flour, baking powder, plus salt in a bowl. In a measuring cup, whisk the buttermilk, honey, and egg until combined. Put the batter into the dry ingredients until just combined.
4. In oven-safe bowls or dishes, spoon out the black bean soup. Distribute dollops of the cornbread batter on top and then spread it out evenly with a spatula. Bake for 30 minutes, until the cornbread is just set.

- Sodium: 409 mg
- Protein: 14 g

95. Mushroom Florentine

15 MIN

20 MIN

4

- Calories: 287
- Carbohydrates: 50.4 g
- Fat: 4.2 g

- 5 oz whole-grain pasta
- 1/4 cup low-sodium vegetable broth
- 1 cup mushrooms, sliced
- 1/4 cup of soy milk
- 1 tsp. olive oil
- 1/2 tsp. Italian seasonings

1. Cook the pasta according to the direction of the manufacturer. Then pour olive oil into the saucepan and heat it. Add mushrooms and Italian seasonings. Stir the mushrooms well and cook for 10 minutes.
2. Then add soy milk and vegetable broth. Add cooked pasta and mix up the mixture well. Cook it for 5 minutes on low heat.

- Sodium: 26 mg
- Protein: 12.4 g

96. Hasselback Eggplant

15 MIN

COOKING TIME

25 MIN

SERVINGS

2

INGREDIENTS

- 2 eggplants, trimmed
- 2 tomatoes, sliced
- 1 tbsp. low-fat yogurt
- 1 tsp. curry powder
- 1 tsp. olive oil

DIRECTIONS

1. Make the cuts in the eggplants in the shape of the Hasselback. Then rub the vegetables with curry powder and fill with sliced tomatoes. Sprinkle the eggplants with olive oil and yogurt and wrap them in the foil (each Hasselback eggplant wrap separately). Bake the vegetables at 375°F for 25 minutes.

NUTRITIONS

- Calories: 188
- Carbohydrates: 38.1 g
- Fat: 3 g

- Sodium: 23 mg
- Protein: 7 g

97. Vegetarian Kebabs

PREPARATION TIME

15 MIN

COOKING TIME

6MIN

SERVINGS

4

INGREDIENTS

- 2 tbsp. balsamic vinegar
- 1 tbsp. olive oil
- 1 tsp. dried parsley
- 2 tbsp. water
- 2 sweet peppers
- 2 red onions, peeled
- 2 zucchinis, trimmed

DIRECTIONS

1. Cut the sweet peppers and onions into medium size squares. Then slice the zucchini. String all vegetables into the skewers. After this, in the shallow bowl, mix up olive oil, dried parsley, water, and balsamic vinegar.
2. Sprinkle the vegetable skewers with olive oil mixture and transfer to the preheated grill to 390°F. Cook the kebabs for 3 minutes per side or until the vegetables are light brown.

NUTRITIONS

- Calories: 88
- Carbohydrates: 13 g
- Fat: 3.9 g

- Sodium: 14 mg
- Protein: 2.4 g

98. White Beans Stew

15 MIN

COOKING TIME

55 MIN

SERVINGS

4

INGREDIENTS

- 1 cup white beans, soaked
- 1 cup low-sodium vegetable broth
- 1 cup zucchini, chopped
- 1 tsp. tomato paste
- 1 tbsp. avocado oil
- 4 cups of water
- 1/2 tsp. peppercorns
- 1/2 tsp. ground black pepper
- 1/4 tsp. ground nutmeg

DIRECTIONS

1. Heat avocado oil in the saucepan, add zucchinis, and roast them for 5 minutes. After this, add white beans, vegetable broth, tomato paste, water, peppercorns, ground black pepper, and ground nutmeg. Simmer the stew for 50 minutes on low heat.

NUTRITIONS

- Calories: 184
- Carbohydrates: 32.6 g
- Fat: 1 g
- Sodium: 55 mg
- Protein: 12.3 g

99. Vegetarian Lasagna

PREPARATION TIME

15 MIN

COOKING TIME

30 MIN

SERVINGS

6

INGREDIENTS

- 1 cup carrot, diced
- 1/2 cup bell pepper, diced
- 1 cup spinach, chopped
- 1 tbsp. olive oil
- 1 tsp. chili powder
- 1 cup tomatoes, chopped
- 4 oz low-fat cottage cheese
- 1 eggplant, sliced
- 1 cup low-sodium vegetable broth

DIRECTIONS

1. Put carrot, bell pepper, and spinach in the saucepan. Add olive oil and chili powder and stir the vegetables well. Cook them for 5 minutes.
2. Make the sliced eggplant layer in the casserole mold and top it with a vegetable mixture. Add tomatoes, vegetable stock, and cottage cheese. Bake the lasagna for 30 minutes at 375°F.

NUTRITIONS

- Calories: 77
- Carbohydrates: 9.7 g
- Fat: 3 g
- Sodium: 124 mg
- Protein: 4.1 g

100. Carrot Cakes

15 MIN

COOKING TIME

10 MIN

SERVINGS

4

INGREDIENTS

- 1 cup carrot, grated
- 1 tbsp. semolina
- 1 egg, beaten
- 1 tsp. Italian seasonings
- 1 tbsp. sesame oil

DIRECTIONS

1. In the mixing bowl, mix up grated carrot, semolina, egg, and Italian seasonings. Heat sesame oil in the skillet. Make the carrot cakes with the help of 2 spoons and put them in the skillet. Roast the cakes for 4 minutes per side.

NUTRITIONS

- Calories: 70
- Carbohydrates: 4.8 g
- Fat: 4.9 g
- Sodium: 35 mg
- Protein: 1.9 g

101. Vegan Chili

PREPARATION TIME

15 MIN

COOKING TIME

25 MIN

SERVINGS

4

INGREDIENTS

- 1/2 cup bulgur
- 1 cup tomatoes, chopped
- 1 chili pepper, chopped
- 1 cup red kidney beans, cooked
- 2 cups low-sodium vegetable broth
- 1 tsp. tomato paste
- 1/2 cup celery stalk, chopped

DIRECTIONS

1. Put all ingredients in the big saucepan and stir well. Close the lid and simmer the chili for 25 minutes over medium-low heat.

NUTRITIONS

- Calories: 234
- Carbohydrates: 44.9 g
- Fat: 0.9 g
- Sodium: 92 mg
- Protein: 13.1 g

102. Aromatic Whole Grain Spaghetti

PREPARATION TIME

15 MIN

COOKING TIME

10 MIN

SERVINGS

2

INGREDIENTS

- 1 tsp. dried basil
- 1/4 cup of soy milk
- 6 oz whole-grain spaghetti
- 2 cups of water
- 1 tsp. ground nutmeg

DIRECTIONS

1. Bring the water to boil, add spaghetti, and cook them for 8 to 10 minutes. Meanwhile, bring the soy milk to a boil. Drain the cooked spaghetti and mix them up with soy milk, ground nutmeg, and dried basil. Stir the meal well.

NUTRITIONS

- Calories: 128
- Carbohydrates: 25 g
- Fat: 1.4 g
- Sodium: 25 mg
- Protein: 5.6 g

Chapter 5

Dinner Dishes

103. Baked Falafel

15 MIN

COOKING TIME

25 MIN

SERVINGS

3

INGREDIENTS

- 2 cups chickpeas, cooked
- 1 yellow onion, diced
- 3 tbsp. olive oil
- 1 cup fresh parsley, chopped
- 1 tsp. ground cumin
- 1/2 tsp. coriander
- 2 garlic cloves, diced

DIRECTIONS

1. Blend all ingredients in the food processor. Preheat the oven to 375°F. Then line the baking tray with the baking paper. Make the balls from the chickpeas mixture and press them gently in the shape of the falafel. Put the falafel in the tray and bake in the oven for 25 minutes.

NUTRITIONS

- Calories: 316
- Carbohydrates: 43.3 g
- Fat: 11.2 g

- Fiber: 12.4 g
- Sodium: 23 mg
- Protein 13.5 g

104. Paella

PREPARATION TIME

15 MIN

COOKING TIME

25 MIN

SERVINGS

6

INGREDIENTS

- 1 tsp. dried saffron
- 1 cup short-grain rice
- 1 tbsp. olive oil
- 2 cups of water
- 1 tsp. chili flakes
- 6 oz artichoke hearts, chopped
- 1/2 cup green peas
- 1 onion, sliced
- 1 cup bell pepper, sliced

DIRECTIONS

1. Pour water into the saucepan. Add rice and cook it for 15 minutes. Meanwhile, heat olive oil in the skillet. Add dried saffron, chili flakes, onion, and bell pepper. Roast the vegetables for 5 minutes.
2. Add them to the cooked rice. Then add artichoke hearts and green peas. Stir the paella well and cook it for 10 minutes over low heat.

NUTRITIONS

- Calories: 170
- Carbohydrates: 32.7 g
- Fat: 2.7 g

- Sodium: 33 mg
- Protein: 4.2 g

105. Chunky Tomatoes

15 MIN

15 MIN

3

INGREDIENTS

- 2 cups plum tomatoes, roughly chopped
- 1/2 cup onion, diced
- 1/2 tsp. garlic, diced
- 1 tsp. Italian seasonings
- 1 tsp. canola oil
- 1 chili pepper, chopped

DIRECTIONS

1. Heat canola oil in the saucepan. Add chili pepper and onion. Cook the vegetables for 5 minutes. Stir them from time to time. After this, add tomatoes, garlic, and Italian seasonings. Close the lid and sauté the dish for 10 minutes.

NUTRITIONS

- Calories: 550
- Carbohydrates: 8.4 g
- Fat: 2.3 g
- Sodium: 17 mg
- Protein: 1.7 g

106. Mushroom Cakes

15 MIN

10 MIN

4

INGREDIENTS

- 2 cups mushrooms, chopped
- 3 garlic cloves, chopped
- 1 tbsp. dried dill
- 1 egg, beaten
- 1/4 cup of rice, cooked
- 1 tbsp. sesame oil
- 1 tsp. chili powder

DIRECTIONS

1. Grind the mushrooms in the food processor. Add garlic, dill, egg, rice, and chili powder. Blend the mixture for 10 seconds. After this, heat sesame oil for 1 minute.
2. Make the medium size mushroom cakes and put them in the hot sesame oil. Cook the mushroom cakes for 5 minutes per side on medium heat.

NUTRITIONS

- Calories: 103
- Carbohydrates: 12 g
- Fat: 4.8 g
- Sodium: 27 mg
- Protein: 3.7 g

107. Glazed Eggplant Rings

15 MIN

COOKING TIME

10 MIN

SERVINGS

4

INGREDIENTS

- 3 eggplants, sliced
- 1 tbsp. liquid honey
- 1 tsp. minced ginger
- 2 tbsp. lemon juice
- 3 tbsp. avocado oil
- 1/2 tsp. ground coriander
- 3 tbsp. water

DIRECTIONS

1. Rub the eggplants with ground coriander. Then heat the avocado oil in the skillet for 1 minute. When the oil is hot, add the sliced eggplant and arrange it in one layer.
2. Cook the vegetables for 1 minute per side. Transfer the eggplant to the bowl. Then add minced ginger, liquid honey, lemon juice, and water in the skillet. Bring it to a boil and add cooked eggplants. Coat the vegetables in the sweet liquid well and cook for 2 minutes more.

NUTRITIONS

- Calories: 136
- Carbohydrates: 29.6 g
- Fat: 2.2 g

- Sodium: 11 mg
- Protein: 4.3 g

108. Sweet Potato Balls

PREPARATION TIME

15 MIN

COOKING TIME

10 MIN

SERVINGS

4

INGREDIENTS

- 1 cup sweet potato, mashed, cooked
- 1 tbsp. fresh cilantro, chopped
- 1 egg, beaten
- 3 tbsp. ground oatmeal
- 1 tsp. ground paprika
- 1/2 tsp. ground turmeric
- 2 tbsp. coconut oil

DIRECTIONS

1. Mix mashed sweet potato, fresh cilantro, egg, ground oatmeal, paprika, and turmeric in a bowl. Stir the mixture until smooth and make the small balls. Heat the coconut oil in the saucepan. Put the sweet potato balls, then cook them until golden brown.

NUTRITIONS

- Calories: 133
- Carbohydrates: 13.1 g
- Fat: 8.2 g

- Sodium: 44 mg
- Protein: 2.8 g

109. Chickpea Curry

15 MIN

COOKING TIME

10 MIN

SERVINGS

4

INGREDIENTS

- 1 1/2 cup chickpeas, boiled
- 1 tsp. curry powder
- 1/2 tsp. garam masala
- 1 cup spinach, chopped
- 1 tsp. coconut oil
- 1/4 cup of soy milk
- 1 tbsp. tomato paste
- 1/2 cup of water

DIRECTIONS

1. Heat coconut oil in the saucepan. Add curry powder, garam masala, tomato paste, and soy milk. Whisk the mixture until smooth and bring it to a boil.
2. Add water, spinach, and chickpeas. Stir the meal and close the lid. Cook it for 5 minutes over medium heat.

NUTRITIONS

- Calories: 298
- Carbohydrates: 47.8 g
- Fat: 6.1 g
- Sodium: 37 mg
- Protein: 15.4 g

110. Pan-Fried Salmon With Salad

PREPARATION TIME

15 MIN

COOKING TIME

10 MIN

SERVINGS

4

INGREDIENTS

- 2 Salmon slices
- A pinch of salt and pepper
- 1 tbsp. extra-virgin olive oil
- 2 tbsp. unsalted butter
- 1/2 tsp. fresh dill
- 1 tbsp. fresh lemon juice
- 100 g. salad leaves, or bag of mixed leaves

Salad dressing:
- 3 tbsp. olive oil
- 2 tbsp. balsamic vinaigrette
- 1/2 tsp. maple syrup (honey)

DIRECTIONS

1. Pat-dry the salmon fillets with a paper towel and season with a pinch of salt and pepper. In a skillet, warm up oil over medium-high heat and add fillets. Cook each side for 5 to 7 minutes until golden brown.
2. Dissolve butter, dill, and lemon juice in a small saucepan. Put the butter mixture onto the cooked salmon. Lastly, combine all the salad dressing ingredients and drizzle to mixed salad leaves in a large bowl. Toss to coat. Serve with fresh salads on the side. Enjoy!

NUTRITIONS

- Calories: 307
- Carbohydrate: 1.7 g
- Fat: 22 g
- Protein: 34.6 g
- Sodium: 80 mg

111. Veggie Variety

PREPARATION TIME

15 MIN

COOKING TIME

15 MIN

SERVINGS

2

INGREDIENTS

- 1/2 onion, diced
- 1 tsp. vegetable oil (corn or sunflower oil)
- 200 g. Tofu/ bean curd
- 4 cherry tomatoes, halved
- 30 ml. vegetable milk (soy or oat milk)
- 1/2 tsp curry powder
- 1/4 tsp paprika
- A pinch of salt and pepper
- 2 slices of Vegan protein bread/ Whole grain bread
- Chives for garnish

DIRECTIONS

1. Dice the onion and fry in a frying pan with the oil. Break the tofu by hand into small pieces and put them in the pan. Sauté 7 to 8 minutes. Season with curry, paprika, salt, and pepper, the cherry tomatoes, and milk, and cook it all over roast for a few minutes. Serve with bread as desired and sprinkle with chopped chives.

NUTRITIONS

- Calories: 216
- Carbohydrate: 24.8 g
- Fat: 8.4 g

- Protein: 14.1 g
- Sodium: 140 mg

112. Vegetable Pasta

PREPARATION TIME

15 MIN

COOKING TIME

15 MIN

SERVINGS

4

INGREDIENTS

- 1 kg. Thin zucchini
- 20 g. fresh ginger
- 350 g. smoked tofu
- 1 lime
- 2 garlic cloves
- 3 tbsp sunflower oil
- 2 tbsp. sesame seeds
- A pinch of salt and pepper
- 4 tbsp. fried onions
- Soy sauce

DIRECTIONS

1. Wash and clean the zucchini and, using a julienne cutter, cut the pulp around the kernel into long thin strips (noodles). Ginger peel and finely chop. Crumble tofu. Halve lime, squeeze juice. Peel and chop garlic.
2. Warm up 1 tbsp oil in a large pan and fry the tofu for about 5 minutes. After about 3 minutes, add ginger, garlic, and sesame. Season with soy sauce. Remove from the pan and keep warm.
3. Wipe out the pan, then warm 2 tbsp. of oil in it. Stir fry zucchini strips for about 4 minutes while turning. Season with salt, pepper, and lime juice. Arrange pasta and tofu. Sprinkle with fried onions.

NUTRITIONS

- Calories: 262
- Carbohydrate: 17.1 g
- Fat: 17.7 g

- Protein: 15.4 g
- Sodium: 62 mg

113. Vegetable Noodles With Bolognese

15 MIN

COOKING TIME

15 MIN

SERVINGS

4

INGREDIENTS

- 1.5 kg. small zucchini (e.g., green and yellow)
- 600 g. carrots
- 1 onion
- 1 tbsp. olive oil
- 250 g. beef steak
- A pinch of Salt and pepper
- 2 tbsp. tomato paste
- 1 tbsp. flour
- 1 tsp. vegetable broth (instant)
- 40 g. pecorino or parmesan
- 1 small potty of basil
- 400 ml. water

DIRECTIONS

1. Clean and peel zucchini and carrots and wash. Using a sharp, long knife, cut first into thin slices, then into long, fine strips. Clean or peel the soup greens, wash and cut into tiny cubes. Peel the onion and chop finely. Heat the Bolognese oil in a large pan. Fry meat in it crumbly. Season with salt and pepper.
2. Briefly sauté the prepared vegetable and onion cubes. Stir in tomato paste. Dust the flour, sweat briefly. Pour in 400 ml of water and stir in the vegetable stock. Boil everything, simmer for 7 to 8 minutes.
3. Meanwhile, cook the vegetable strips in plenty of salted water for 3 to 5 minutes. Drain, collecting some cooking water. Add the vegetable strips to the pan and mix well. If the sauce is not liquid enough, stir in some vegetable cooking water and season everything again.
4. Slicing cheese into fine shavings. Wash the basil, shake dry, peel off the leaves, and cut roughly. Arrange vegetable noodles, sprinkle with parmesan and basil

NUTRITIONS

- Calories: 269
- Carbohydrate: 21.7 g
- Fat: 9.7 g

- Protein: 25.6 g
- Sodium: 253 mg

114. Harissa Bolognese With Vegetable Noodles

15 MIN

COOKING TIME

30 MIN

SERVINGS

4

INGREDIENTS

- 2 onions
- 1 garlic clove
- 3–4 tbsp. oil
- 400 g. ground beef
- A pinch of salt, pepper, cinnamon
- 1 tsp. Harissa (Arabic seasoning paste, tube)
- 1 tbsp. tomato paste
- 2 sweet potatoes
- 2 medium Zucchini
- 3 stems/basil
- 100 g. feta
- 200 ml. water

DIRECTIONS

1. Peel onions and garlic, finely dice. Warm-up 1 tbsp. oil in a wide saucepan. Fry meat in it crumbly. Fry onions and garlic for a short time. Season with salt, pepper, and 1/2 tsp. cinnamon. Stir in Harissa and tomato paste.
2. Add tomatoes and 200 ml of water, bring to the boil and simmer for about 15 minutes with occasional stirring. Peel sweet potatoes and zucchini or clean and wash. Cut vegetables into spaghetti with a spiral cutter.
3. Warm-up 2–3 tbsp. oil in a large pan. Braise sweet potato spaghetti in it for about 3 minutes. Add the zucchini spaghetti and continue to simmer for 3–4 minutes while turning.
4. Season with salt and pepper. Wash the basil, shake dry and peel off the leaves. Garnish vegetable spaghetti and Bolognese on plates. Feta crumbles over. Sprinkle with basil.

NUTRITIONS

- Calories: 452
- Carbohydrate: 27.6 g
- Fat: 22.3 g

- Protein: 37.1 g
- Sodium: 253 mg

115. Curry Vegetable Noodles With Chicken

15 MIN

COOKING TIME

15 MIN

SERVINGS

2

INGREDIENTS

- 600 g. zucchini
- 500 g. chicken fillet
- A pinch of salt and pepper
- 2 tbsp. oil
- 150 g. red and yellow cherry tomatoes
- 1 tsp. curry powder
- 150 g. fat-free cheese
- 200 ml. vegetable broth
- 4 stalk (s) of fresh basil

DIRECTIONS

1. 1.   Wash the zucchini, clean, and cut into long thin strips with a spiral cutter. Wash meat, pat dry, and season with salt. Heat 1 tbsp. oil in a pan. Roast chicken in it for about 10 minutes until golden brown.
2. 2.   Wash cherry tomatoes and cut them in half. Approximately 3 minutes before the end of the cooking time to the chicken in the pan. Heat 1 tbsp. oil in another pan. Sweat curry powder into it then stirs in cream cheese and broth. Flavor the sauce with salt plus pepper and simmer for about 4 minutes.
3. 3.   Wash the basil, shake it dry and pluck the leaves from the stems. Cut small leaves of 3 stems. Remove meat from the pan and cut it into strips. Add tomatoes, basil, and zucchini to the sauce and heat for 2 to 3 minutes. Serve vegetable noodles and meat on plates and garnish with basil.

NUTRITIONS

- Calories: 376
- Carbohydrate: 9.5 g
- Fat: 17.2 g

- Protein: 44.9 g
- Sodium: 352 mg
- Cholesterol: 53 mg

116. Sweet and Sour Vegetable Noodles

PREPARATION TIME

15 MIN

COOKING TIME

30 MIN

SERVINGS

4

INGREDIENTS

- 4 chicken fillets (75 g. each)
- 300 g. whole-wheat spaghetti
- 750 g. carrots
- 1/4 liter clear chicken broth (instant)
- 1 tbsp. sugar
- 1 tbsp. green peppercorns
- 2–3 tbsp. balsamic vinegar
- Capuchin flowers
- A pinch of salt
- Water

DIRECTIONS

1. Cook spaghetti in boiling water for about 8 minutes. Then drain. In the meantime, peel and wash carrots. Cut into long strips (best with a special grater). Blanch for 2 minutes in boiling salted water, drain. Wash chicken fillets. Add to the boiling chicken soup and cook for about 15 minutes.
2. Melt the sugar until golden brown. Measure 1/4 liter of chicken stock and deglaze the sugar with it. Add peppercorns, cook for 2 minutes. Season with salt and vinegar. Add the fillets, then cut into thin slices. Then turn the pasta and carrots in the sauce and serve garnished with capuchin flowers. Serve and enjoy.

NUTRITIONS

- Calories: 374
- Carbohydrate: 23.1 g
- Fat: 21 g

- Protein: 44 g
- Sodium: 295 mg

117. Farro Cucumber-Mint Salad

PREPARATION TIME

15 MIN

COOKING TIME

30 MIN

SERVINGS

4-6

INGREDIENTS

- 1 cup baby arugula
- 1 English cucumber, halved along the length, seeded, and cut into 1/4-inch pieces
- 1 1/2 cups whole farro
- 2 tbsp. lemon juice
- 2 tbsp. minced shallot
- 2 tbsp. plain Greek yogurt
- 3 tbsp. chopped fresh mint
- 3 tbsp. extra-virgin olive oil
- 6 oz. cherry tomatoes, halved
- Salt and pepper
- 4 quarts of water

DIRECTIONS

1. Bring 4 quarts of water to boil in a Dutch oven. Put in farro and 1 tbsp. salt, return to boil, and cook until grains are soft with a slight chew, 15 to 30 minutes.
2. Drain farro, spread in rimmed baking sheet, and allow to cool completely for about 15 minutes.
3. Beat oil, lemon juice, shallot, yogurt, 1/4 tsp. salt, and 1/4 tsp. pepper together in a big container.
4. Put in farro, cucumber, tomatoes, arugula, and mint and toss gently to combine. Sprinkle with salt and pepper to taste. Serve.

NUTRITIONS

- Calories: 97
- Carbohydrates: 15 g
- Fat: 4 g

- Protein: 2 g

118. Chorizo-Kidney Beans Quinoa Pilaf

PREPARATION TIME

15 MIN

COOKING TIME

37 MIN

SERVINGS

4

INGREDIENTS

- 1/4 lb. dried Spanish chorizo diced (about 2/3 cup)
- 1/4 tsp. red pepper flakes
- 1/4 tsp. smoked paprika
- 1/2 tsp. cumin
- 1/2 tsp. sea salt
- 1 3/4 cups water
- 1 cup quinoa
- 1 large clove garlic minced
- 1 small red bell pepper finely diced
- 1 small red onion finely diced
- 1 tbsp. tomato paste
- 1 (15 oz.) can of kidney beans rinsed and drained

DIRECTIONS

1. Place a nonstick pot on medium-high fire and heat for 2 minutes. Add chorizo and sauté for 5 minutes until lightly browned. Stir in peppers and onion. Sauté for 5 minutes.
2. Add tomato paste, red pepper flakes, salt, paprika, cumin, and garlic. Sauté for 2 minutes. Stir in quinoa and mix well. Sauté for 2 minutes.
3. Add water and beans. Mix well. Cover and simmer for 20 minutes or until liquid is fully absorbed. Turn off fire and fluff quinoa. Let it sit for 5 minutes more while uncovered. Serve and enjoy.

NUTRITIONS

- Calories: 260
- Carbohydrates: 40.9 g
- Fat: 6.8 g

- Protein: 9.6 g

119. Goat Cheese 'N Red Beans Salad

PREPARATION TIME

15 MIN

COOKING TIME

0 MIN

SERVINGS

6

NUTRITIONS

- Calories: 385
- Carbohydrates: 44.0 g
- Fat: 15.0 g
- Protein: 22.5 g

INGREDIENTS

- 2 cans of Red Kidney Beans, drained and rinsed well
- Water or vegetable broth to cover beans
- 1 bunch parsley, chopped
- 1 1/2 cups red grape tomatoes, halved
- 3 cloves garlic, minced
- 3 tbsp. olive oil
- 3 tbsp. lemon juice
- 1/2 tsp. salt
- 1/2 tsp. white pepper
- 6 oz. goat cheese, crumbled

DIRECTIONS

1. In a large bowl, combine beans, parsley, tomatoes, and garlic. Add olive oil, lemon juice, salt, and pepper.
2. Mix well and refrigerate until ready to serve. Spoon into individual dishes topped with crumbled goat cheese.

120. Greek Farro Salad

PREPARATION TIME

15 MIN

COOKING TIME

20 MIN

SERVINGS

4

NUTRITIONS

- Calories: 428
- Carbohydrates: 47.6 g
- Fat: 24.5 g
- Protein: 17.7 g

INGREDIENTS

- Farro:
- 1/2 tsp. fine-grain sea salt
- 1 cup farro, rinsed
- 1 tbsp. olive oil
- 2 garlic cloves, pressed or minced
- Salad:
- 1/2 small red onion, chopped and then rinsed under water to mellow the flavor
- 1 avocado, sliced into strips
- 1 cucumber, sliced into thin rounds
- 15 pitted Kalamata olives, sliced into rounds
- 1-pint cherry tomatoes, sliced into rounds
- 2 cups cooked chickpeas (or one 14-oz. can rinse and drained)
- 5 oz. mixed greens
- Lemon wedges
- Herbed yogurt ingredients:
- 1/8 tsp. salt
- 1 1/4 cups plain Greek yogurt
- 1 1/2 tbsp. lightly packed fresh dill, roughly chopped
- 1 1/2 tbsp. lightly packed fresh mint, torn into pieces
- 1 tbsp. lemon juice (about 1/2 lemon)
- 1 tbsp. olive oil

DIRECTIONS

1. In a blender, blend and puree all herbed yogurt ingredients and set aside. Then cook the farro by placing it in a pot filled halfway with water.
2. Bring to a boil, reduce fire to a simmer and cook for 15 minutes or until farro is tender. Drain well. Mix in salt, garlic, and olive oil, and fluff to coat.
3. Evenly divide the cooled farro into 4 bowls. Evenly divide the salad ingredients on the 4 farro bowl. Top with 1/4 of the yogurt dressing. Serve and enjoy.

121. White Bean and Tuna Salad

15 MIN

8 MIN

4

INGREDIENTS

- 1 (12 oz.) can solid white albacore tuna, drained
- 1 (16 oz.) can Great Northern beans, drained and rinsed
- 1 (2.25 oz.) can slice black olives, drained
- 1 tsp. dried oregano
- 1/2 tsp. finely grated lemon zest
- 1/4 medium red onion, thinly sliced
- 3 tbsp. lemon juice
- 3/4 lb. green beans, trimmed and snapped in half
- 4 large hard-cooked eggs, peeled and quartered
- 6 tbsp. extra-virgin olive oil
- Salt and ground black pepper, to taste
- 1 cup of water

DIRECTIONS

1. Place a saucepan on the medium-high fire. Add a cup of water and the green beans. Cover and cook for 8 minutes. Drain immediately once tender.
2. In a salad bowl, whisk well oregano, olive oil, lemon juice, and lemon zest. Season generously with pepper and salt and mix until salt is dissolved.
3. Stir in drained green beans, tuna, beans, olives, and red onion. Mix thoroughly to coat. Adjust seasoning to taste. Spread eggs on top. Serve and enjoy.

NUTRITIONS

- Calories: 551
- Carbohydrates: 33.4 g
- Fat: 30.3 g

- Protein: 36.3 g

122. Spicy Sweet Red Hummus

15 MIN

0 MIN

8

INGREDIENTS

- 1 (15 oz.) can garbanzo beans, drained
- 1 (4 oz.) jar roasted red peppers
- 1 1/2 tbsp. tahini
- 1 clove garlic, minced
- 1 tbsp. chopped fresh parsley
- 1/2 tsp. cayenne pepper
- 1/2 tsp. ground cumin
- 1/4 tsp. salt
- 3 tbsp. lemon juice

DIRECTIONS

1. In a blender, add all ingredients and process until smooth and creamy. Adjust seasoning to taste if needed. Can be stored in an airtight container for up to 5 days.

NUTRITIONS

- Calories: 64
- Carbohydrates: 9.6 g
- Fat: 2.2 g

- Protein: 2.5 g

123. Black Bean Chili with Mangoes

PREPARATION TIME

15 MIN

COOKING TIME

10 MIN

SERVINGS

4

INGREDIENTS

- 2 tbsp. coconut oil
- 1 onion, chopped
- 2 (15 oz. /425 g.) cans of black beans, drained and rinsed
- 1 tbsp. chili powder
- 1 tsp. sea salt
- 1/4 tsp. freshly ground black pepper
- 1 cup of water
- 2 ripe mangoes, sliced thinly
- 1/4 cup chopped fresh cilantro, divided
- 1/4 cup sliced scallions, divided

DIRECTIONS

1. Heat the coconut oil in a pot over high heat until melted. Put the onion in the pot and sauté for 5 minutes or until translucent.
2. Add the black beans to the pot. Sprinkle with chili powder, salt, and ground black pepper. Pour in the water. Stir to mix well.
3. Bring to a boil. Reduce the heat to low, then simmering for 5 minutes or until the beans are tender. Turn off the heat and mix in the mangoes, then garnish with scallions and cilantro before serving.

NUTRITIONS

- Calories: 430
- Carbohydrates: 71.9 g
- Fat: 9.1 g
- Protein: 20.2 g

124. Israeli Style Eggplant and Chickpea Salad

PREPARATION TIME

5 MIN

COOKING TIME

20 MIN

SERVINGS

6

INGREDIENTS

- 2 tbsp. balsamic vinegar
- 2 tbsp. freshly squeezed lemon juice
- 1 tsp. ground cumin
- 1/4 tsp. sea salt
- 2 tbsp. olive oil, divided
- 1 (1 lb. / 454 g.) medium globe eggplant, stem removed, cut into flat cubes (about 1/2 inch thick)
- 1 (15 oz. / 425 g.) can chickpeas, drained and rinsed
- 1/4 cup chopped mint leaves
- 1 cup sliced sweet onion
- 1 garlic clove, finely minced
- 1 tbsp. sesame seeds, toasted

DIRECTIONS

1. Preheat the oven to 550ºF (288ºC) or the highest level of your oven or broiler. Grease a baking sheet with 1 tbsp. olive oil.
2. Combine the balsamic vinegar, lemon juice, cumin, salt, and 1 tbsp. of olive oil in a small bowl. Stir to mix well.
3. Arrange the eggplant cubes on the baking sheet, then brush with 2 tbsp. the balsamic vinegar mixture on both sides.
4. Broil in the preheated oven for 8 minutes or until lightly browned. Flip the cubes halfway through the cooking time.
5. Meanwhile, combine the chickpeas, mint, onion, garlic, and sesame seeds in a large serving bowl. Drizzle with the remaining balsamic vinegar mixture. Stir to mix well.
6. Remove the eggplant from the oven. Allow to cool for 5 minutes, then slice them into 1/2-inch strips on a clean work surface.
7. Add the eggplant strips to the serving bowl, then toss to combine well before serving.

NUTRITIONS

- Calories: 125
- Carbohydrates: 20.9 g
- Fat: 2.9 g
- Protein: 5.2 g

125. Italian Saut'ed Cannellini Beans

15 MIN

COOKING TIME

15 MIN

SERVINGS

6

NUTRITIONS

- Calories: 435
- Carbohydrates: 80.3 g
- Fat: 2.1 g

- Protein: 26.2 g

INGREDIENTS

- 2 tsp. extra-virgin olive oil
- 1/2 cup minced onion
- 1/4 cup red wine vinegar
- 1 (12 oz. / 340 g.) can no-salt-added tomato paste
- 2 tbsp. raw honey
- 1/2 cup of water
- 1/4 tsp. ground cinnamon
- 2 (15 oz. / 425 g.) cans cannellini beans

DIRECTIONS

1. Heat the olive oil in a saucepan over medium heat until shimmering. Add the onion and sauté for 5 minutes or until translucent.
2. Pour in the red wine vinegar, tomato paste, honey, and water. Sprinkle with cinnamon. Stir to mix well.
3. Reduce the heat to low, then pour all the beans into the saucepan. Cook for 10 more minutes. Stir constantly. Serve immediately.

126. Lentil and Vegetable Curry Stew

PREPARATION TIME

15 MIN

COOKING TIME

4H 7 MIN

SERVINGS

8

INGREDIENTS

- 1 tbsp. coconut oil
- 1 yellow onion, diced
- 1/4 cup yellow Thai curry paste
- 2 cups unsweetened coconut milk
- 2 cups dry red lentils, rinsed well, and drained
- 3 cups bite-sized cauliflower florets
- 2 golden potatoes, cut into chunks
- 2 carrots, peeled and diced
- 8 cups low-sodium vegetable soup, divided
- 1 bunch kale, stems removed and roughly chopped
- Sea salt, to taste
- 1/2 cup fresh cilantro, chopped
- A pinch crushed red pepper flakes

DIRECTIONS

1. Heat the coconut oil in a nonstick skillet over medium-high heat until melted. Add the onion and sauté for 5 minutes or until translucent.
2. Pour in the curry paste and sauté for another 2 minutes, then fold in the coconut milk and stir to combine well. Bring to a simmer and turn off the heat.
3. Put the lentils, cauliflower, potatoes, and carrot in the slow cooker. Pour in 6 cups of vegetable soup and the curry mixture. Stir to combine well.
4. Cover and cook on high for 4 hours or until the lentils and vegetables are soft. Stir periodically.
5. During the last 30 minutes, fold the kale in the slow cooker and pour in the remaining vegetable soup. Sprinkle with salt.
6. Pour the stew in a large serving bowl and spread the cilantro and red pepper flakes on top before serving hot.

NUTRITIONS

- Calories: 530
- Carbohydrates: 75.2 g
- Fat: 19.2 g

- Protein: 20.3 g

127. Lush Moroccan Chickpea, Vegetable, and Fruit Stew

PREPARATION TIME

15 MIN

COOKING TIME

6H 4 MIN

SERVINGS

6

NUTRITIONS

- Calories: 611
- Carbohydrates: 107.4 g
- Fat: 9.0 g

INGREDIENTS

- 1 large bell pepper, any color, chopped
- 6 oz. (170 g.) green beans, trimmed and cut into bite-size pieces
- 3 cups canned chickpeas, rinsed and drained
- 1 (15 oz. / 425 g.) can diced tomatoes, with the juice
- 1 large carrot, cut into 1/4-inch rounds
- 2 large potatoes, peeled and cubed
- 1 large yellow onion, chopped
- 1 tsp. grated fresh ginger
- 2 garlic cloves, minced
- 1 3/4 cups low-sodium vegetable soup
- 1 tsp. ground cumin
- 1 tbsp. ground coriander
- 1/4 tsp. ground red pepper flakes
- Sea salt and ground black pepper, to taste
- 8 oz. (227 g.) fresh baby spinach
- 1/4 cup diced dried figs
- 1/4 cup diced dried apricots
- 1 cup plain Greek yogurt

- Protein: 30.7 g

DIRECTIONS

1. Place the bell peppers, green beans, chicken peas, tomatoes and juice, carrot, potatoes, onion, ginger, and garlic in the slow cooker.
2. Pour in the vegetable soup and sprinkle with cumin, coriander, red pepper flakes, salt, and ground black pepper. Stir to mix well.
3. Put the slow cooker lid on and cook on high for 6 hours or until the vegetables are soft. Stir periodically. Open the lid and fold in the spinach, figs, apricots, and yogurt. Stir to mix well.
4. Cook for 4 minutes or until the spinach is wilted. Pour them into a large serving bowl. Allow to cool for at least 20 minutes, then serve warm.

128. Simple Pork Stir Fry

PREPARATION TIME

10 MIN

COOKING TIME

15 MIN

SERVINGS

4

NUTRITIONS

- Calories: 343
- Carbohydrates: 21 g
- Fat: 31 g

INGREDIENTS

- 4 oz. bacon, chopped
- 4 oz. snow peas
- 2 tbsp. butter
- 1 lb. pork loin, cut into thin strips
- 2 cups mushrooms, sliced
- 3/4 cup white wine
- 1/2 cup yellow onion, chopped
- 3 tbsp. sour cream
- Salt and white pepper to taste
- Water

- Protein: 23 g

DIRECTIONS

1. Put snow peas in a saucepan, add water to cover, add a pinch of salt, bring to a boil over medium heat, cook until they are soft, drain and leave aside.
2. Heat a pan over medium-high heat, add bacon, cook for a few minutes, drain grease, transfer to a bowl and leave aside.
3. Heat a pan with 1 tbsp. butter over medium heat, add pork strips, salt, and pepper to taste, brown for a few minutes, and transfer to a plate as well.
4. Return pan to medium heat, add remaining butter and melt it. Add onions and mushrooms, stir and cook for 4 minutes.
5. Add wine, and simmer until it's reduced. Add cream, peas, pork, salt, and pepper to taste, stir, heat up, divide between plates, top with bacon, and serve.

129. Pork and Lentil Soup

10 MIN

1 HOUR

6

- Calories: 343
- Carbohydrates: 21 g
- Fat: 31 g

INGREDIENTS

- 1 small yellow onion, chopped
- 1 tbsp. olive oil
- 1 1/2 tsp. basil, chopped
- 1 1/2 tsp. ginger, grated
- 3 garlic cloves, chopped
- Salt and black pepper to taste
- 1/2 tsp. cumin, ground
- 1 carrot, chopped
- 1 lb. pork chops, bone-in 3 oz. brown lentils, rinsed
- 3 cups chicken stock
- 2 tbsp. tomato paste
- 2 tbsp. lime juice
- 1 tsp. red chili flakes, crushed

DIRECTIONS

1. Heat a saucepan with the oil over medium heat, add garlic, onion, basil, ginger, salt, pepper, and cumin, stir well and cook for 6 minutes.
2. Add carrots, stir and cook for 5 more minutes. Add pork and brown for a few minutes. Add lentils, tomato paste, and stock, stir, bring to a boil, cover pan and simmer for 50 minutes.
3. Transfer pork to a plate, discard bones, shred it and return to pan. Add chili flakes and lime juice, stir, ladle into bowls and serve.

- Protein: 23 g

130. Simple Braised Pork

40 MIN

1 HOUR

4

- Calories: 320
- Carbohydrates: 21 g
- Fat: 31 g

INGREDIENTS

- 2 lb. pork loin roast, boneless and cubed
- 5 tbsp. butter
- Salt and black pepper to taste
- 2 cups chicken stock
- 1/2 cup dry white wine
- 2 garlic cloves, minced
- 1 tsp. thyme, chopped
- 1 thyme spring
- 1 bay leaf
- 1/2 yellow onion, chopped
- 2 tbsp. white flour
- 3/4 lb. pearl onions
- 1/2 lb. red grapes

DIRECTIONS

1. Heat a pan with 2 tbsp. butter over high heat, add pork loin, some salt, and pepper, stir, brown for 10 minutes, and transfer to a plate.
2. Add wine to the pan, bring to a boil over high heat and cook for 3 minutes.
3. Add stock, garlic, thyme spring, bay leaf, yellow onion and return meat to the pan, bring to a boil, cover, reduce heat to low, cook for 1 hour, strain liquid into another saucepan, and transfer pork to a plate.
4. Put pearl onions in a small saucepan, add water to cover, bring to a boil over medium-high heat, boil them for 5 minutes, drain, peel them and leave aside for now.
5. In a bowl, mix 2 tbsp. butter with flour and stir well. Add 1/2 cup of the strained cooking liquid and whisk well.
6. Pour this into cooking liquid, bring to a simmer over medium heat and cook for 5 minutes. Add salt and pepper, chopped thyme, pork, and pearl onions, cover, and simmer for a few minutes.
7. Meanwhile, heat a pan with 1 tbsp. butter, add grapes, stir and cook them for 1 to 2 minutes. Divide pork meat on plates, drizzle the sauce all over, and serve with onions and grapes on the side.

- Protein: 23 g

131. Pork and Chickpea Stew

20 MIN

COOKING TIME

8 HOURS

SERVINGS

4

INGREDIENTS

- 2 tbsp. white flour
- 1/2 cup chicken stock
- 1 tbsp. ginger, grated
- 1 tsp. coriander, ground
- 2 tsp. cumin, ground
- Salt and black pepper to taste
- 2 1/2 lb. pork butt, cubed
- 28 oz. canned tomatoes, drained and chopped
- 4 oz. carrots, chopped
- 1 red onion cut in wedges
- 4 garlic cloves, minced
- 1/2 cup apricots, cut in quarters
- 1 cup couscous, cooked
- 15 oz. canned chickpeas, drained
- Cilantro, chopped for serving

DIRECTIONS

1. Put stock in your slow cooker. Add flour, cumin, ginger, coriander, salt, and pepper and stir. Add tomatoes, pork, carrots, garlic, onion, and apricots, cover the cooker and cook on Low for 7 hours and 50 minutes.
2. Add chickpeas and couscous, cover, and cook for 10 more minutes. Divide on plates, sprinkle cilantro, and serve right away.

NUTRITIONS

- Calories: 216
- Carbohydrates: 21 g
- Fat: 31 g

- Protein: 23 g

132. Pork and Greens Salad

PREPARATION TIME

10 MIN

COOKING TIME

15 MIN

SERVINGS

4

INGREDIENTS

- 1 lb. pork chops, boneless and cut into strips
- 8 oz. white mushrooms, sliced
- 1/2 cup Italian dressing
- 6 cups mixed salad greens
- 6 oz. jarred artichoke hearts, drained
- Salt and black pepper to the taste
- 1/2 cup basil, chopped
- 1 tbsp. olive oil

DIRECTIONS

1. Heat a pan with the oil over medium-high heat, add the pork, and brown for 5 minutes. Add the mushrooms, stir and sauté for 5 minutes more.
2. Add the dressing, artichokes, salad greens, salt, pepper, and basil, cook for 4 to 5 minutes, divide everything into bowls and serve.

NUTRITIONS

- Calories: 320
- Carbohydrates: 21 g
- Fat: 31 g

- Protein: 23 g

133. Pork Strips and Rice

10 MIN

25 MIN

4

INGREDIENTS

- 1/2 lb. pork loin, cut into strips
- Salt and black pepper to taste
- 2 tbsp. olive oil
- 2 carrots, chopped
- 1 red bell pepper, chopped
- 3 garlic cloves, minced
- 2 cups veggie stock
- 1 cup basmati rice
- 1/2 cup garbanzo beans
- 10 black olives, pitted and sliced
- 1 tbsp. parsley, chopped

DIRECTIONS

1. Heat a pan with the oil over medium-high heat. Add the pork fillets, stir, salt, and black pepper cook for 5 minutes, and transfer them to a plate.
2. Add the carrots, bell pepper, and garlic, stir and cook for 5 more minutes.
3. Add the rice, the stock, beans, and the olives, stir, cook for 14 minutes, divide between plates, sprinkle the parsley on top, and serve.

NUTRITIONS

- Calories: 220
- Carbohydrates: 21 g
- Fat: 31 g

- Protein: 23 g

134. Pork and Bean Stew

20 MIN

4 HOURS

4

INGREDIENTS

- 2 lb. pork neck
- 1 tbsp. white flour
- 1 1/2 tbsp. olive oil
- 2 eggplants, chopped
- 1 brown onion, chopped
- 1 red bell pepper, chopped
- 3 garlic cloves, minced
- 1 tbsp. thyme, dried
- 2 tsp. sage, dried
- 4 oz. canned white beans, drained
- 1 cup chicken stock
- 12 oz. zucchinis, chopped
- Salt and pepper to taste
- 2 tbsp. tomato paste

DIRECTIONS

1. In a bowl, mix flour with salt, pepper, pork neck, and toss. Heat a pan with 2 tsp. oil over medium-high heat, add pork, and cook for 3 minutes on each side.
2. Transfer pork to a slow cooker and leave aside. Heat the remaining oil in the same pan over medium heat, add eggplant, onion, bell pepper, thyme, sage, and garlic, stir and cook for 5 minutes.
3. Add reserved flour, stir and cook for 1 more minute. Add to pork, then add beans, stock, tomato paste, and zucchinis. Cover and cook on high for 4 hours. Uncover, transfer to plates and serve.

NUTRITIONS

- Calories: 310
- Carbohydrates: 21 g
- Fat: 31 g

- Protein: 23 g

135. Pork With Couscous

10 MIN

COOKING TIME

7 HOURS

SERVINGS

6

NUTRITIONS

- Calories: 320
- Carbohydrates: 21 g
- Fat: 31 g

INGREDIENTS

- 2 1/2 lb. pork loin boneless and trimmed
- 3/4 cup chicken stock
- 2 tbsp. olive oil
- 1/2 tbsp. sweet paprika
- 2 1/4 tsp. sage, dried
- 1/2 tbsp. garlic powder
- 1/4 tsp. rosemary, dried
- 1/4 tsp. marjoram, dried
- 1 tsp. basil, dried
- 1 tsp. oregano, dried
- Salt and black pepper to taste
- 2 cups couscous, cooked
- 1 tsp Thyme

- Protein: 23 g

DIRECTIONS

1. In a bowl, mix oil with stock, paprika, garlic powder, sage, rosemary, thyme, marjoram, oregano, salt, and pepper to taste and whisk well. Put pork loin in your crockpot.
2. Add stock and spice mix, stir, cover, and cook on Low for 7 hours. Slice pork return to pot and toss with cooking juices. Divide between plates and serve with couscous on the side.

136. Grilled Steak, Mushroom, and Onion Kebabs

PREPARATION TIME

10 MIN

COOKING TIME

10 MIN

SERVINGS

2

NUTRITIONS

- Calories: 410
- Carbohydrates: 12 g
- Fat: 14 g

INGREDIENTS

- 1 lb. boneless top sirloin steak
- 8 oz. White button mushrooms
- 1 medium red onion
- 4 peeled garlic cloves
- 2 rosemary sprigs
- 2 tbsp. Extra-virgin olive oil
- 1/4 tsp. black pepper
- 2 tbsp. Red wine vinegar
- 1/4 tsp. sea salt
- Cooking spray

- Protein: 36 g

DIRECTIONS

1. Soak 12 (10-inch) wooden skewers in water. Spray the cold grill with nonstick cooking spray, and heat the grill to medium-high.
2. Cut a piece of aluminum foil into a 10-inch square. Place the garlic and rosemary sprigs in the center, drizzle with 1 tbsp. oil, and wrap tightly to form a foil packet.
3. Arrange it on the grill, and seal the grill cover.
4. Cut the steak into 1-inch cubes. Thread the beef onto the wet skewers, alternating with whole mushrooms and onion wedges. Spray the kebabs thoroughly with nonstick cooking spray, and sprinkle with pepper.
5. Cook the kebabs on the covered grill for 5 minutes.
6. Flip and grill for 5 more minutes while covered.
7. Unwrap foil packets with garlic and rosemary sprigs and put them into a small bowl.
8. Carefully strip the rosemary sprigs of their leaves into the bowl and pour in any accumulated juices and oil from the foil packet.
9. Mix in the remaining 1 tbsp. of oil and the vinegar and salt.
10. Mash the garlic with a fork, and mix all ingredients in the bowl together. Pour over the finished steak kebabs and serve.

137. Kale Sprouts & Lamb

PREPARATION TIME

10 MIN

COOKING TIME

30 MIN

SERVINGS

2

INGREDIENTS

- 2 lbs. lamb, cut into chunks
- 1 tbsp. parsley, chopped
- 2 tbsp. olive oil
- 1 cup kale, chopped
- 1 cup Brussels sprouts, halved
- 1 cup beef stock
- Pepper
- Salt

DIRECTIONS

1. Add all ingredients into the inner pot of the instant pot and stir well.
2. Seal pot with lid and cook on high for 30 minutes.
3. Once done, allow to release pressure naturally. Remove lid.
4. Serve and enjoy.

NUTRITIONS

- Calories: 504
- Carbohydrates: 3.9 g
- Fat: 23.8 g

- Sugar: 0.5 g
- Protein: 65.7 g
- Cholesterol 204 mg

138. Shrimp With Garlic and Mushrooms

PREPARATION TIME

15 MIN

COOKING TIME

15 MIN

SERVINGS

4

INGREDIENTS

- 1 lb. (454 g.) peeled and deveined fresh shrimp
- 1 tsp. salt
- 1 cup extra-virgin olive oil
- 8 large garlic cloves, thinly sliced
- 4 oz. (113 g.) sliced mushrooms (shiitake, baby Bella, or button)
- 1/2 tsp. red pepper flakes
- 1/4 cup chopped fresh flat-leaf Italian parsley
- Zucchini noodles or riced cauliflower, for serving

DIRECTIONS

1. Rinse the shrimp and pat dry. Place in a small bowl and sprinkle with salt. In a large rimmed, thick skillet, heat the olive oil over medium-low heat.
2. Add the garlic and heat until very fragrant, 3 to 4 minutes, reducing the heat if the garlic starts to burn.
3. Add the mushrooms and sauté for 5 minutes, until softened. Add the shrimp and red pepper flakes and sauté until the shrimp begins to turn pink for another 3 to 4 minutes.
4. Remove from the heat and stir in the parsley. Serve over zucchini noodles or riced cauliflower.

NUTRITIONS

- Calories: 620
- Carbohydrates: 4 g
- Fat: 56 g

- Protein: 24 g

139. Pistachio-Crusted Whitefish

PREPARATION TIME

10 MIN

COOKING TIME.

20 MIN

SERVINGS

2

INGREDIENTS

- 1/4 cup shelled pistachios
- 1 tbsp. fresh parsley
- 1 tbsp. grated Parmesan cheese
- 1 tbsp. panko bread crumbs
- 2 tbsp. olive oil
- 1/4 tsp. salt
- 10 oz. skinless whitefish (1 large piece or 2 smaller ones)

DIRECTIONS

1. Preheat the oven to 350°F and set the rack to the middle position. Line a sheet pan with foil or parchment paper.
2. Combine all of the ingredients except the fish in a mini food processor, and pulse until the nuts are finely ground.
3. Alternatively, you can mince the nuts with a chef's knife and combine the ingredients by hand in a small bowl.
4. Place the fish on the sheet pan. Spread the nut mixture evenly over the fish and pat it down lightly.
5. Bake the fish for 20 to 30 minutes, depending on the thickness, until it flakes easily with a fork.
6. Keep in mind that a thicker cut of fish takes a bit longer to bake. You'll know it's done when it's opaque, flakes apart easily with a fork, or reaches an internal temperature of 145°F

NUTRITIONS

- Calories: 185
- Carbohydrates : 23.8 g
- Fat: 5.2 g

- Protein: 10.1 g

140. Crispy Homemade Fish Sticks Recipe

PREPARATION TIME

10 MIN

COOKING TIME

15 MIN

SERVINGS

2

INGREDIENTS

- 1 beaten egg
- 1 1/2 cup of flour
- 1/2 cup of parmesan cheese
- 1/2 cup of bread crumbs.
- Zest of 1 lemon juice
- Parsley
- Salt
- 1 tsp. black pepper
- 1 tbsp. sweet paprika
- 1 tsp. oregano
- 1 1/2 lb. salmon
- Extra virgin olive oil

DIRECTIONS

1. Preheat your oven to about 450°F. Get a bowl, dry your salmon, and season its two sides with the salt.
2. Then chop into small sizes of 1 1/2 inch length each. Get a bowl and mix black pepper with oregano.
3. Add paprika to the mixture and blend it. Then spice the fish stick with the mixture you have just made. Get another dish and pour your flour.
4. You will need a different bowl again to pour your egg wash into. Pick yet the fourth dish, mix your breadcrumb with your parmesan and add lemon zest to the mixture.
5. Return to the fish sticks and dip each fish into flour such that both sides are coated with flour. As you dip each fish into flour, take it out and dip it into the egg wash and lastly, dip it in the breadcrumb mixture.
6. Do this for all fish sticks and arrange them on a baking sheet. Ensure you oil the baking sheet before arranging the stick thereon and drizzle the top of the fish sticks with extra virgin olive oil.
7. Caution: allow excess flours to fall off a fish before dipping it into other ingredients.
8. Also, ensure that you do not let the coating peel while you add extra virgin olive oil on top of the fishes.
9. Fix the baking sheet in the middle of the oven and allow it to cook for 13 min. By then, the fishes should be golden brown and you can collect them from the oven, and you can serve them immediately.
10. Top it with your lemon zest, parsley, and fresh lemon juice.

- Sodium: 293.1 mg
- Protein: 13.5 g

NUTRITIONS

- Calories: 119
- Carbohydrates: 9.3 g
- Fat: 3.4 g

141. Sauced Shellfish in White Wine

10 MIN

10 MIN

2

INGREDIENTS

- 2 lb. fresh cuttlefish
- 1/2 cup olive oil
- 1 piece large onion, finely chopped
- 1 cup of Robola white wine
- 1/4 cup lukewarm water
- 1 piece bay leaf
- 1/2 bunch parsley, chopped
- 4 pieces tomatoes, grated
- Salt and pepper

DIRECTIONS

1. Take out the hard centerpiece of cartilage (cuttlebone), the bag of ink, and the intestines from the cuttlefish.
2. Wash the cleaned cuttlefish with running water. Slice it into small pieces, and drain excess water.
3. Heat the oil in a saucepan placed over medium-high heat and sauté the onion for 3 minutes until tender.
4. Add the sliced cuttlefish and pour in the white wine. Cook for 5 minutes until it simmers.
5. Pour in the water, and add the tomatoes, bay leaf, parsley, tomatoes, salt, and pepper. Simmer the mixture over low heat until the cuttlefish slices are tender and left with their thick sauce. Serve them warm with rice.
6. Be careful not to overcook the cuttlefish as its texture becomes very hard. A safe rule of thumb is grilling the cuttlefish over a raging fire for 3 minutes before using it in any recipe.

NUTRITIONS

- Calories: 308
- Carbohydrates: 8 g
- Fats: 18.1 g

- Fiber: 1.5 g
- Protein: 25.6 g

142. Pistachio Sole Fish

5 MIN

10 MIN

2

INGREDIENTS

- 4 (5 oz.) boneless sole fillets
- 1/2 cup pistachios, finely chopped
- Juice of 1 lemon
- 1 tsp. extra virgin olive oil
- Salt and pepper to taste

DIRECTIONS

1. Preheat your oven to 350°F
2. Wrap baking sheet using parchment paper and keep it on the side
3. Pat fish dry with kitchen towels and lightly season with salt and pepper
4. Take a small bowl and stir in pistachios
5. Place sol on the prepped sheet and press 2 tbsp. pistachio mixture on top of each fillet
6. Rub the fish with lemon juice and olive oil
7. Bake for 10 minutes until the top is golden and fish flakes with a fork

NUTRITIONS

- Calories: 166
- Carbohydrates: 2 g
- Fat: 6 g

- Protein 32 g

143. Speedy Tilapia With Red Onion and Avocado

10 MIN

COOKING TIME

5 MIN

SERVINGS

2

INGREDIENTS

- 1 tbsp. extra-virgin olive oil
- 1 tbsp. freshly squeezed orange juice
- 1/4 tsp. kosher or sea salt
- 4 (4-oz.) tilapia fillets, more oblong than square, skin-on or skinned
- 1/4 cup chopped red onion (about 1/8 onion)
- 1 avocado, pitted, skinned, and sliced

DIRECTIONS

1. In a 9-inch glass pie dish, use a fork to mix together the oil, orange juice, and salt. Working with one fillet at a time, place each in the pie dish and turn to coat on all sides.
2. Arrange the fillets in a wagon-wheel formation, so that one end of each fillet is in the center of the dish and the other end is temporarily draped over the edge of the dish.
3. Top each fillet with 1 tbsp. onion, then fold the end of the fillet that's hanging over the edge in half over the onion.
4. When finished, you should have 4 folded-over fillets with the fold against the outer edge of the dish and the ends all in the center.
5. Cover the dish with plastic wrap, leaving a small part open at the edge to vent the steam. Microwave on high for about 3 minutes.
6. The fish is done when it just begins to separate into flakes (chunks) when pressed gently with a fork. Top the fillets with the avocado and serve.

NUTRITIONS

- Calories: 155
- Carbohydrates: 4 g
- Fiber: 3 g

- Protein: 22 g

144. Steamed Mussels in White Wine Sauce

PREPARATION TIME

5 MIN

COOKING TIME

10 MIN

SERVINGS

2

INGREDIENTS

- 2 lb. small mussels
- 1 tbsp. extra-virgin olive oil
- 1 cup thinly sliced red onion
- 3 garlic cloves, sliced
- 1 cup dry white wine
- 2 (1/4-inch-thick) lemon slices
- 1/4 tsp. freshly ground black pepper
- 1/4 tsp. kosher or sea salt
- Fresh lemon wedges, for serving (optional)

DIRECTIONS

1. In a large colander in the sink, run cold water over the mussels (but don't let the mussels sit in standing water).
2. All the shells should be closed tight; discard any shells that are a little bit open or any shells that are cracked. Leave the mussels in the colander until you're ready to use them.
3. In a large skillet over medium-high heat, heat the oil. Add the onion and cook for 4 minutes, stirring occasionally.
4. Add the garlic and cook for 1 minute, stirring constantly. Add the wine, lemon slices, pepper, and salt, and bring to a simmer. Cook for 2 minutes.
5. Add the mussels and cover. Cook for 3 minutes, or until the mussels open their shells. Gently shake the pan two or three times while they are cooking.
6. All the shells should now be wide open. Using a slotted spoon, discard any mussels that are still closed. Spoon the opened mussels into a shallow serving bowl, and pour the broth over the top. Serve with additional fresh lemon slices, if desired.

NUTRITIONS

- Calories: 22
- Fat: 7 g
- Fiber: 1 g

- Protein 18 g
- Carbohydrates: 10 g

145. Orange and Garlic Shrimp

20 MIN

10 MIN

2

INGREDIENTS

- 1 large orange
- 3 tbsp. extra-virgin olive oil, divided
- 1 tbsp. chopped fresh Rosemary
- 1 tbsp. chopped fresh thyme
- 3 garlic cloves, minced (about 11/2 tsp.)
- 1/4 tsp. freshly ground black pepper
- 1/4 tsp. kosher or sea salt
- 1 1/2 lb. fresh raw shrimp, shells, and tails removed

DIRECTIONS

1. Zest the entire orange using a citrus grater. In a large zip-top plastic bag, combine the orange zest and 2 tbsp. oil with the Rosemary, thyme, garlic, pepper, and salt.
2. Add the shrimp, seal the bag, and gently massage the shrimp until all the ingredients are combined and the shrimp is completely covered with the seasonings. Set aside.
3. Heat a grill, grill pan, or a large skillet over medium heat. Brush on or swirl in the remaining 1 tbsp. of oil.
4. Add half the shrimp, and cook for 4 to 6 minutes, or until the shrimp turn pink and white, flipping halfway through if on the grill or stirring every minute if in a pan. Transfer the shrimp to a large serving bowl.
5. Repeat with the remaining shrimp, and add them to the bowl.
6. While the shrimp cook, peel the orange and cut the flesh into bite-size pieces. Add to the serving bowl, and toss with the cooked shrimp. Serve immediately or refrigerate and serve cold.

NUTRITIONS

- Calories: 190
- Fat: 8 g
- Fiber: 1 g
- Protein: 24 g

146. Roasted Shrimp-Gnocchi Bake

10 MIN

20 MIN

2

INGREDIENTS

- 1 cup chopped fresh tomato
- 2 tbsp. extra-virgin olive oil
- 2 garlic cloves, minced
- 1/2 tsp. freshly ground black pepper
- 1/4 tsp. crushed red pepper
- 1 (12 oz.) jar roasted red peppers
- 1 lb. fresh raw shrimp, shells, and tails removed
- 1 lb. frozen gnocchi (not thawed)
- 1/2 cup cubed feta cheese
- 1/3 cup fresh torn basil leaves

DIRECTIONS

1. Preheat the oven to 425°F. In a baking dish, mix the tomatoes, oil, garlic, black pepper, and crushed red pepper. Roast in the oven for 10 minutes.
2. Stir in the roasted peppers and shrimp. Roast for 10 more minutes, until the shrimp turn pink and white.
3. While the shrimp cooks, cook the gnocchi on the stovetop according to the package directions.
4. Drain in a colander and keep warm. Remove the dish from the oven. Mix in the cooked gnocchi, feta, and basil, and serve.

NUTRITIONS

- Calories: 227
- Fat: 7 g
- Fiber: 1 g
- Protein: 20 g

147. Tuna Sandwich

INGREDIENTS

- 2 slices whole-grain bread
- 16 oz. can low sodium tuna in water, in its juice
- 2 tsp. yogurt (1.5% fat) or low-fat mayonnaise
- 1 medium tomato, diced
- 1/2 small sweet onion, finely diced
- Lettuce leaves

DIRECTIONS

1. Toast whole grain bread slices. Mix tuna, yogurt, or mayonnaise, diced tomato, and onion. Cover a toasted bread with lettuce leaves and spread the tuna mixture on the sandwich. Spread tuna mixed on toasted bread with lettuce leaves. Place another disc as a cover on top. Enjoy the sandwich.

NUTRITIONS

- Calories: 235
- Carbohydrate: 25.9 g
- Fat: 3 g
- Protein: 27.8 g
- Sodium: 350 mg

148. Fruited Quinoa Salad

INGREDIENTS

- 2 cups cooked quinoa
- 1 mango, sliced and peeled
- 1 cup strawberry, quartered
- 1/2 cup blueberries
- 2 tbsp. pine nuts
- Chopped mint leave for garnish
- Lemon vinaigrette:
- 1/4 cup olive oil
- 1/4 cup apple cider vinegar
- Zest of lemon
- 3 tbsp. lemon juice
- 1 tsp. sugar

DIRECTIONS

1. For the Lemon Vinaigrette, whisk olive oil, apple cider vinegar, lemon zest and juice, and sugar to a bowl; set aside. Combine quinoa, mango, strawberries, blueberries, and pine nuts in a large bowl. Stir the lemon vinaigrette and garnish with mint. Serve and enjoy!

NUTRITIONS

- Calories: 425
- Carbohydrates: 76.1 g
- Proteins: 11.3 g
- Fat: 10.9 g
- Sodium: 16 mg

149. Turkey Wrap

PREPARATION TIME

15 MIN

COOKING TIME

0 MIN

SERVINGS

2

INGREDIENTS

- 2 slices of low-fat Turkey breast (deli-style)
- 4 tbsp. non-fat cream cheese
- 1/2 cup lettuce leaves
- 1/2 cup carrots, slice into a stick
- 2 Homemade wraps or store-bought whole-wheat tortilla wrap

DIRECTIONS

1. Prepare all the ingredients. Spread 2 tbsp. of non-fat cream cheese on each wrap. Arrange lettuce leaves, then add a slice of turkey breast; a slice of carrots stick on top. Roll and cut into half. Serve and enjoy!

NUTRITIONS

- Calories: 224
- Carbohydrates: 35 g
- Fat: 3.8 g

- Sodium: 293 mg
- Protein: 10.3 g

150. Chicken Wrap

PREPARATION TIME

15 MIN

COOKING TIME

15 MIN

SERVINGS

2

INGREDIENTS

- 1 tbsp. extra-virgin olive oil
- Lemon juice, divided into 3 parts
- 2 cloves garlic, minced
- 1 lb. boneless skinless chicken breasts
- 1/2 cup non-fat plain Greek yogurt
- 1/2 tsp. paprika
- A pinch of salt and pepper
- Hot sauce to taste
- Pita bread
- Tomato slice
- Lettuce

DIRECTIONS

1. For the marinade, whisk 1 tbsp. olive oil, juice of 2 lemons, garlic, salt, and pepper in a bowl. Add chicken breasts to the marinade and place them into a large Ziploc. Let marinate for 30 minutes to 4 hours.
2. For the yogurt sauce, mix yogurt, hot sauce, and the remaining lemon juice season with paprika and a pinch of salt and pepper.
3. Warm skillet over medium heat and coat it with oil. Add chicken breast and cook until golden brown and cook about 8 minutes per side. Remove from pan and rest for few minutes, then slice.
4. To a piece of pita bread, add lettuce, tomato, and chicken slices. Drizzle with the prepared spicy yogurt sauce. Serve and enjoy!

NUTRITIONS

- Calories: 348
- Carbohydrates: 8.7 g
- Proteins: 56 g

- Fat 10.2 g
- Sodium: 198 mg

151. Veggie Wrap

15 MIN

COOKING TIME

0 MIN

SERVINGS

2

INGREDIENTS

- 2 Homemade wraps or any flour tortillas
- 1/2 cup spinach
- 1/2 cup alfalfa sprouts
- 1/2 cup avocado, sliced thinly
- 1 medium tomato, sliced thinly
- 1/2 cup cucumber, sliced thinly
- A pinch of salt and pepper
- 2 tbsp. of cream cheese

DIRECTIONS

1. Put 2 tbsp. of cream cheese on each tortilla. Layer each veggie according to your liking. A pinch of salt and pepper. Roll and cut into half. Serve and Enjoy!

NUTRITIONS

- Calories: 249
- Carbohydrates: 12.3 g
- Fat: 21.5 g

- Sodium: 169 mg
- Protein: 5.7 g

152. Salmon Wrap

PREPARATION TIME

15 MIN

COOKING TIME

0 MIN

SERVINGS

1

INGREDIENTS

- 2 oz. Smoke Salmon
- 2 tsp. low-fat cream cheese
- 1/2 medium-size red onion, finely sliced
- 1/2 tsp. fresh basil or dried basil
- A pinch of pepper
- Arugula leaves
- 1 Homemade wrap or any whole-meal tortilla

DIRECTIONS

1. Warm wraps or tortillas into a heated pan or oven. Combine cream cheese, basil, pepper, and spread into the tortilla. Top with salmon, arugula, and sliced onion. Roll up and slice. Serve and Enjoy!

NUTRITIONS

- Calories: 151
- Carbohydrates: 19.2 g
- Fat: 3.4 g

- Sodium: 316 mg
- Protein: 10.4 g

153. Dill Chicken Salad

15 MIN

COOKING TIME

15 MIN

SERVINGS

3

INGREDIENTS

- 1 tbsp. unsalted butter
- 1 small onion, diced
- 2 cloves garlic, minced
- 500 g. boneless skinless chicken breasts

Salad:
- 2/3 cup Fat-free yogurt
- 1/4 cup mayonnaise light
- 2 large shallots, minced
- 1/2 cup fresh dill, finely chopped

DIRECTIONS

1. Dissolve the butter over medium heat in a wide pan. Sauté onion and garlic in the butter and chicken breasts. Put water to cover the chicken breasts by 1 inch. Bring to boil. Cover and reduce the heat to a bare simmer.
2. Cook for 8 to 10 minutes or until the chicken is cooked through. Cool thoroughly. The shred chicken finally using 2 forks. Set aside. Whisk yogurt and mayonnaise. Then toss with the chicken. Add shallots and dill. Mix again all. Serve and Enjoy!

NUTRITIONS

- Calories: 253
- Carbohydrates: 9 g
- Fat: 9.5 g

- Sodium: 236 mg
- Protein: 33.1 g

Chapter 6
Poultry

154. Parmesan and Chicken Spaghetti Squash

15 MIN

COOKING TIME

20 MIN

SERVINGS

6

INGREDIENTS

- 16 oz. mozzarella
- 1 cup Parmesan
- 1 spaghetti squash piece
- 1 lb. cooked cube chicken
- 1 cup marinara sauce

DIRECTIONS

1. Split up the squash in halves and remove the seeds. Arrange or put one cup of water in your pot, then put a trivet on top.
2. Add the squash halves to the trivet. Cook for 20 minutes at high pressure. Remove the squashes and shred them using a fork into spaghetti portions
3. Pour sauce over the squash and give it a nice mix. Top them up with the cubed-up chicken and top with mozzarella and parmesan . Broil for 1-2 minutes and broil until the cheese has melted

NUTRITIONS

- Calories: 237
- Carbohydrates:32 g
- Fat:10 g

- Protein:11 g
- Sodium: 500 mg

155. Apricot Chicken

PREPARATION TIME

15 MIN

COOKING TIME

6 MIN

SERVINGS

4

INGREDIENTS

- 1 bottle creamy French dressing
- 1/4 cup flavorless oil
- White cooked rice
- 1 large jar Apricot preserve
- 4 lb. boneless and skinless chicken
- 1 package onion soup mix

DIRECTIONS

1. Rinse and pat dry the chicken. Dice into bite-size pieces. In a large bowl, mix the apricot preserve, creamy dressing, and onion soup mix. Stir until thoroughly combined. Place the chicken in the bowl. Mix until coated.
2. In a large skillet, heat the oil. Place the chicken in the oil gently. Cook 4 to 6 minutes on each side, until golden brown. Serve over rice.

NUTRITIONS

- Calories: 202
- Carbohydrates:75 g
- Fat:12 g

- Protein:20 g
- Sugars:10 g
- Sodium: 630 mg

156. Oven-Fried Chicken Breasts

15 MIN

COOKING TIME

30 MIN

SERVINGS

8

INGREDIENTS

- 1/2 pack Ritz crackers
- 1 cup plain non-fat yogurt
- 8 boneless, skinless, and halved chicken breasts

DIRECTIONS

1. Preheat the oven to 350°F. Rinse and pat dry the chicken breasts. Pour the yogurt into a shallow bowl. Dip the chicken pieces in the yogurt, then roll in the cracker crumbs. Place the chicken in a single layer in a baking dish. Bake for 15 minutes per side. Serve.

NUTRITIONS

- Calories: 200
- Carbohydrates:98 g
- Fat:13 g

- Protein:19 g
- Sodium:217 mg

157 Rosemary Roasted Chicken

PREPARATION TIME

15 MIN

COOKING TIME

20 MIN

SERVINGS

8

INGREDIENTS

- 8 rosemary springs
- 1 minced garlic clove
- Black pepper
- 1 tbsp. chopped rosemary
- 1 chicken
- 1 tbsp. organic olive oil

DIRECTIONS

1. In a bowl, mix garlic with rosemary, rub the chicken with black pepper, the oil, and rosemary mix, place it inside roasting pan, introduce inside the oven at 350°F, and roast for sixty minutes and 20 min. Carve chicken, divide between plates and serve using a side dish. Enjoy!

NUTRITIONS

- Calories: 325
- Carbohydrates:15 g
- Fat:5 g

- Protein:14 g
- Sodium: 950 mg

158. Artichoke and Spinach Chicken

PREPARATION TIME

15 MIN

COOKING TIME

5 MIN

SERVINGS

4

INGREDIENTS

- 10 oz. baby spinach
- 1/2 tsp. crushed red pepper flakes
- 14 oz. chopped artichoke hearts
- 28 oz. no-salt-added tomato sauce
- 2 tbsps. Essential olive oil
- 4 boneless and skinless chicken breasts

DIRECTIONS

1. Heat up a pan with the oil over medium-high heat, add chicken and red pepper flakes and cook for 5 minutes on them. Add spinach, artichokes, and tomato sauce, toss, cook for ten minutes more, divide between plates and serve. Enjoy!

NUTRITIONS

- Calories: 212
- Carbohydrates:16 g
- Fat:3 g

- Protein:20 g
- Sugar:5 g
- Sodium:418 mg

159. Pumpkin and Black Beans Chicken

PREPARATION TIME

15 MIN

COOKING TIME

25 MIN

SERVINGS

4

INGREDIENTS

- 1 tbsp. essential olive oil
- 1 tbsp. Chopped cilantro
- 1 cup coconut milk
- 15 oz canned black beans, drained
- 1 lb. skinless and boneless chicken breasts
- 2 cups of water
- 1/2 cup pumpkin flesh

DIRECTIONS

1. Heat a pan when using oil over medium-high heat, add the chicken and cook for 5 minutes. Add the water, milk, pumpkin, and black beans toss, cover the pan, reduce heat to medium and cook for 20 minutes. Add cilantro, toss, divide between plates and serve. Enjoy!

NUTRITIONS

- Calories: 254
- Carbohydrates:16 g
- Fat:6 g

- Protein:22 g
- Sodium:92 mg

160. Chicken Thighs and Apples Mix

PREPARATION TIME

15 MIN

COOKING TIME

60 MIN

SERVINGS

4

INGREDIENTS

- 3 cored and sliced apples
- 1 tbsp. apple cider vinegar treatment
- 3/4 cup natural apple juice
- 1/4 tsp. pepper and salt
- 1 tbsp. grated ginger
- 8 chicken thighs
- 3 tbsp. Chopped onion

DIRECTIONS

1. In a bowl, mix chicken with salt, pepper, vinegar, onion, ginger, and apple juice, toss well, cover, keep for the fridge for ten minutes, transfer with a baking dish, and include apples. Introduce inside the oven at 400°F for just 1 hour. Divide between plates and serve. Enjoy!

NUTRITIONS

- Calories: 214
- Carbohydrates:14 g
- Fat:3 g

- Protein:15 g
- Sodium:405 mg

161. Thai Chicken Thighs

PREPARATION TIME

15 MIN

COOKING TIME

1H 5 MIN

SERVINGS

6

INGREDIENTS

- 1/2 cup Thai chili sauce
- 1 chopped green onions bunch
- 4 lb. chicken thighs

DIRECTIONS

1. Heat a pan over medium-high heat. Add chicken thighs, brown them for 5 minutes on both sides Transfer to some baking dish, then add chili sauce and green onions and toss.
2. Introduce into the oven and bake at 400°F for 60 minutes. Divide everything between plates and serve. Enjoy!

NUTRITIONS

- Calories: 220
- Carbohydrates:12 g
- Fat:4 g

- Protein:10 g
- Sodium: 870 mg

162. Falling "Off" The Bone Chicken

PREPARATION TIME

15 MIN

COOKING TIME

40 MIN

SERVINGS

4

INGREDIENTS

- 6 peeled garlic cloves
- 1 tbsp. organic extra virgin coconut oil
- 2 tbsp. Lemon juice
- 1 1/2 cup pacific organic bone chicken broth
- 1/4 tsp. freshly ground black pepper
- 1/2 tsp. sea flavored vinegar
- 1 whole organic chicken piece
- 1 tsp. paprika
- 1 tsp. dried thyme

DIRECTIONS

1. Take a small bowl and toss in the thyme, paprika, pepper, and flavored vinegar and mix them. Use the mixture to season the chicken properly. Pour down the oil in your instant pot and heat it to shimmering; toss in the chicken with breast downward and let it cook for about 6–7 minutes
2. After 7 minutes, flip over the chicken pour down the broth, garlic cloves, and lemon juice. Cook for 25 minutes on a high setting. Remove the dish from the cooker and let it stand for about 5 minutes before serving.

NUTRITIONS

- Calories: 664
- Carbohydrates:44 g
- Fat:44 g

- Protein:27 g
- Sugars:0.1 g
- Sodium:800 mg

163. Feisty Chicken Porridge

PREPARATION TIME

15 MIN

COOKING TIME

30 MIN

SERVINGS

4

INGREDIENTS

- 1 1/2 cup fresh ginger
- 1 lb. cooked chicken legs
- Green onions
- Toasted cashew nuts
- 5 cups chicken broth
- 1 cup jasmine rice
- 4 cups water

DIRECTIONS

1. Place the rice in your fridge and allow it to chill 1 hour before cooking. Take the rice out and add them to your Instant Pot. Pour broth and water. Lock up the lid and cook on Porridge mode.
2. Separate the meat from the chicken legs and add the meat to your soup. Stir well over sauté mode. Season with a bit of fresh ginger and enjoy with a garnish of nuts and onion

NUTRITIONS

- Calories: 206
- Carbohydrates:8 g
- Fat:8 g

- Protein:23 g
- Sugars:0 g
- Sodium:950 mg

164. The Ultimate Faux-Tisserie Chicken

15 MIN

35 MIN

5

- 2 tbsp. Olive oil
- 1/2 quartered medium onion
- 2 tbsp. Favorite seasoning
- 2 1/2 lbs. whole chicken
- Black pepper
- 5 large fresh garlic cloves

1. Massage the chicken with 1 tbsp. of olive oil and sprinkle pepper on top. Place onion wedges and garlic cloves inside the chicken. Take a butcher's twin and secure the legs
2. Set your pot to Sauté mode. Put olive oil in your pan on medium heat, allow the oil to heat up. Add chicken and sear on both sides for 4 minutes per side. Sprinkle your seasoning over the chicken, remove the chicken and place a trivet at the bottom of your pot
3. Sprinkle seasoning over the chicken, making sure to rub it. Transfer the chicken to the trivet with the breast side facing up, lock up the lid. Cook on high pressure for 25 minutes. Allow it to rest and serve!

- Calories: 1010
- Carbohydrates:47 g
- Fat:64 g

- Protein:60 g
- Sodium:209 mg

165. Oregano Chicken Thighs

15 MIN

20 MIN

6

- 12 chicken thighs
- 1 tsp. dried parsley
- 1/4 tsp. pepper and salt.
- 1/2 cup extra virgin essential olive oil
- 4 minced garlic cloves
- 1 cup chopped oregano
- 1/4 cup low-sodium veggie stock

1. In your food processor, mix parsley with oregano, garlic, salt, pepper, and stock and oil. Put chicken thighs into the bowl, add oregano paste, toss, cover, and then leave aside in the fridge for 10 minutes.
2. Heat the kitchen grill over medium heat, add chicken pieces, close the lid and cook for twenty or so minutes with them. Divide between plates and serve!

- Calories: 254
- Carbohydrates:7 g
- Fat:3 g

- Protein:17 g
- Sugars:0.9 g
- Sodium:730 mg

166. Pesto Chicken Breasts With Summer Squash

15 MIN

COOKING TIME

10 MIN

SERVINGS

4

INGREDIENTS

- 4 medium boneless, skinless chicken breast halves
- 1 tbsp. olive oil
- 2 tbsp. Homemade pesto
- 2 cups finely chopped zucchini
- 2 tbsp. Finely shredded Asiago

DIRECTIONS

1. Cook your chicken in hot oil on medium heat for 4 minutes in a large nonstick skillet. Flip the chicken then put the zucchini.
2. Cook for 4 to 6 minutes more or until the chicken is tender and no longer pink (170°F), and squash is crisp-tender, stirring squash gently once or twice. Transfer chicken and squash to 4 dinner plates. Spread pesto over chicken; sprinkle with Asiago.

NUTRITIONS

- Calories: 230
- Carbohydrates:8 g
- Fat:9 g

- Protein:30 g
- Sodium:578 mg

167. Chicken, Tomato and Green Beans

PREPARATION TIME

15 MIN

COOKING TIME

25 MIN

SERVINGS

4

INGREDIENTS

- 6 oz. low-sodium canned tomato paste
- 2 tbsp. olive oil
- 1/4 tsp. black pepper
- 2 lb. trimmed green beans
- 2 tbsp. Chopped parsley
- 1 1/2 lb. boneless, skinless, and cubed chicken breasts
- 25 oz. no-salt-added canned tomato sauce

DIRECTIONS

1. Heat a pan with 50% of the oil over medium heat, add chicken, stir, cover, cook for 5 minutes on both sides and transfer to a bowl. Heat inside the same pan while using rest through the oil over medium heat, add green beans, stir and cook for 10 minutes.
2. Return chicken for that pan, add black pepper, tomato sauce, tomato paste, and parsley, stir, cover, cook for 10 minutes more, divide between plates and serve. Enjoy!

NUTRITIONS

- Calories: 190
- Carbohydrates:12 g
- Fat:4 g

- Protein:9 g
- Sodium:168 mg

168. Chicken Tortillas

15 MIN

COOKING TIME

5 MIN

SERVINGS

4

INGREDIENTS

- 6 oz. boneless, skinless, and cooked chicken breasts
- Black pepper
- 1/3 cup fat-free yogurt
- 4 heated up whole-wheat tortillas
- 2 chopped tomatoes

DIRECTIONS

1. Heat up a pan over medium heat, add one tortilla during those times, heat up, and hang them on the working surface. Spread yogurt on each tortilla, add chicken and tomatoes, roll, and black pepper divide between plates, and serve. Enjoy!

NUTRITIONS

- Calories:190
- Carbohydrates:12 g
- Fat:2 g

- Protein:6 g
- Sodium:300 mg

169. Chicken With Potatoes Olives & Sprouts

PREPARATION TIME

15 MIN

COOKING TIME

35 MIN

SERVINGS

4

INGREDIENTS

- 1 lb. chicken breasts, skinless, boneless, and cut into pieces
- 1/4 cup olives, quartered
- 1 tsp. oregano
- 1 1/2 tsp. Dijon mustard
- 1 lemon juice
- 1/3 cup vinaigrette dressing
- 1 medium onion, diced
- 3 cups potatoes cut into pieces
- 4 cups Brussels sprouts, trimmed and quartered
- 1/4 tsp. pepper
- 1/4 tsp. salt

DIRECTIONS

1. Warm-up oven to 400°F. Place chicken in the center of the baking tray, then place potatoes, sprouts, and onions around the chicken.
2. In a small bowl, mix vinaigrette, oregano, mustard, lemon juice, and salt and pour over chicken and veggies. Sprinkle olives and season with pepper.
3. Bake in preheated oven for 20 minutes. Transfer chicken to a plate. Stir the vegetables and roast for 15 minutes more. Serve and enjoy.

NUTRITIONS

- Calories: 397
- Carbohydrates: 31.4 g
- Fat: 13 g

- Protein: 38.3 g
- Sodium: 175 mg

170. Garlic Mushroom Chicken

15 MIN

15 MIN

4

INGREDIENTS

- 4 chicken breasts, boneless and skinless
- 3 garlic cloves, minced
- 1 onion, chopped
- 2 cups mushrooms, sliced
- 1 tbsp. olive oil
- 1/2 cup chicken stock
- 1/4 tsp. pepper
- 1/2 tsp. salt

DIRECTIONS

1. Season chicken with pepper and salt. Warm oil in a pan on medium heat, then put season chicken in the pan and cook for 5 to 6 minutes on each side. Remove and place on a plate.
2. Add onion and mushrooms to the pan and sauté until tender, about 2–3 minutes. Add garlic and sauté for a minute. Add stock and bring to boil. Stir well and cook for 1–2 minutes. Pour over chicken and serve.

NUTRITIONS

- Calories: 331
- Carbohydrates: 4.6g
- Fat: 14.5g

- Protein: 43.9g
- Sodium 420 mg

171. Grilled Chicken

15 MIN

15 MIN

4

INGREDIENTS

- 4 chicken breasts, skinless and boneless
- 1 1/2 tsp. dried oregano
- 1 tsp. paprika
- 5 garlic cloves, minced
- 1/2 cup fresh parsley, minced
- 1/2 cup olive oil
- 1/2 cup fresh lemon juice
- Pepper
- Salt

DIRECTIONS

1. Add lemon juice, oregano, paprika, garlic, parsley, and olive oil to a large zip-lock bag. Season chicken with pepper and salt and add to bag. Seal bag and shake well to coat chicken with marinade. Let sit chicken in the marinade for 20 minutes.
2. Remove chicken from marinade and grill over medium-high heat for 5-6 minutes on each side. Serve and enjoy.

NUTRITIONS

- Calories: 512
- Fat: 36.5 g
- Protein: 43.1 g

- Carbohydrates: 3 g
- Sodium: 110 mg

172. Delicious Lemon Chicken Salad

INGREDIENTS

- 1 lb. chicken breast, cooked and diced
- 1 tbsp. fresh dill, chopped
- 2 tsp. olive oil
- 1/4 cup low-fat yogurt
- 1 tsp. lemon zest, grated
- 2 tbsp. onion, minced
- 1/4 tsp. pepper
- 1/4 tsp. salt

DIRECTIONS

1. Put all your ingredients into the large mixing bowl and toss well. Season with pepper and salt. Cover and place in the refrigerator. Serve chilled and enjoy.

NUTRITIONS

- Calories: 165
- Carbohydrates: 2.2 g
- Fat: 5.4 g

- Protein: 25.2 g
- Sodium: 153 mg

173. Healthy Chicken Orzo

INGREDIENTS

- 1 cup whole wheat orzo
- 1 lb. chicken breasts, sliced
- 1/2 tsp. red pepper flakes
- 1/2 cup feta cheese, crumbled
- 1/2 tsp. oregano
- 1 tbsp. fresh parsley, chopped
- 1 tbsp. fresh basil, chopped
- 1/4 cup pine nuts
- 1 cup spinach, chopped
- 1/4 cup white wine
- 1/2 cup olives, sliced
- 1 cup grape tomatoes, cut in half
- 1/2 tbsp. garlic, minced
- 2 tbsp. olive oil
- 1/2 tsp. pepper
- 1/2 tsp. salt

DIRECTIONS

1. Add water in a small saucepan and bring to boil. Heat 1 tbsp. olive oil in a pan over medium heat. Season chicken with pepper and salt and cook in the pan for 5–7 minutes on each side. Remove from pan and set aside.
2. Add orzo to boiling water and cook according to the packet directions. Heat remaining olive oil in a pan on medium heat, then put garlic in the pan and sauté for a minute. Stir in white wine and cherry tomatoes and cook on high for 3 minutes.
3. Add cooked orzo, spices, spinach, pine nuts, and olives and stir until well combined. Add chicken on top of orzo and sprinkle with feta cheese. Serve and enjoy.

NUTRITIONS

- Calories: 518
- Carbohydrates: 26.2 g
- Fat: 27.7 g

- Protein: 40.6 g
- Sodium 121 mg

174. Lemon Garlic Chicken

15 MIN

COOKING TIME

12 MIN

SERVINGS

3

INGREDIENTS

- 3 chicken breasts, cut into thin slices
- 2 lemon zest, grated
- 1/4 cup olive oil
- 4 garlic cloves, minced
- Pepper
- Salt

DIRECTIONS

1. Warm-up olive oil in a pan over medium heat. Add garlic to the pan and sauté for 30 seconds. Put the chicken in the pan and sauté for 10 minutes. Add lemon zest and lemon juice and bring to boil. Remove from heat and season with pepper and salt. Serve and enjoy.

NUTRITIONS

- Calories: 439
- Carbohydrates: 4.9 g
- Fat: 27.8 g
- Protein: 42.9 g
- Sodium: 306 mg

175. Simple Mediterranean Chicken

PREPARATION TIME

15 MIN

COOKING TIME

15 MIN

SERVINGS

12

INGREDIENTS

- 2 chicken breasts, skinless and boneless
- 1 1/2 cup grape tomatoes, cut in half
- 1/2 cup olives
- 2 tbsp. olive oil
- 1 tsp. Italian seasoning
- 1/4 tsp. pepper
- 1/4 tsp. salt

DIRECTIONS

1. Season chicken with Italian seasoning, pepper, and salt. Warm-up olive oil in a pan over medium heat. Add season chicken to the pan and cook for 4–6 minutes on each side. Transfer chicken on a plate.
2. Put tomatoes plus olives in the pan and cook for 2–4 minutes. Pour olive and tomato mixture on top of the chicken and serve.

NUTRITIONS

- Calories: 468
- Carbohydrates: 7.8g
- Fat: 29.4g
- Protein: 43.8g
- Sodium 410 mg

176. Roasted Chicken Thighs

PREPARATION TIME

15 MIN

COOKING TIME

55 MIN

SERVINGS

4

INGREDIENTS

- 8 chicken thighs
- 3 tbsp. fresh parsley, chopped
- 1 tsp. dried oregano
- 6 garlic cloves, crushed
- 1/4 cup capers, drained
- 10 oz. roasted red peppers, sliced
- 2 cups grape tomatoes
- 1 1/2 lbs. potatoes, cut into small chunks
- 4 tbsp. olive oil
- Pepper
- Salt

DIRECTIONS

1. Heat the oven to 200°C / 400°F. Season chicken with pepper and salt. Heat up 2 tbsp. olive oil in a pan over medium heat. Add chicken to the pan and sear until lightly golden brown from all the sides.
2. Transfer chicken onto a baking tray. Add tomato, potatoes, capers, oregano, garlic, and red peppers around the chicken. Season with pepper and salt and drizzle with remaining olive oil. Bake in preheated oven for 45–55 minutes. Garnish with parsley and serve.

NUTRITIONS

- Calories: 848
- Carbohydrates: 45.2 g
- Fat: 29.1 g

- Protein: 91.3 g
- Sodium: 110 mg

177. Olive Capers Chicken

PREPARATION TIME

15 MIN

COOKING TIME

16 MIN

SERVINGS

4

INGREDIENTS

- 2 lb. chicken
- 1/3 cup chicken stock
- 3.5 oz. Capers
- 6 oz. olives
- 1/4 cup fresh basil
- 1 tbsp. olive oil
- 1 tsp. oregano
- 2 garlic cloves, minced
- 2 tbsp. red wine vinegar
- 1/8 tsp. pepper
- 1/4 tsp. salt

DIRECTIONS

1. Put olive oil in your instant pot and set the pot on sauté mode. Add chicken to the pot and sauté for 3-4 minutes. Add remaining ingredients and stir well. Seal pot with the lid and select manual, and set timer for 12 minutes. Serve and enjoy.

NUTRITIONS

- Calories: 433
- Carbohydrates: 4.8 g
- Fat: 15.2 g

- Protein: 66.9 g
- Sodium: 244 mg

178. Classic Chicken Cooking With Tomatoes & Tapenade

25 MIN

COOKING TIME

25 MIN

SERVINGS

2

INGREDIENTS

- 4–5 oz. Chicken breasts, boneless and skinless
- 1/4 tsp. salt (divided)
- 3 tbsp. fresh basil leaves, chopped (divided)
- 1 tbsp. olive oil
- 1 1/2 cups cherry tomatoes halved
- 1/4 cup olive tapenade

DIRECTIONS

1. Arrange the chicken on a sheet of glassine or waxed paper. Sprinkle half of the salt and a third of the basil evenly over the chicken.
2. Press lightly, and flip over the chicken pieces. Sprinkle the remaining salt and another third of the basil. Cover the seasoned chicken with another sheet of waxed paper.
3. By using a meat mallet or rolling pin, lb. the chicken to a half-inch thickness.
4. Heat the olive oil in a 12-inch skillet placed over medium-high heat. Add the pounded chicken breasts.
5. Cook for 6 minutes on each side until the chicken turns golden brown with no traces of pink in the middle. Transfer the browned chicken breasts to a platter, and cover to keep them warm.
6. In the same skillet, add the olive tapenade and tomatoes. Cook for 3 minutes until the tomatoes just begin to be tender.
7. To serve, pour over the tomato-tapenade mixture over the cooked chicken breasts, and top with the remaining basil.

NUTRITIONS

- Calories: 190
- Carbohydrates: 6 g
- Fats: 7 g
- Fiber: 1 g
- Protein: 26 g

179. Grilled Grapes & Chicken Chunks

PREPARATION TIME

15 MIN

COOKING TIME

30 MIN

SERVINGS

2

INGREDIENTS

- 2 cloves garlic, minced
- 1/4 cup extra-virgin olive oil
- 1 tbsp. rosemary, minced
- 1 tbsp. oregano, minced
- 1 tsp. lemon zest
- 1/2 tsp. red chili flakes, crushed
- 1 lb. Chicken breast, boneless and skinless
- 1 3/4 cups green grapes, seedless and rinsed
- 1/2 tsp. salt
- 1 tbsp. lemon juice
- 2 tbsp. extra-virgin olive oil

DIRECTIONS

1. Combine and mix all the marinade ingredients in a small mixing bowl. Mix well until fully combined. Set aside.
2. Cut the chicken breast into 3/4-inch cubes. Alternately thread the chicken and grapes onto 12 skewers. Place the skewers in a large baking dish to hold them for marinating.
3. Pour the marinade over the skewers, coating them thoroughly. Marinate for 4 to 24 hours.
4. Remove the skewers from the marinade and allow dripping off any excess oil. Sprinkle over with salt.
5. Grill the chicken and grape skewers for 3 minutes on each side until cooked through.
6. To serve, arrange the skewers on a serving platter and drizzle with lemon juice and olive oil.

NUTRITIONS

- Calories: 230
- Carbohydrates: 14 g
- Fats: 20 g
- Fiber: 1 g
- Protein: 1 g

180. Turkish Turkey Mini Meatloaves

15 MIN

COOKING TIME

20 MIN

SERVINGS

2

NUTRITIONS

- Calories: 130
- Carbohydrates: 14 g
- Fat: 7 g

INGREDIENTS

- 1 lb. Ground turkey breast
- 1 piece egg
- 1/4 cup whole-wheat breadcrumbs, crushed
- 1/4 cup feta cheese, plus more for topping
- 1/4 cup Kalamata olives halved
- 1/4 cup fresh parsley, chopped
- 1/4 cup red onion, minced
- 1/4 cup + 2 tbsp. hummus (refer to Homemade Hummus recipe)
- 2 cloves garlic, minced
- 1/2 tsp. dried basil
- 1/4 tsp. Dried oregano
- Salt and pepper
- 1/2 piece small cucumber, peeled, seeded, and chopped
- 1 piece large tomato, chopped
- 3 tbsp. fresh basil, chopped
- 1/2 lemon, juice
- 1 tsp. extra-virgin olive oil

DIRECTIONS

1. Preheat your oven to 425°F.
2. Line a 5-inch x 9-inch baking sheet with foil, and spray the surfaces with non-stick grease. Set aside.
3. Except for the 1/4 cup hummus, combine and mix all the turkey meatloaf ingredients in a large mixing bowl. Mix well until fully combined.
4. Divide the mixture equally into 4 portions. Form the portions into loaves. Spread a tablespoon of the remaining hummus on each meatloaf. Place the loaves on the greased baking sheet.
5. Bake for 20 minutes until the loaves no longer appear pink in the center. (Ensure the meatloaf cooks through by inserting a meat thermometer and the reading reaches 165°F.)
6. Combine and mix all the topping ingredients in a small mixing bowl. Mix well until fully combined.
7. To serve, spoon the topping over the cooked meatloaves.

- Fiber: 4
- Protein: 6 g

181. Charred Chicken Souvlaki Skewers

20 MIN

COOKING TIME

15 MIN

SERVINGS

2

NUTRITIONS

- Calories: 360
- Carbohydrates: 3 g
- Fats: 26 g

INGREDIENTS

- 1/2 cup olive oil
- 1/2 cup fresh squeezed lemon juice
- 1 tbsp. red wine vinegar
- 1 tbsp. finely minced garlic (or garlic puree from a jar)
- 1 tbsp. dried Greek oregano
- 1 tsp. dried thyme
- 6 pieces chicken breasts, boneless, skinless, with trimmed off tendons and fats
- Fresh cucumber and cherry tomatoes for garnish

DIRECTIONS

1. Combine and mix all the marinade ingredients in a small mixing bowl. Mix well until fully combined.
2. Slice each chicken breast crosswise into six 1-inch strips.
3. Place the chicken strips into a large plastic container with a tight-fitting lid.
4. Pour the marinade into the plastic container, and seal with its lid. Gently shake the container and turn it over so that the marinade evenly coats all of the meat. Refrigerate the sealed plastic container to marinate for 8 hours or more.
5. Spray the grill's surfaces with non-stick grease. Preheat your charcoal or gas barbecue grill to medium-high heat.
6. Take the chicken out and let it cool to room temperature. Drain the chicken pieces and thread them onto skewers. (Try to thread six pieces for each skewer and fold over each chicken piece so it will not spin around the skewer.)
7. Grill the chicken souvlaki skewers for 15 minutes, turning once after seeing the appearance of desirable grill marks.
8. To serve, place the souvlaki on a serving plate alongside the cucumber and tomato garnish.

- Fiber: 0 g
- Protein: 30 g

182. Lemon Caper Chicken

10 MIN

COOKING TIME

15 MIN

SERVINGS

2

INGREDIENTS

- 2 tbsp. virgin olive oil
- 2 chicken breasts (boneless, skinless, cut in half, lb. to 3/4 an inch thick)
- 1/4 cup capers
- 2 lemons (wedges)
- 1 tsp. oregano
- 1 tsp. basil
- 1/2 tsp. black pepper

DIRECTIONS

1. Take a large skillet and place it on your stove and add the olive oil to it. Turn the heat to medium and allow it to warm up.
2. As the oil heats up season your chicken breast with the oregano, basil, and black pepper on each side.
3. Place your chicken breast into the hot skillet and cook on each side for five minutes.
4. Transfer the chicken from the skillet to your dinner plate. Top with capers and serve with a few lemon wedges.

NUTRITIONS

- Calories: 182
- Carbohydrates: 3.4 g
- Protein: 26.6 g
- Fat: 8.2 g

183. Herb Roasted Chicken

PREPARATION TIME

20 MIN

COOKING TIME

45 MIN

SERVINGS

2

INGREDIENTS

- 1 tbsp. virgin olive oil
- 1 whole chicken
- 2 rosemary springs
- 3 garlic cloves (peeled)
- 1 lemon (cut in half)
- 1 tsp. sea salt
- 1 tsp. black pepper

DIRECTIONS

1. Turn your oven to 450°F.
2. Take your whole chicken and pat it dry using paper towels. Then rub in the olive oil. Remove the leaves from one of the springs of rosemary and scatter them over the chicken. Sprinkle the sea salt and black pepper over top. Place the other whole sprig of rosemary into the cavity of the chicken. Then add in the garlic cloves and lemon halves.
3. Place the chicken into a roasting pan and then place it into the oven. Allow the chicken to bake for 1 hour, then check that the internal temperature should be at least 165 degrees F. If the chicken begins to brown too much, cover it with foil and return it to the oven to finish cooking.
4. When the chicken has cooked to the appropriate temperature remove it from the oven. Let it rest for at least 20 minutes before carving.
5. Serve with a large side of roasted or steamed vegetables or your favorite salad.

NUTRITIONS

- Calories: 309
- Carbohydrates: 1.5 g
- Protein: 27.2 g
- Fat: 21.3 g

184. Grilled Chicken Breasts

10 MIN

COOKING TIME

15 MIN

SERVINGS

2

INGREDIENTS

- 4 Boneless skinless chicken breast
- 3 tbsp. Lemon juice
- 3 tbsp. olive oil
- 3 tbsp. Chopped fresh parsley
- 3 Minced garlic cloves
- 1 tsp. Paprika
- 1/2 tsp. dried oregano
- Salt and pepper, to taste.

DIRECTIONS

1. In a large Ziploc bag, mix well oregano, paprika, garlic, parsley, olive oil, and lemon juice.
2. Pierce chicken with a knife several times and sprinkle with salt and pepper.
3. Add chicken to bag and marinate 20 minutes or up to two days in the fridge.
4. Remove chicken from bag and grill for 5 minutes per side in a 350°F preheated grill.
5. When cooked, transfer to a plate for 5 minutes before slicing.
6. Serve and enjoy with a side of rice or salad

NUTRITIONS

- Calories: 238
- Carbohydrates: 2 g
- Fats: 19 g

- Protein: 24 g

185. Turkey Meatballs

PREPARATION TIME

10 MIN

COOKING TIME

25 MIN

SERVINGS

2

INGREDIENTS

- 1/4 diced yellow onion
- 14 oz. diced artichoke hearts
- 1 lb. ground turkey
- 1 tsp. dried parsley
- 1 tsp. oil
- 4 tbsp. Chopped basil
- Pepper and salt, to taste.

DIRECTIONS

1. Grease the baking sheet and preheat the oven to 350°F.
2. On medium heat, place a nonstick medium saucepan, sauté artichoke hearts, pepper, salt, and diced onions for 5 minutes or until onions are soft.
3. Meanwhile, in a big bowl, mix parsley, basil, and ground turkey with your hands. Season to taste.
4. Once the onion mixture has cooled, add it into the bowl and mix thoroughly.
5. With an ice cream scooper, scoop ground turkey and form balls.
6. Place on a prepared cooking sheet, pop in the oven, and bake until cooked around 15–20 minutes.
7. Remove from pan, serve and enjoy

NUTRITIONS

- Calories: 283
- Carbohydrates: 30 g
- Fat: 12 g

- Protein: 12 g

186. Chicken Marsala

10 MIN

COOKING TIME

45 MIN

SERVINGS

2

INGREDIENTS

- 2 tbsp. olive oil
- 4 skinless, boneless chicken breast cutlets
- 3/4 tbsp. black pepper, divided
- 1/2 tsp. kosher salt, divided
- 8 oz. Mushrooms, sliced
- 4 thyme sprigs
- 1/4-quart unsalted chicken stock
- 2-quarts Marsala wine
- 2 tbsp. olive oil
- 1 tbsp. fresh thyme, chopped

DIRECTIONS

1. Heat oil in a pan and fry chicken for 4–5 minutes per side. Remove chicken from the pan and set it aside.
2. In the same pan add thyme, mushrooms, salt, and pepper; stir fry for 1–2 minutes.
3. Add Marsala wine, chicken broth, and cooked chicken. Let simmer for 10–12 minutes on low heat.
4. Add to a serving dish. Enjoy.

NUTRITIONS

- Calories: 206
- Carbohydrates: 3 g
- Fat: 17 g

- Protein: 8 g

187. Buttery Garlic Chicken

PREPARATION TIME

5 MIN

COOKING TIME

40 MIN

SERVINGS

2

INGREDIENTS

- 2 tbsp. ghee, melted
- 2 boneless skinless chicken breasts
- 1 tbsp. dried Italian seasoning
- 4 tbsp. butter
- 1/4 cup grated Parmesan cheese
- 1 clove Garlic
- Pink Himalayan salt
- Pepper

DIRECTIONS

1. Preheat the oven to 375°F. Select a baking dish that fits both chicken breasts and coat it with ghee. Dries the chicken breasts. Season with pink Himalayan salt, pepper, and Italian seasoning. Place the chicken in the baking dish.
2. In a medium skillet over medium heat, melt the butter. Sauté minced garlic, for about 5 minutes.
3. Remove the butter-garlic mixture from the heat, and pour it over the chicken breasts.
4. Roast in the oven for 30 to 35 minutes. Sprinkle some of the Parmesan cheese on top of each chicken breast. Let the chicken rest in the baking dish for 5 minutes.
5. Divide the chicken between two plates, spoon the butter sauce over the chicken, and serve.

NUTRITIONS

- Calories: 642
- Carbohydrates: 37 g
- Fat: 45 g

- Protein: 57 g

188. Creamy Chicken-Spinach Skillet

10 MIN

COOKING TIME

17 MIN

SERVINGS

2

INGREDIENTS

- 1 lb. Boneless skinless chicken breast
- 1 medium diced onion
- 12 oz. diced roasted red peppers
- 2 1/2 cup Chicken stock
- 2 cups baby spinach leaves
- 2 cups cooked pasta
- 2 tbsp. Butter
- 4 minced garlic cloves
- 7 oz. cream cheese
- Salt and pepper, to taste.

DIRECTIONS

1. Place a saucepan on medium-high heat for 2 minutes. Add butter and melt for a minute, swirling to coat the pan.
2. Add chicken to a pan, season with pepper and salt to taste. Cook chicken on high heat for 3 minutes per side.
3. Lower heat to medium and stir in onions, red peppers, and garlic. Sauté for 5 minutes and deglaze the pot with a little bit of stock.
4. Whisk in chicken stock and cream cheese. Cook and mix until thoroughly combined.
5. Stir in spinach and adjust seasoning to taste. Cook for 2 minutes or until spinach is wilted.
6. Serve and enjoy.

NUTRITIONS

- Calories: 484
- Carbohydrates: 33 g
- Fats: 22 g

- Protein: 36 g

189. Creamy Chicken Breasts

PREPARATION TIME

10 MIN

COOKING TIME

12 MIN

SERVINGS

4

INGREDIENTS

- 4 chicken breasts, skinless and boneless
- 1 tbsp. basil pesto
- 1 1/2 tbsp. cornstarch
- 1/4 cup roasted red peppers, chopped
- 1/3 cup heavy cream
- 1 tsp. Italian seasoning
- 1 tsp. garlic, minced
- 1 cup chicken broth
- Pepper
- Salt

DIRECTIONS

1. Add chicken into the instant pot. Season chicken with Italian seasoning, pepper, and salt. Sprinkle with garlic. Pour broth over chicken. Seal pot with lid and cook on high for 8 minutes.
2. Once done, allow to release pressure naturally for 5 minutes then release remaining using quick release. Remove lid. Transfer chicken to a plate and clean the instant pot.
3. Set instant pot on sauté mode. Add heavy cream, pesto, cornstarch, and red pepper to the pot and stir well and cook for 3–4 minutes.
4. Return chicken to the pot and coat well with the sauce. Serve and enjoy.

NUTRITIONS

- Calories: 341
- Carbohydrates: 4.4 g
- Fat: 15.2 g

- Protein: 43.8 g

190. Cheese Garlic Chicken & Potatoes

INGREDIENTS

- 2 lb. Chicken breasts, skinless, boneless, cut into chunks
- 1 tbsp. olive oil
- 3/4 cup chicken broth
- 1 tbsp. Italian seasoning
- 1 tbsp. garlic powder
- 1 tsp. garlic, minced
- 1 1/2 cup parmesan cheese, shredded
- 1 lb. potatoes, chopped
- Pepper
- Salt

DIRECTIONS

1. Add oil into the inner pot of the instant pot and set the pot on sauté mode. Add chicken and cook until browned. Add remaining ingredients except for cheese and stir well.
2. Seal pot with lid and cook on high for 8 minutes. Once done, release pressure using quick release. Remove lid. Top with cheese and cover with lid for 5 minutes or until cheese is melted. Serve and enjoy.

NUTRITIONS

- Calories: 674
- Carbohydrates: 21.4 g
- Fat: 29 g
- Protein: 79.7 g

191. Easy Chicken Scampi

INGREDIENTS

- 3 chicken breasts, skinless, boneless, and sliced
- 1 tsp. garlic, minced
- 1 tbsp. Italian seasoning
- 2 cups chicken broth
- 1 bell pepper, sliced
- 1/2 onion, sliced
- Pepper
- Salt

DIRECTIONS

1. Add chicken into the instant pot and top with remaining ingredients. Seal pot with lid and cook on high for 25 minutes. Once done, release pressure using quick release. Remove lid.
2. Remove chicken from pot and shred using a fork. Return shredded chicken to the pot and stir well. Serve over cooked whole grain pasta and top with cheese.

NUTRITIONS

- Calories: 254
- Carbohydrates: 4.6 g
- Fat: 9.9 g
- Protein: 34.6 g

192. Protein-Packed Chicken Bean Rice

10 MIN

COOKING TIME

15 MIN

SERVINGS

6

INGREDIENTS

- 1 lb. Chicken breasts, skinless, boneless, and cut into chunks
- 14 oz can cannellini beans, rinsed and drained
- 4 cups chicken broth
- 2 cups brown rice
- 1 tbsp. Italian seasoning
- 1 small onion, chopped
- 1 tbsp. garlic, chopped
- 1 tbsp. olive oil
- Pepper
- Salt

DIRECTIONS

1. Add oil into the inner pot of the instant pot and set the pot on sauté mode. Add garlic and onion and sauté for 3 minutes. Add remaining ingredients and stir everything well.
2. Seal pot with a lid and select manual and set timer for 12 minutes. Once done, release pressure using quick release. Remove lid. Stir well and serve.

NUTRITIONS

- Calories: 494
- Carbohydrates: 61.4 g
- Fat: 11.3 g

- Protein: 34.2 g

193. Pesto Vegetable Chicken

PREPARATION TIME

10 MIN

COOKING TIME

25 MIN

SERVINGS

4

INGREDIENTS

- 1 1/2 lb. Chicken thighs, skinless, boneless, and cut into pieces
- 1/2 cup chicken broth
- 1/4 cup fresh parsley, chopped
- 2 cups cherry tomatoes, halved
- 1 cup basil pesto
- 3/4 lb. Asparagus, trimmed and cut in half
- 2/3 cup sun-dried tomatoes, drained and chopped
- 2 tbsp. olive oil
- Pepper
- Salt

DIRECTIONS

1. Add oil into the inner pot of the instant pot and set the pot on sauté mode. Add chicken and sauté for 5 minutes. Add remaining ingredients except for tomatoes and stir well.
2. Seal pot with a lid and select manual and set timer for 15 minutes. Once done, release pressure using quick release. Remove lid.
3. Add tomatoes and stir well. Again, seal the pot and select the manual, and set the timer for 5 minutes. Release pressure using quick release. Remove lid. Stir well and serve.

NUTRITIONS

- Calories: 459
- Carbohydrates: 14.9 g
- Fat: 20.5 g

- Protein: 9.2 g

194. Greek Chicken Rice

10 MIN

COOKING TIME

14 MIN

SERVINGS

4

INGREDIENTS

- 3 chicken breasts, skinless, boneless, and cut into chunks
- 1/4 fresh parsley, chopped
- 1 zucchini, sliced
- 2 bell peppers, chopped
- 1 cup rice, rinsed and drained
- 1 1/2 cup chicken broth
- 1 tbsp. oregano
- 3 tbsp. fresh lemon juice
- 1 tbsp. garlic, minced
- 1 onion, diced
- 2 tbsp. olive oil
- Pepper
- Salt

DIRECTIONS

1. Add oil into the inner pot of the instant pot and set the pot on sauté mode. Add onion and chicken and cook for 5 minutes. Add rice, oregano, lemon juice, garlic, broth, pepper, and salt, and stir everything well.
2. Seal pot with lid and cook on high for 4 minutes. Once done, release pressure using quick release. Remove lid. Add parsley, zucchini, and bell peppers and stir well.
3. Seal pot again with lid and select manual and set timer for 5 minutes. Release pressure using quick release. Remove lid. Stir well and serve.

NUTRITIONS

- Calories: 500
- Carbohydrates: 48 g
- Fat: 16.5 g
- Protein: 38.7 g

195. Flavorful Chicken Tacos

PREPARATION TIME

10 MIN

COOKING TIME

10 MIN

SERVINGS

3

INGREDIENTS

- 2 chicken breasts, skinless and boneless
- 1 tbsp. chili powder
- 1/2 tsp. ground cumin
- 1/2 tsp. garlic powder
- 1/4 tsp. onion powder
- 1/2 tsp. paprika
- 4 oz. can green chilis, diced
- 1/4 cup chicken broth
- 14 oz. can tomato, diced
- Pepper
- Salt

DIRECTIONS

1. Add all ingredients except chicken into the instant pot and stir well. Add chicken and stir. Seal pot with lid and cook on high for 10 minutes.
2. Once done, allow to release pressure naturally for 5 minutes then release remaining using quick release. Remove lid.
3. Remove chicken from pot and shred using a fork. Return shredded chicken to the pot and stir well. Serve and enjoy.

NUTRITIONS

- Calories: 237
- Carbohydrates: 10.8 g
- Fat: 8 g
- Protein: 30.5 g

196. Quinoa Chicken Bowls

PREPARATION TIME

10 MIN

COOKING TIME

6 MIN

SERVINGS

4

INGREDIENTS

- 1 lb. Chicken breasts, skinless, boneless, and cut into chunks
- 14 oz. can chickpeas, drained and rinsed
- 1 cup olives, pitted and sliced
- 1 cup cherry tomatoes, halved
- 1 cucumber, sliced
- 2 tsp. Greek seasoning
- 1 1/2 cup. chicken broth
- 1 cup quinoa, rinsed and drained
- Pepper
- Salt

DIRECTIONS

1. Add broth and quinoa into the instant pot and stir well. Season chicken with Greek seasoning, pepper, and salt and place into the instant pot.
2. Seal pot with lid and cook on high for 6 minutes. Once done, release pressure using quick release. Remove lid. Stir quinoa and chicken mixture well.
3. Add remaining ingredients and stir everything well. Serve immediately and enjoy it.

NUTRITIONS

- Calories: 566
- Carbohydrates: 57.4 g
- Fat: 16.4 g

- Protein: 46.8 g

197. Quick Chicken With Mushrooms

PREPARATION TIME

10 MIN

COOKING TIME

22 MIN

SERVINGS

6

INGREDIENTS

- 2 lb. Chicken breasts, skinless and boneless
- 1/2 cup heavy cream
- 1/3 cup water
- 3/4 lb. Mushrooms, sliced
- 3 tbsp. olive oil
- 1 tsp. Italian seasoning
- Pepper
- Salt

DIRECTIONS

1. Add oil into the inner pot of the instant pot and set the pot on sauté mode. Season chicken with Italian seasoning, pepper, and salt.
2. Add chicken to the pot and sauté for 5 minutes. Remove chicken from pot and set aside. Add mushrooms and sauté for 5 minutes or until mushrooms are lightly brown.
3. Return chicken to the pot. Add water and stir well. Seal pot with a lid and select manual and set timer for 12 minutes.
4. Once done, release pressure using quick release. Remove lid. Remove chicken from pot and place on a plate.
5. Set pot on sauté mode. Add heavy cream and stir well and cook for 5 minutes. Pour mushroom sauce over chicken and serve.

NUTRITIONS

- Calories: 396
- Carbohydrates: 2.2 g
- Fat: 22.3 g

- Protein: 45.7 g

198. Herb Garlic Chicken

10 MIN

COOKING TIME

12 MIN

SERVINGS

8

INGREDIENTS

- 4 lb. Chicken breasts, skinless and boneless
- 1 tbsp. garlic powder
- 2 tbsp. dried Italian herb mix
- 2 tbsp. olive oil
- 1/4 cup chicken stock
- Pepper
- Salt

DIRECTIONS

1. Coat chicken with oil and season with dried herb, garlic powder, pepper, and salt. Place chicken into the instant pot. Pour stock over the chicken. Seal pot with a lid and select manual and set timer for 12 minutes.
2. Once done, allow to release pressure naturally for 5 minutes then release remaining using quick release. Remove lid. Shred chicken using a fork and serve.

NUTRITIONS

- Calories: 502
- Carbohydrates: 7.8 g
- Fat: 20.8 g

- Protein: 66.8 g

199. Chicken with Mushrooms

PREPARATION TIME

15 MIN

COOKING TIME

6 HOURS

SERVINGS

2

INGREDIENTS

- 2 chicken breasts, skinless and boneless
- 1 cup mushrooms, sliced
- 1 onion, sliced
- 1 cup chicken stock
- 1/2 tsp. thyme, dried
- Pepper
- Salt

DIRECTIONS

1. Add all ingredients to the slow cooker. Cook on low for 6 hours. Serve and enjoy.

NUTRITIONS

- Calories: 313
- Carbohydrates: 6.9 g
- Fat: 11.3 g

- Protein: 44.3 g
- Sodium: 541 mg

200. Baked Chicken

15 MIN

COOKING TIME

35 MIN

SERVINGS

4

INGREDIENTS

- 2 lbs. chicken tenders
- 1 large zucchini
- 1 cup grape tomatoes
- 2 tbsp. olive oil
- 3 dill sprigs

For topping:
- 2 tbsp. feta cheese, crumbled
- 1 tbsp. olive oil
- 1 tbsp. fresh lemon juice
- 1 tbsp. fresh dill, chopped

DIRECTIONS

1. Warm oven to 200°C / 400°F. Drizzle the olive oil on a baking tray, then place chicken, zucchini, dill, and tomatoes on the tray. Season with salt. Bake chicken for 30 minutes.
2. Meanwhile, in a small bowl, stir all topping ingredients. Place chicken on the serving tray, then top with veggies and discard dill sprigs. Sprinkle topping mixture on top of chicken and vegetables. Serve and enjoy.

NUTRITIONS

- Calories: 557
- Carbohydrates: 5.2 g
- Fat: 28.6 g

- Protein: 67.9 g
- Sodium 760 mg

201. Garlic Pepper Chicken

PREPARATION TIME

15 MIN

COOKING TIME

21 MIN

SERVINGS

2

INGREDIENTS

- 2 chicken breasts, cut into strips
- 2 bell peppers, cut into strips
- 5 garlic cloves, chopped
- 3 tbsp. water
- 2 tbsp. olive oil
- 1 tbsp. paprika
- 2 tsp. black pepper
- 1/2 tsp. salt

DIRECTIONS

1. Heat olive oil in a large saucepan over medium heat. Add garlic and sauté for 2-3 minutes. Add peppers and cook for 3 minutes. Add chicken and spices and stir to coat. Add water and stir well. Bring to boil. Cover and simmer for 10-15 minutes. Serve and enjoy.

NUTRITIONS

- Calories: 462
- Carbohydrates: 14.8 g
- Fat: 25.7 g

- Protein: 44.7 g
- Sodium: 720 mg

202. Mustard Chicken Tenders

15 MIN

COOKING TIME

20 MIN

SERVINGS

4

INGREDIENTS

- 1 lb. chicken tenders
- 2 tbsp. fresh tarragon, chopped
- 1/2 cup whole grain mustard
- 1/2 tsp. paprika
- 1 garlic clove, minced
- 1/2 oz. fresh lemon juice
- 1/2 tsp. pepper
- 1/4 tsp. kosher salt

DIRECTIONS

1. Warm oven to 425°F. Add all ingredients except chicken to the large bowl and mix well. Put the chicken in the bowl, then stir until well coated. Place chicken on a baking dish and cover. Bake for 15–20 minutes. Serve and enjoy.

NUTRITIONS

- Calories: 242
- Carbohydrates: 3.1 g
- Fat: 9.5 g

- Protein: 33.2 g
- Sodium 240 mg

203. Salsa Chicken Chili

PREPARATION TIME

15 MIN

COOKING TIME

20 MIN

SERVINGS

8

INGREDIENTS

- 2 1/2 lb. chicken breasts, skinless and boneless
- 1/2 tsp. cumin powder
- 3 garlic cloves, minced
- 1 onion, diced
- 16 oz. salsa
- 1 tsp. oregano
- 1 tbsp. olive oil

DIRECTIONS

1. Add oil into the instant pot and set the pot on sauté mode. Add onion to the pot and sauté until softened, about 3 minutes. Add garlic and sauté for a minute. Add oregano and cumin and sauté for a minute. Add half salsa and stir well. Place chicken and pour remaining salsa over chicken.
2. Seal pot with the lid and select manual, and set timer for 10 minutes. Remove chicken and shred. Move it back to the pot, then stir well to combine. Serve and enjoy.

NUTRITIONS

- Calories: 308
- Carbohydrates: 5.4 g
- Fat: 12.4 g

- Protein: 42.1 g
- Sodium 656 mg

Chapter 7
Vegetables

204. Moroccan-Inspired Tagine With Chickpeas & Vegetables

15 MIN

COOKING TIME

45 MIN

SERVINGS

3

INGREDIENTS

- 2 tsp. olive oil
- 1 cup chopped carrots
- 1/2 cup finely chopped onion
- 1 sweet potato, diced
- 1 cup low-sodium vegetable broth
- 1/4 tsp. ground cinnamon
- 1/8 tsp. salt
- 1 1/2 cups chopped bell peppers, any color
- 3 ripe plum tomatoes, chopped
- 1 tbsp. tomato paste
- 1 garlic clove, pressed or minced
- 1 (15 oz.) can chickpeas, drained and rinsed
- 1/2 cup chopped dried apricots
- 1 tsp. curry powder
- 1/2 tsp. paprika
- 1/2 tsp. turmeric

DIRECTIONS

1. Heat oil over medium heat in a large Dutch oven or saucepan. Add the carrots and onion and cook until the onion is translucent about 4 minutes. Add the sweet potato, broth, cinnamon, and salt and cook for 5 to 6 minutes, until the broth is slightly reduced.
2. Add the peppers, tomatoes, tomato paste, and garlic. Stir and cook for another 5 minutes. Add the chickpeas, apricots, curry powder, paprika, and turmeric to the pot. Bring all to a boil, then reduce the heat to low, cover, simmer for about 30 minutes, and serve.

NUTRITIONS

- Calories: 469
- Carbohydrates: 88 g
- Fat: 9 g
- Protein: 16 g
- Sodium: 256 mg

205. Spaghetti Squash With Maple Glaze & Tofu Crumbles

15 MIN

COOKING TIME

22 MIN

SERVINGS

3

INGREDIENTS

- 2 oz. firm tofu, well-drained
- 1 small spaghetti squash, halved lengthwise
- 2 1/2 tsp. olive oil, divided
- 1/8 tsp. salt
- 1/2 cup chopped onion
- 1 tsp. dried rosemary
- 1/4 cup dry white wine
- 2 tbsp. maple syrup
- 1/2 tsp. garlic powder
- 1/4 cup shredded Gruyère cheese

DIRECTIONS

1. Put the tofu in a large mesh colander and place it over a large bowl to drain. Score the squash using a paring knife so the steam can vent while it cooks. Place the squash in a medium microwave-safe dish and microwave on high for 5 minutes. Remove the squash from the microwave and allow it to cool.
2. Cut the cooled squash in half on a cutting board. Remove the seeds, then put the squash halves into a 9-by-11-inch baking dish.
3. Drizzle the squash with half a tsp. olive oil and season it with the salt, then wrap it using wax paper and put it back in the microwave for 5 more minutes on high. Once it's cooked, scrape the squash strands with a fork into a small bowl and cover it to keep it warm.
4. While the squash is cooking, heat 1 tsp. oil in a large skillet over medium-high heat. Put the onion and sauté for 2 minutes. Add the rosemary and stir for 1 minute, until fragrant.
5. Put the rest of the oil in the same skillet. Crumble the tofu into the skillet, stir fry until lightly browned, about 4 minutes, and transfer it to a small bowl.
6. Add the wine, maple syrup, and garlic powder to the skillet and stir to combine. Cook for 2 minutes until slightly reduced and thickened. Remove from the heat. Evenly divide the squash between two plates, then top it with the tofu mixture. Drizzle the maple glaze over the top, then add the grated cheese.

NUTRITIONS

- Calories: 330
- Carbohydrates: 36 g
- Fat: 15 g
- Fiber: 5 g
- Protein: 12 g
- Sodium: 326 mg
- Potassium: 474 mg

206. Stuffed Tex-Mex Baked Potatoes

15 MIN

COOKING TIME

45 MIN

SERVINGS

2

NUTRITIONS

- Calories: 624
- Carbohydrates: 91 g
- Fat: 21 g

- Fiber: 21 g
- Protein: 24 g
- Sodium: 366 mg

- Potassium: 2134 mg

INGREDIENTS

- 2 large Idaho potatoes
- 1/2 cup black beans, rinsed and drained
- 1/4 cup store-bought salsa
- 1 avocado, diced
- 1 tsp. freshly squeezed lime juice
- 1/2 cup nonfat plain Greek yogurt
- 1/4 tsp. reduced-sodium taco seasoning
- 1/4 cup shredded sharp cheddar cheese

DIRECTIONS

1. Preheat the oven to 400°F. Scrub the potatoes, then slice an "X" into the top of each using a paring knife. Put the potatoes on the oven rack, then bake for 45 minutes until they are tender.
2. In a small bowl, stir the beans and salsa and set aside. In another small bowl, mix the avocado and lime juice and set aside. In a third small bowl, stir the yogurt and the taco seasoning until well blended.
3. When the potatoes are baked, carefully open them up. Top each potato with the bean and salsa mixture, avocado, seasoned yogurt, and cheddar cheese, evenly dividing each component, and serve.

207. Lentil-Stuffed Zucchini Boats

PREPARATION TIME

15 MIN

COOKING TIME

45 MIN

SERVINGS

2

INGREDIENTS

- 2 medium zucchinis, halved lengthwise and seeded
- 2 1/4 cups water, divided
- 1 cup green or red lentils, dried & rinsed
- 2 tsp. olive oil
- 1/3 cup diced onion
- 2 tbsp. tomato paste
- 1/2 tsp. oregano
- 1/4 tsp. garlic powder
- A pinch salt
- 1/4 cup grated part-skim mozzarella cheese

DIRECTIONS

1. Preheat the oven to 375°F. Line a baking sheet with parchment paper. Place the zucchini, hollow sides up, on the baking sheet, and set aside.
2. Boil 2 cups of water to a boil over high heat in a medium saucepan and add the lentils. Lower the heat, then simmer for 20 to 25 minutes. Drain and set aside.
3. Heat up the olive oil in a medium skillet over medium-low heat. Sauté the onions until they are translucent, about 4 minutes. Lower the heat and add the cooked lentils, tomato paste, oregano, garlic powder, and salt.
4. Add the last quarter cup of water and simmer for 3 minutes, until the liquid reduces and forms a sauce. Remove from heat.
5. Stuff each zucchini half with the lentil mixture, dividing it evenly, top with cheese, bake for 25 minutes, and serve. The zucchini should be fork-tender, and the cheese should be melted.

NUTRITIONS

- Calories: 479
- Carbohydrates: 74 g
- Fat: 9 g

- Fiber: 14 g
- Protein: 31 g
- Sodium: 206 mg

- Potassium: 1389 mg

208. Baked Eggplant Parmesan

15 MIN

COOKING TIME

35 MIN

SERVINGS

3

INGREDIENTS

- 1 small to medium eggplant, cut into 1/4-inch slices
- 1/2 tsp. salt-free Italian seasoning blend
- 1 tbsp. olive oil
- 1/4 cup diced onion
- 1/2 cup diced yellow or red bell pepper
- 2 garlic cloves, pressed or minced
- 1 (8 oz.) can tomato sauce
- 3 oz. fresh mozzarella, cut into 6 pieces
- 1 tbsp. grated Parmesan cheese, divided
- 5–6 fresh basil leaves, chopped
- Cooking spray

DIRECTIONS

1. Preheat an oven-style air fryer to 400°F.
2. Working in two batches, place the eggplant slices onto the air-fryer tray and sprinkle them with Italian seasoning. Bake for 7 minutes. Repeat with the remaining slices, then set them aside on a plate.
3. In a medium skillet, heat the oil over medium heat and sauté the onion and peppers until softened for about 5 minutes. Add the garlic and sauté for 1 to 2 more minutes. Add the tomato sauce and stir to combine. Remove the sauce from the heat.
4. Spray a 9-by-6-inch casserole dish with cooking spray. Spread one-third of the sauce into the bottom of the dish. Layer eggplant slices onto the sauce. Sprinkle with half of the Parmesan cheese.
5. Continue layering the sauce and eggplant, ending with the sauce. Place the mozzarella pieces on the top. Sprinkle the remaining Parmesan evenly over the entire dish. Bake in the oven for 20 minutes. Garnish with fresh basil, cut into four servings, and serve.

NUTRITIONS

- Calories: 213
- Carbohydrates: 20 g
- Fat: 12 g

- Fiber: 7 g
- Protein: 10 g
- Sodium: 222 mg

- Potassium: 763 mg

209. Sweet Potato Rice With Spicy Peanut Sauce

PREPARATION TIME

15 MIN

COOKING TIME

25 MIN

SERVINGS

2

INGREDIENTS

- 1/2 cup basmati rice
- 2 tsp. olive oil, divided
- 1 (8 oz.) can chickpeas, drained and rinsed
- 2 medium sweet potatoes, small cubes
- 1/4 tsp. ground cumin
- 1 cup of water
- 1/8 tsp. salt
- 2 tbsp. chopped cilantro
- 3 tbsp. peanut butter
- 1 tbsp. sriracha
- 2 tsp. reduced-sodium soy sauce
- 1/2 tsp. garlic powder
- 1/4 tsp. ground ginger

DIRECTIONS

1. Heat up 1 tsp. oil in a large nonstick skillet over medium-high heat. Add the chickpeas and heat for 3 minutes. Stir and cook until lightly browned. Transfer the chickpeas to a small bowl.
2. Put the rest of the 1 tsp. oil into the skillet, then add the potatoes and cumin, distributing them evenly. Cook the potatoes until they become lightly browned before turning them.
3. While the potatoes are cooking, boil the water with the salt in a large saucepan over medium-high heat. Put the rice in the boiling water, adjust the heat to low, cover, and simmer for 20 minutes.
4. When the potatoes have fully cooked, about 10 minutes in total, remove the skillet from the heat. Transfer the potatoes and chickpeas to the rice, folding them all gently. Add the chopped cilantro.
5. In a small bowl, whisk the peanut butter, sriracha, soy sauce, garlic powder, and ginger until well blended. Divide the rice mixture between two serving bowls. Drizzle with the sauce and serve.

NUTRITIONS

- Calories: 667
- Carbohydrates: 100 g
- Fat: 22 g

- Fiber: 14 g
- Protein: 20 g
- Sodium: 563 mg

- Potassium: 963 mg

210. Vegetable Red Curry

15 MIN

25 MIN

2

- 2 tsp. olive oil
- 1 cup sliced carrots
- 1/2 cup chopped onion
- 1 garlic clove, pressed or minced
- 2 bell peppers, seeded and thinly sliced
- 1 cup chopped cauliflower
- 2/3 cup light coconut milk
- 1/2 cup low-sodium vegetable broth
- 1 tbsp. tomato paste
- 1 tsp. curry powder
- 1/2 tsp. ground cumin
- 1/2 tsp. ground coriander
- 1/4 tsp. turmeric
- 2 cups fresh baby spinach
- 1 cup quick-cooking brown rice

1. Heat oil in a large nonstick skillet over medium heat. Add the carrots, onion, and garlic and cook for 2 to 3 minutes. Reduce the heat to medium-low, add the peppers and cauliflower to the skillet, cover, and cook for 5 minutes.
2. Add the coconut milk, broth, tomato paste, curry powder, cumin, coriander, and turmeric, stirring to combine. Simmer, covered (vent the lid slightly), for 10 to 15 minutes until the curry is slightly reduced and thickened.
3. Uncover, add the spinach, and stir for 2 minutes until it is wilted and mixed into the vegetables. Remove from the heat. Cook the rice as stated in the package instructions. Serve the curry over the rice.

- Calories: 584
- Carbohydrates: 101 g
- Fat: 16 g

- Fiber: 10 g
- Protein: 13 g
- Sodium: 102 mg

- Potassium: 1430 mg

211. Black Bean Burgers

15 MIN

20 MIN

4

- 1/2 cup quick-cooking brown rice
- 2 tsp. canola oil, divided
- 1/2 cup finely chopped carrots
- 1/4 cup finely chopped onion
- 1 can black beans, drained
- 1 tbsp. salt-free mesquite seasoning blend
- 4 small, hard rolls

1. Cook the rice as stated in the package directions and set aside. Heat up 1 tsp. oil in a large nonstick skillet over medium heat. Add the carrots and onions and cook until the onions are translucent about 4 minutes. Adjust the heat to low, and cook again for 5 to 6 minutes, until the carrots are tender.
2. Add the beans and seasoning to the skillet and continue cooking for 2 to 3 more minutes. Pulse bean mixture in a food processor 3 to 4 times or until the mixture is coarsely blended. Put the batter in a medium bowl and fold in the brown rice until well combined.
3. Divide the mixture evenly and form it into 4 patties with your hands. Heat the remaining oil in the skillet. Cook the patties for 4 to 5 minutes per side, turning once. Serve the burgers on the rolls with your choice of toppings.

- Calories: 368
- Carbohydrates: 66 g
- Fat: 6 g

- Fiber: 8 g
- Protein: 13 g
- Sodium: 322 mg

- Potassium: 413 mg

212. Summer Barley Pilaf With Yogurt Dill Sauce

PREPARATION TIME

15 MIN

COOKING TIME

30 MIN

SERVINGS

3

INGREDIENTS

- 2 2/3 cups low-sodium vegetable broth
- 2 tsp. avocado oil
- 1 small zucchini, diced
- 1/3 cup slivered almonds
- 2 scallions, sliced
- 1 cup barley
- 1/2 cup plain nonfat Greek yogurt
- 2 tsp. grated lemon zest
- 1/4 tsp. dried dill

DIRECTIONS

1. Boil the broth in a large saucepan. Heat up the oil in a skillet. Add the zucchini and sauté for 3 to 4 minutes. Add the almonds and the white parts of the scallions and sauté for 2 minutes. Remove, and transfer it to a small bowl.
2. Add the barley to the skillet and sauté for 2 to 3 minutes to toast. Transfer the barley to the boiling broth and reduce the heat to low, cover, and simmer for 25 minutes or until tender. Remove, and let stand for 10 minutes or until the liquid is absorbed.
3. Simultaneously, mix the yogurt, lemon zest, and dill in a small bowl and set aside. Fluff the barley with a fork. Add the zucchini, almond, and onion mixture and mix gently. To serve, divide the pilaf between two bowls and drizzle the yogurt over each bowl.

NUTRITIONS

- Calories: 545
- Carbohydrates: 87 g
- Fat: 15 g
- Fiber: 19 g
- Protein: 21 g
- Sodium: 37 mg
- Potassium: 694 mg

213. Lentil Quinoa Gratin With Butternut Squash

PREPARATION TIME

15 MIN

COOKING TIME

1H 15 MIN

SERVINGS

3

INGREDIENTS

- For the lentils and squash:
- Nonstick cooking spray
- 2 cups of water
- 1/2 cup dried green or red lentils, rinsed
- A pinch of salt
- 1 tsp. olive oil, divided
- 1/2 cup quinoa
- 1/4 cup diced shallot
- 2 cups frozen cubed butternut squash
- 1/4 cup low-fat milk
- 1 tsp. chopped fresh rosemary
- Freshly ground black pepper
- For the gratin topping:
- 1/4 cup panko bread crumbs
- 1 tsp. olive oil
- 1/3 cup shredded Gruyère cheese

DIRECTIONS

1. Preheat the oven to 400°F. Spray 1 1/2-quart casserole dish or an 8-by-8-inch baking dish with cooking spray.
2. In a medium saucepan, stir the water, lentils, and salt and boil over medium-high heat. Lower the heat once the water is boiling, cover, and simmer for 20 to 25 minutes. Then drain and transfer the lentils to a large bowl and set aside.
3. In the same saucepan, heat up 1/2 tsp. oil over medium heat. Add the quinoa and quickly stir for 1 minute to toast it lightly. Cook according to the package directions, about 20 minutes.
4. While the quinoa cooks, heat the remaining olive oil in a medium skillet over medium-low heat, add the shallots, and sauté them until they are translucent for about 3 minutes. Add the squash, milk, and rosemary and cook for 1 to 2 minutes.
5. Remove, then transfer to the lentil bowl. Add in the quinoa and gently toss all. Season with pepper to taste. Transfer the mixture to the casserole dish.
6. For the gratin topping, mix the panko bread crumbs with the olive oil in a small bowl. Put the bread crumbs over the casserole and top them with the cheese. Bake the casserole for 25 minutes and serve.

NUTRITIONS

- Calories: 576
- Carbohydrates: 87 g
- Fat: 15 g
- Fiber: 12 g
- Protein: 28 g
- Sodium: 329 mg
- Potassium: 1176 mg

214. Brown Rice Casserole With Cottage Cheese

15 MIN

45 MIN

SERVINGS

3

NUTRITIONS

- Calories: 334
- Carbohydrates: 47 g
- Fat: 9 g
- Fiber: 5 g
- Protein: 19 g
- Sodium: 425 mg
- Potassium: 553 mg

INGREDIENTS

- Nonstick cooking spray
- 1 cup quick-cooking brown rice
- 1 tsp. olive oil
- 1/2 cup diced sweet onion
- 1 (10 oz.) bag of fresh spinach
- 1 1/2 cups low-fat cottage cheese
- 1 tbsp. grated Parmesan cheese
- 1/4 cup sunflower seed kernels

DIRECTIONS

1. Preheat the oven to 375°F. Spray a small 1 1/2-quart casserole dish with cooking spray. Cook the rice, as stated in the package directions. Set aside.
2. Warm-up oil in a large nonstick skillet over medium-low heat. Add the onion and sauté for 3 to 4 minutes. Add the spinach and cover the skillet, cooking for 1 to 2 minutes until the spinach wilts. Remove the skillet from the heat.
3. In a medium bowl, mix the rice, spinach mixture, and cottage cheese. Transfer the mixture to the prepared casserole dish. Top with the Parmesan cheese and sunflower seeds, bake for 25 minutes until lightly browned, and serve.

215. Quinoa-Stuffed Peppers Squash

PREPARATION TIME

15 MIN

COOKING TIME

35 MIN

SERVINGS

2

NUTRITIONS

- Calories: 292
- Carbohydrates: 45 g
- Fat: 9 g
- Fiber: 8 g
- Protein: 12 g
- Sodium: 154 mg
- Potassium: 929 mg

INGREDIENTS

- 2 large green bell peppers, halved
- 1 1/2 tsp. olive oil, divided
- 1/2 cup quinoa
- 1/2 cup minced onion
- 1 garlic clove, pressed or minced
- 1 cup chopped portobello mushrooms
- 3 tbsp. grated Parmesan cheese, divided
- 4 oz. tomato sauce

DIRECTIONS

1. Preheat the oven to 400°F. Put the pepper halves on your prepared baking sheet. Brush the insides of peppers with 1/2 tsp. olive oil and bake for 10 minutes.
2. Remove the baking sheet, then set aside. While the peppers bake, cook the quinoa in a large saucepan over medium heat according to the package directions and set aside.
3. Heat the rest of the oil in a medium-size skillet over medium heat. Add the onion and sauté until it's translucent about 3 minutes. Put the garlic and cook for 1 minute.
4. Put the mushrooms in the skillet, adjust the heat to medium-low, cover, and cook for 5 to 6 minutes. Uncover, and if there's still liquid in the pan, reduce the heat and cook until the liquid evaporates.
5. Add the mushroom mixture, 1 tbsp. of Parmesan, and the tomato sauce to the quinoa and gently stir to combine. Carefully spoon the quinoa mixture into each pepper half and sprinkle with the remaining Parmesan. Return the peppers to the oven, bake for 10 to 15 more minutes until tender, and serve.

216. Greek Flatbread With Spinach, Tomatoes & Feta

PREPARATION TIME

5 MIN

COOKING TIME

9 MIN

SERVINGS

2

INGREDIENTS

- 2 cups fresh baby spinach, coarsely chopped
- 2 tsp. olive oil
- 2 slices naan, or another flatbread
- 1/4 cup sliced black olives
- 2 plum tomatoes, thinly sliced
- 1 tsp. salt-free Italian seasoning blend
- 1/4 cup crumbled feta
- 3 tbsp. water

DIRECTIONS

1. Preheat the oven to 400°F. Heat 3 tbsp. water in a small skillet over medium heat. Add the spinach, cover, and steam until wilted, about 2 minutes. Drain off any excess water, then put it aside.
2. Drizzle the oil evenly onto both flatbreads. Top each evenly with spinach, olives, tomatoes, seasoning, and feta. Bake the flatbreads for 5 to 7 minutes, or until lightly browned. Cut each into four pieces and serve hot.

NUTRITIONS

- Calories: 411
- Carbohydrates: 53 g
- Fat: 15 g

- Fiber: 7 g
- Protein: 15 g
- Sodium: 621 mg

- Potassium: 522 mg

217. Mushroom Risotto With Peas

PREPARATION TIME

15 MIN

COOKING TIME

20 MIN

SERVINGS

2

INGREDIENTS

- 2 cups low-sodium vegetable or chicken broth
- 1 tsp. olive oil
- 8 oz. baby portobello mushrooms, thinly sliced
- 1/2 cup frozen peas
- 1 tsp. butter
- 1 cup arborio rice
- 1 tbsp. grated Parmesan cheese

DIRECTIONS

1. Pour the broth into a microwave-proof glass measuring cup. Microwave on high for 1 1/2 minutes or until hot. Heat oil over medium heat in a large saucepan. Add the mushrooms and stir for 1 minute. Cover and cook until soft, about 3 more minutes. Stir in the peas and reduce the heat to low.
2. Put the mushroom batter to the saucepan's sides and add the butter to the middle, heating until melted. Put the rice in the saucepan and stir for 1 to 2 minutes to lightly toast. Add the hot broth, 1/2 cup at a time, and stir gently.
3. As the broth is cooked into the rice, continue adding more broth, 1/2 cup at a time, stirring after each addition, until all broth is added. Once all of the liquid is absorbed (this should take 15 minutes), remove it from the heat. Serve immediately, topped with Parmesan cheese.

NUTRITIONS

- Calories: 430
- Carbohydrates: 83 g
- Fat: 6 g

- Fiber: 5 g
- Protein: 10 g
- Sodium: 78 mg

- Potassium: 558 mg

218. Loaded Tofu Burrito With Black Beans

15 MIN

20 MIN

2

INGREDIENTS

- 4 oz. extra-firm tofu, pressed and cut into 2-inch cubes
- 2 tsp. mesquite salt-free seasoning, divided
- 2 tsp. canola oil
- 1 cup thinly sliced bell peppers
- 1/2 cup diced onions
- 2/3 cup of black beans, drained
- 2 (10-inch) whole-wheat tortillas
- 1 tbsp. sriracha
- Nonfat Greek yogurt, for serving

DIRECTIONS

1. Put the tofu and 1 tsp. seasoning in a medium zip-top plastic freezer bag and toss until the tofu is well coated.
2. Heat up the oil in a medium skillet over medium-high heat. Put the tofu in the skillet. Don't stir; allow the tofu to brown before turning. When lightly browned, about 6 minutes, transfer the tofu from the skillet to a small bowl and set aside.
3. Put the peppers plus onions in the skillet and sauté until tender, about 5 minutes. Lower the heat to medium-low, then put the beans and the remaining seasoning. Cook for 5 minutes.
4. For the burritos, lay each tortilla flat on a work surface. Place half of the tofu in the center of each tortilla, top with half of the pepper-bean mixture, and drizzle with the sriracha.
5. Fold the bottom portion of each tortilla up and over the tofu mixture. Then fold each side into the middle, tuck in, and tightly roll it up toward the open end. Serve with a dollop of yogurt.

NUTRITIONS

- Calories: 327
- Carbohydrates: 41 g
- Fat: 12 g

- Fiber: 11 g
- Protein: 16 g
- Sodium: 282 mg

219. Southwest Tofu Scramble

15 MIN

15 MIN

1

INGREDIENTS

- 1/2 tbsp. olive oil
- 1/2 red onion, chopped
- 2 cups chopped spinach
- 8 oz. firm tofu, drained well
- 1 tsp. ground cumin
- 1/2 tsp. garlic powder
- Optional for serving: sliced avocado or sliced tomatoes

DIRECTIONS

1. Heat up the olive oil in a medium skillet over medium heat. Put the onion and cook for 5 minutes. Add the spinach and cover to steam for 2 minutes.
2. Using a spatula, move the veggies to one side of the pan. Crumble the tofu into the open area in the pan, breaking it up with a fork. Add the cumin and garlic to the crumbled tofu and mix well. Sauté for 5 to 7 minutes until the tofu is slightly browned.
3. Serve immediately with whole-grain bread, fruit, or beans. Top with optional sliced avocado and tomato, if using.

NUTRITIONS

- Calories: 267
- Carbohydrate: 13 g
- Fat: 17 g

- Sodium: 75 mg
- Protein: 23 g

220. Black-Bean and Vegetable Burrito

15 MIN

COOKING TIME

15 MIN

SERVINGS

4

INGREDIENTS

- 1/2 tbsp. olive oil
- 2 red or green bell peppers, chopped
- 1 zucchini or summer squash, diced
- 1/2 tsp. chili powder
- 1 tsp. cumin
- Freshly ground black pepper
- 2 cans black beans drained and rinsed
- 1 cup cherry tomatoes, halved
- 4 (8-inch) whole-wheat tortillas
- Optional for serving: spinach, sliced avocado, chopped scallions, or hot sauce

DIRECTIONS

1. Heat up the oil in a large sauté pan over medium heat. Add the bell peppers and sauté until crisp-tender, about 4 minutes. Add the zucchini, chili powder, cumin, and black pepper to taste, and continue to sauté until the vegetables are tender about 5 minutes.
2. Add the black beans and cherry tomatoes and cook for 5 minutes. Divide between 4 burritos and serve topped with optional ingredients as desired. Enjoy immediately.

NUTRITIONS

- Calories: 311
- Carbohydrate: 52 g
- Fat: 6 g

- Sodium: 499 mg
- Protein: 19 g

221. Baked Eggs in Avocado

PREPARATION TIME

15 MIN

COOKING TIME

15 MIN

SERVINGS

2

INGREDIENTS

- 2 avocados
- Juice of 2 limes
- Freshly ground black pepper
- 4 eggs
- 2 (8-inch) whole-wheat or corn tortillas, warmed
- Optional for serving: halved cherry tomatoes and chopped cilantro

DIRECTIONS

1. Adjust the oven rack to the middle position and preheat the oven to 450°F. Scrape out the center of halved avocado using a spoon of about 1 1/2 tablespoon.
2. Press lime juice over the avocados and season with black pepper to taste, and then place it on a baking sheet. Crack an egg into the avocado.
3. Bake for 10 to 15 minutes. Remove from oven and garnish with optional cilantro and cherry tomatoes and serve with warm tortillas.

NUTRITIONS

- Calories: 534
- Carbohydrate: 30 g
- Fat: 39 g

- Sodium: 462 mg
- Potassium: 1095 mg
- Fiber: 20 g

- Sugar: 3 g
- Protein: 23 g

222. Red Beans and Rice

15 MIN

COOKING TIME

45 MIN

SERVINGS

2

INGREDIENTS

- 1/2 cup dry brown rice
- 1 cup of water, plus 1/4 cup
- 1 can red beans, drained
- 1 tbsp. ground cumin
- Juice of 1 lime
- 4 handfuls of fresh spinach
- Optional toppings: avocado, chopped tomatoes, Greek yogurt, onions

DIRECTIONS

1. Mix rice plus water in a pot and bring to a boil. Cover and reduce heat to a low simmer. Cook for 30 to 40 minutes or according to package directions.
2. Meanwhile, add the beans, 1/4 cup of water, cumin, and lime juice to a medium skillet. Simmer for 5 to 7 minutes.
3. Once the liquid is mostly gone, remove it from the heat and add spinach. Cover and let spinach wilt slightly, 2 to 3 minutes. Mix in with the beans. Serve beans with rice. Add toppings, if using.

NUTRITIONS

- Calories: 232
- Carbohydrate: 41 g
- Fat: 2 g

- Sodium: 210 mg
- Protein: 13 g

223. Hearty Lentil Soup

PREPARATION TIME

15 MIN

COOKING TIME

30 MIN

SERVINGS

4

INGREDIENTS

- 1 tbsp. olive oil
- 2 carrots, peeled and chopped
- 2 celery stalks, diced
- 1 onion, chopped
- 1 tsp. dried thyme
- 1/2 tsp. garlic powder
- Freshly ground black pepper
- 1 (28 oz.) can no-salt diced tomatoes, drained
- 1 cup dry lentils
- 5 cups of water
- Salt

DIRECTIONS

1. Heat up the oil in a large Dutch oven or pot over medium heat. Once the oil is simmering, add the carrot, celery, and onion. Cook, often stirring for 5 minutes.
2. Add the thyme, garlic powder, and black pepper. Cook for 30 seconds. Pour in the drained diced tomatoes and cook for a few more minutes, often stirring to enhance their flavor.
3. Put the lentils, water, plus a pinch of salt. Raise the heat and bring to a boil, then partially cover the pot and reduce heat to maintain a gentle simmer.
4. Cook for 30 minutes, or until lentils are tender but still hold their shape. Ladle into serving bowls and serve with a fresh green salad and whole-grain bread.

NUTRITIONS

- Calories: 168
- Carbohydrate: 35 g
- Fat: 4 g

- Sodium: 130 mg
- Protein: 10 g

224. Black-Bean Soup

PREPARATION TIME

15 MIN

COOKING TIME

20 MIN

SERVINGS

4

INGREDIENTS

- 1 yellow onion
- 1 tbsp. olive oil
- 2 cans black beans, drained
- 1 cup diced fresh tomatoes
- 5 cups low-sodium vegetable broth
- 1/4 tsp. freshly ground black pepper
- 1/4 cup chopped fresh cilantro

DIRECTIONS

1. Cook or sauté the onion in the olive oil for 4 to 5 minutes in a large saucepan over medium heat. Put the black beans, tomatoes, vegetable broth, and black pepper. Boil, then adjust heat to simmer for 15 minutes.
2. Remove, then working in batches, ladle the soup into a blender, and process until somewhat smooth. Put it back in the pot, add the cilantro, and heat until warmed through. Serve immediately.

NUTRITIONS

- Calories: 234
- Carbohydrate: 37 g
- Fat: 5 g

- Sodium: 363 mg
- Protein: 11 g

225. Loaded Baked Sweet Potatoes

PREPARATION TIME

15 MIN

COOKING TIME

20 MIN

SERVINGS

4

INGREDIENTS

- 4 sweet potatoes
- 1/2 cup nonfat or low-fat plain Greek yogurt
- Freshly ground black pepper
- 1 tsp. olive oil
- 1 red bell pepper, cored and diced
- 1/2 red onion, diced
- 1 tsp. ground cumin
- 1 (15 oz.) can chickpeas, drained and rinsed

DIRECTIONS

1. Prick the potatoes using a fork and cook on your microwave's potato setting until potatoes are soft and cooked through, about 8 to 10 minutes for 4 potatoes. If you don't have a microwave, bake at 400°F for about 45 minutes.
2. Combine the yogurt and black pepper in a small bowl and mix well. Heat the oil in a medium pot over medium heat. Add bell pepper, onion, cumin, and additional black pepper to taste.
3. Add the chickpeas, stir to combine, and heat through about 5 minutes. Slice the potatoes lengthwise down the middle and top each half with a portion of the bean mixture followed by 1 to 2 tbsp. of the yogurt. Serve immediately.

NUTRITIONS

- Calories: 264
- Carbohydrate: 51 g
- Fat: 2 g

- Sodium: 124 mg
- Protein: 11 g

226. White Beans With Spinach and Pan-Roasted Tomatoes

15 MIN

COOKING TIME

10 MIN

SERVINGS

4

INGREDIENTS

- 1 tbsp. olive oil
- 4 small plum tomatoes, halved lengthwise
- 10 oz. frozen spinach, defrosted and squeezed of excess water
- 2 garlic cloves, thinly sliced
- 2 tbsp. water
- 1/4 tsp. freshly ground black pepper
- 1 can white beans, drained
- Juice of 1 lemon

DIRECTIONS

1. Heat up the oil in a large skillet over medium-high heat. Put the tomatoes, cut-side down, and cook for 3 to 5 minutes; turn and cook for 1 minute more. Transfer to a plate.
2. Reduce heat to medium and add the spinach, garlic, water, and pepper to the skillet. Cook, tossing until the spinach is heated through, 2 to 3 minutes.
3. Return the tomatoes to the skillet, put the white beans and lemon juice, and toss until heated through 1 to 2 minutes.

NUTRITIONS

- Calories: 293
- Carbohydrate: 43 g
- Fat: 9 g

- Sodium: 267 mg
- Protein: 15 g

227. Black-Eyed Peas and Greens Power Salad

PREPARATION TIME

15 MIN

COOKING TIME

6 MIN

SERVINGS

2

INGREDIENTS

- 1 tbsp. olive oil
- 3 cups purple cabbage, chopped
- 5 cups baby spinach
- 1 cup shredded carrots
- 1 can black-eyed peas, drained
- Juice of 1/2 lemon
- Salt
- Freshly ground black pepper

DIRECTIONS

1. In a medium pan, add the oil and cabbage and sauté for 1 to 2 minutes on medium heat. Add in your spinach, cover for 3 to 4 minutes on medium heat, until greens are wilted. Remove from the heat and add to a large bowl.
2. Add in the carrots, black-eyed peas, and a splash of lemon juice. Season with salt and pepper, if desired. Toss and serve.

NUTRITIONS

- Calories: 320
- Carbohydrate: 49 g
- Fat: 9 g

- Sodium: 351 mg
- Potassium: 544 mg
- Protein: 16 g

228. Butternut-Squash Macaroni and Cheese

PREPARATION TIME

15 MIN

COOKING TIME

20 MIN

SERVINGS

2

INGREDIENTS

- 1 cup whole-wheat ziti macaroni
- 2 cups peeled and cubed butternut squash
- 1 cup nonfat or low-fat milk, divided
- Freshly ground black pepper
- 1 tsp. Dijon mustard
- 1 tbsp. olive oil
- 1/4 cup shredded low-fat cheddar cheese

DIRECTIONS

1. Cook the pasta al dente. Put the butternut squash plus 1/2 cup milk in a medium saucepan and place over medium-high heat. Season with black pepper. Bring it to a simmer. Lower the heat, then cook until fork-tender, 8 to 10 minutes.
2. To a blender, add squash and Dijon mustard. Purée until smooth. Meanwhile, place a large sauté pan over medium heat and add olive oil. Add the squash purée and the remaining 1/2 cup of milk. Simmer for 5 minutes. Add the cheese and stir to combine.
3. Add the pasta to the sauté pan and stir to combine. Serve immediately.

NUTRITIONS

- Calories: 373
- Carbohydrate: 59 g
- Fat: 10 g

- Sodium: 193 mg
- Protein: 14 g

229. Pasta With Tomatoes and Peas

PREPARATION TIME

15 MIN

COOKING TIME

15 MIN

SERVINGS

2

INGREDIENTS

- 1/2 cup whole-grain pasta of choice
- 8 cups water, plus 1/4 for finishing
- 1 cup frozen peas
- 1 tbsp. olive oil
- 1 cup cherry tomatoes, halved
- 1/4 tsp. freshly ground black pepper
- 1 tsp. dried basil
- 1/4 cup grated Parmesan cheese (low-sodium)

DIRECTIONS

1. Cook the pasta al dente. Add the water to the same pot you used to cook the pasta, and when it's boiling, add the peas. Cook for 5 minutes. Drain and set aside.
2. Heat up the oil in a large skillet over medium heat. Add the cherry tomatoes, put a lid on the skillet and let the tomatoes soften for about 5 minutes, stirring a few times.
3. Season with black pepper and basil. Toss in the pasta, peas, and 1/4 cup of water, stir and remove from the heat. Serve topped with Parmesan.

NUTRITIONS

- Calories: 266
- Carbohydrate: 30 g
- Fat: 12 g

- Sodium: 320 mg
- Protein: 13 g

230. Healthy Vegetable Fried Rice

15 MIN

COOKING TIME

10 MIN

SERVINGS

4

INGREDIENTS

For the sauce:
- 1/3 cup garlic vinegar
- 1 1/2 tbsp. dark molasses
- 1 tsp. onion powder

For the fried rice:
- 1 tsp. olive oil
- 2 lightly beaten whole eggs + 4 egg whites
- 1 cup of frozen mixed vegetables
- 1 cup frozen edamame
- 2 cups cooked brown rice

DIRECTIONS

1. Prepare the sauce by combining the garlic vinegar, molasses, and onion powder in a glass jar. Shake well.
2. Heat up oil in a large wok or skillet over medium-high heat. Add eggs and egg whites, let cook until the eggs set, for about 1 minute.
3. Break up eggs with a spatula or spoon into small pieces. Add frozen mixed vegetables and frozen edamame. Cook for 4 minutes, stirring frequently.
4. Add the brown rice and sauce to the vegetable-and-egg mixture. Cook for 5 minutes or until heated through. Serve immediately.

NUTRITIONS

- Calories: 210
- Carbohydrate: 28 g
- Fat: 6 g

- Sodium: 113 mg
- Protein: 13 g

231. Portobello-Mushroom Cheeseburgers

PREPARATION TIME

15 MIN

COOKING TIME

10 MIN

SERVINGS

4

INGREDIENTS

- 4 portobello mushrooms, caps removed and brushed clean
- 1 tbsp. olive oil
- 1/2 tsp. freshly ground black pepper
- 1 tbsp. red wine vinegar
- 4 slices reduced-fat Swiss cheese, sliced thin
- 4 whole-wheat 100-calorie sandwich thins
- 1/2 avocado, sliced thin

DIRECTIONS

1. Heat up a skillet or grill pan over medium-high heat. Clean the mushrooms and remove the stems. Brush each cap with olive oil and sprinkle with black pepper. Place in skillet cap-side up and cook for about 4 minutes. Flip and cook for another 4 minutes.
2. Sprinkle with the red wine vinegar and flip. Add the cheese and cook for 2 more minutes. For optimal melting, place a lid loosely over the pan. Meanwhile, toast the sandwich thins. Create your burgers by topping each with sliced avocado. Enjoy immediately.

NUTRITIONS

- Calories: 245
- Carbohydrate: 28 g
- Fat: 12 g

- Sodium: 266 mg
- Protein: 14 g

232. Baked Chickpea and Rosemary Omelet

PREPARATION TIME

15 MIN

COOKING TIME

15 MIN

SERVINGS

2

INGREDIENTS

- 1/2 tbsp. olive oil
- 4 eggs
- 1/4 cup grated Parmesan cheese
- 1 (15 oz.) can chickpeas, drained and rinsed
- 2 cups packed baby spinach
- 1 cup button mushrooms, chopped
- 2 sprigs rosemary, leaves picked (or 2 tsp. dried rosemary)
- Salt
- Freshly ground black pepper

DIRECTIONS

1. Warm oven to 400°F and puts a baking tray on the middle shelf. Line an 8-inch springform pan with baking paper and grease generously with olive oil. If you don't have a springform pan, grease an oven-safe skillet (or cast-iron skillet) with olive oil.
2. Lightly whisk the eggs and Parmesan. Place chickpeas in the prepared pan. Layer the spinach and mushrooms on top of the beans. Pour the egg mixture on top and scatter the rosemary. Season to taste with salt and pepper.
3. Place the pan on the preheated tray and bake until golden and puffy and the center feels firm and springy for about 15 minutes. Remove from the oven, slice, and serve immediately.

NUTRITIONS

- Calories: 418
- Carbohydrate: 33 g
- Fat: 19 g

- Sodium: 595 mg
- Protein: 30 g

233. Chilled Cucumber-and-Avocado Soup With Dill

PREPARATION TIME

15 MIN

COOKING TIME

30 MIN

SERVINGS

4

INGREDIENTS

- 2 English cucumbers, peeled and diced, plus 1/4 cup reserved for garnish
- 1 avocado, peeled, pitted, and chopped, plus 1/4 cup reserved for garnish
- 1 1/2 cups nonfat or low-fat plain Greek yogurt
- 1/2 cup of cold water
- 1/3 cup loosely packed dill, plus sprigs for garnish
- 1 tbsp. freshly squeezed lemon juice
- 1/4 tsp. freshly ground black pepper
- 1/4 tsp. salt
- 1 clove garlic

DIRECTIONS

1. Purée ingredients in a blender until smooth. If you prefer a thinner soup, add more water until you reach the desired consistency. Divide soup among 4 bowls. Cover with plastic wrap and refrigerate for 30 minutes. Garnish with cucumber, avocado, and dill sprigs, if desired.

NUTRITIONS

- Calories: 142
- Carbohydrate: 12 g
- Fat: 7 g

- Sodium: 193 mg
- Protein: 11 g

234. Turmeric Endives

10 MIN

COOKING TIME

20 MIN

SERVINGS

4

INGREDIENTS

- 2 endives, halved lengthwise
- 2 tbsp. olive oil
- 1 tsp. rosemary, dried
- 1/2 tsp. turmeric powder
- A pinch of black pepper

DIRECTIONS

1. Mix the endives with the oil and the other ingredients in a baking pan, toss gently, bake at 400°F for 20 minutes. Serve as a side dish.

NUTRITIONS

- Calories: 64
- Carbohydrates: 0.8 g
- Fat: 7.1 g
- Fiber: 0.6 g
- Sodium: 3 mg
- Potassium: 50 mg
- Protein: 0.2 g

235. Parmesan Endives

PREPARATION TIME

10 MIN

COOKING TIME

20 MIN

SERVINGS

4

INGREDIENTS

- 4 endives, halved lengthwise
- 1 tbsp. lemon juice
- 1 tbsp. lemon zest, grated
- 2 tbsp. fat-free parmesan, grated
- 2 tbsp. olive oil
- A pinch of black pepper

DIRECTIONS

1. In a baking dish, combine the endives with the lemon juice and the other ingredients except for the parmesan and toss. Sprinkle the parmesan on top, bake the endives at 400°F for 20 minutes, and serve.

NUTRITIONS

- Calories: 71
- Carbohydrates: 2.2 g
- Fat: 7.1 g
- Fiber: 0.9 g
- Sodium: 71 mg
- Potassium: 88 mg
- Protein: 0.9 g

236. Lemon Asparagus

10 MIN

COOKING TIME

20 MIN

SERVINGS

4

INGREDIENTS

- 1 lb. asparagus, trimmed
- 2 tbsp. basil pesto
- 1 tbsp. lemon juice
- A pinch of black pepper
- 3 tbsp. olive oil
- 2 tbsp. cilantro, chopped

DIRECTIONS

1. Arrange the asparagus n a lined baking sheet, add the pesto and the other ingredients, toss, bake at 400°F for 20 minutes. Serve as a side dish.

NUTRITIONS

- Calories: 114
- Carbohydrates: 4.5 g
- Fat: 10.7 g

- Fiber: 2.4 g
- Sodium: 3 mg
- Potassium: 240 mg

- Protein: 2.6 g

237. Lime Carrots

PREPARATION TIME

10 MIN

COOKING TIME

30 MIN

SERVINGS

4

INGREDIENTS

- 1 lb. baby carrots, trimmed
- 1 tbsp. sweet paprika
- 1 tsp. lime juice
- 3 tbsp. olive oil
- A pinch of black pepper
- 1 tsp. sesame seeds

DIRECTIONS

1. Arrange the carrots on a lined baking sheet, add the paprika and the other ingredients except for the sesame seeds, toss, bake at 400°F for 30 minutes. Divide the carrots between plates, sprinkle sesame seeds on top and serve as a side dish.

NUTRITIONS

- Calories: 139
- Carbohydrates: 10.5 g
- Fat 11.2 g

- Fiber: 4 g
- Sodium: 89 mg
- Potassium: 313 mg

- Protein: 1.1 g

238. Garlic Potato Pan

10 MIN

COOKING TIME

1 HOUR

SERVINGS

8

INGREDIENTS

- 1 lb. gold potatoes, peeled and cut into wedges
- 2 tbsp. olive oil
- 1 red onion, chopped
- 2 garlic cloves, minced
- 2 cups coconut cream
- 1 tbsp. thyme, chopped
- 1/4 tsp. nutmeg, ground
- 1/2 cup low-fat parmesan, grated

DIRECTIONS

1. Heat a pan with the oil over medium heat put the onion plus the garlic, and sauté for 5 minutes. Add the potatoes and brown them for 5 minutes more.
2. Add the cream and the rest of the ingredients, toss gently, bring to a simmer and cook over medium heat for 40 minutes more. Divide the mix between plates and serve as a side dish.

NUTRITIONS

- Calories: 230
- Carbohydrates: 14.3 g
- Fat: 19.1 g

- Fiber: 3.3 g
- Cholesterol: 6 mg
- Sodium: 105 mg

- Potassium 426mg
- Protein: 3.6 g

239. Balsamic Cabbage

PREPARATION TIME

10 MIN

COOKING TIME

20 MIN

SERVINGS

4

INGREDIENTS

- 1 lb. green cabbage, roughly shredded
- 2 tbsp. olive oil
- A pinch of black pepper
- 1 shallot, chopped
- 2 garlic cloves, minced
- 2 tbsp. balsamic vinegar
- 2 tsp. hot paprika
- 1 tsp. sesame seeds

DIRECTIONS

1. Heat up a pan with the oil over medium heat, add the shallot and the garlic, and sauté for 5 minutes. Add the cabbage and the other ingredients, toss, cook over medium heat for 15 minutes, divide between plates and serve.

NUTRITIONS

- Calories: 100
- Carbohydrates: 8.2 g
- Fat: 7.5 g

- Fiber: 3 g
- Sodium: 22 mg
- Potassium: 225 mg

- Protein: 1.8 g

240. Chili Broccoli

10 MIN

COOKING TIME

30 MIN

SERVINGS

4

INGREDIENTS

- 2 tbsp. olive oil
- 1 lb. broccoli florets
- 2 garlic cloves, minced
- 2 tbsp. chili sauce
- 1 tbsp. lemon juice
- A pinch of black pepper
- 2 tbsp. cilantro, chopped

DIRECTIONS

1. In a baking pan, combine the broccoli with the oil, garlic, and the other ingredients, toss a bit, and bake at 400°F for 30 minutes. Divide the mix between plates and serve as a side dish.

NUTRITIONS

- Calories: 103
- Carbohydrates: 8.3 g
- Fat: 7.4 g

- Fiber: 3 g
- Sodium: 229 mg
- Potassium: 383 mg

- Protein: 3.4 g

241. Hot Brussels Sprouts

PREPARATION TIME

10 MIN

COOKING TIME

25 MIN

SERVINGS

4

INGREDIENTS

- 1 tbsp. olive oil
- 1 lb. Brussels sprouts, trimmed and halved
- 2 garlic cloves, minced
- 1/2 cup low-fat mozzarella, shredded
- A pinch of pepper flakes, crushed

DIRECTIONS

1. In a baking dish, combine the sprouts with the oil and the other ingredients except for the cheese and toss. Sprinkle the cheese on top, introduce it in the oven, and bake at 400°F for 25 minutes. Divide between plates and serve as a side dish.

NUTRITIONS

- Calories: 111
- Carbohydrates: 11.6 g
- Fat: 3.9 g

- Fiber: 5 g
- Cholesterol: 4 mg
- Sodium: 209 mg

- Potassium: 447 mg
- Protein: 10 g

242. Paprika Brussels Sprouts

10 MIN

25 MIN

4

- 2 tbsp. olive oil
- 1 lb. Brussels sprouts, trimmed and halved
- 3 green onions, chopped
- 2 garlic cloves, minced
- 1 tbsp. balsamic vinegar
- 1 tbsp. sweet paprika
- A pinch of black pepper

1. In a baking pan, combine the Brussels sprouts with the oil and the other ingredients, toss and bake at 400°F for 25 minutes. Divide the mix between plates and serve.

- Calories: 121
- Carbohydrates: 12.6 g
- Fat: 7.6 g
- Fiber: 5.2 g
- Sodium: 31 mg
- Potassium: 521 mg
- Protein: 4.4 g

243. Creamy Cauliflower Mash

10 MIN

25 MIN

4

- 2 lb. cauliflower florets
- 1/2 cup of coconut milk
- A pinch of black pepper
- 1/2 cup low-fat sour cream
- 1 tbsp. cilantro, chopped
- 1 tbsp. chives, chopped
- Water

1. Put the cauliflower in a pot, add water to cover, bring to a boil over medium heat, cook for 25 minutes and drain. Mash the cauliflower, add the milk, black pepper, and the cream, whisk well, divide between plates, sprinkle the rest of the ingredients on top, and serve.

- Calories: 188
- Carbohydrates: 15 g
- Fat: 13.4 g
- Fiber: 6.4 g
- Cholesterol: 13 mg
- Sodium: 88 mg
- Potassium: 811 mg
- Protein: 6.1 g

244. Avocado, Tomato, and Olives Salad

PREPARATION TIME

5 MIN

COOKING TIME

0 MIN

SERVINGS

4

INGREDIENTS

- 2 tbsp. olive oil
- 2 avocados, cut into wedges
- 1 cup kalamata olives, pitted and halved
- 1 cup tomatoes, cubed
- 1 tbsp. ginger, grated
- A pinch of black pepper
- 2 cups baby arugula
- 1 tbsp. balsamic vinegar

DIRECTIONS

1. In a bowl, combine the avocados with the kalamata and the other ingredients, toss and serve as a side dish.

NUTRITIONS

- Calories: 320
- Carbohydrates: 13.9 g
- Fat: 30.4 g

- Fiber: 8.7 g
- Sodium: 305 mg
- Potassium: 655 mg

- Protein: 3 g

245. Radish and Olives Salad

PREPARATION TIME

5 MIN

COOKING TIME

0 MIN

SERVINGS

4

INGREDIENTS

- 2 green onions, sliced
- 1 lb. radishes, cubed
- 2 tbsp. balsamic vinegar
- 2 tbsp. olive oil
- 1 tsp. chili powder
- 1 cup black olives, pitted and halved
- A pinch of black pepper

DIRECTIONS

1. Mix radishes with the onions and the other ingredients in a large salad bowl, toss, and serve as a side dish.

NUTRITIONS

- Calories: 123
- Carbohydrates: 6.9 g
- Fat: 10.8 g

- Fiber: 3.3 g
- Sodium: 345 mg
- Potassium: 306 mg

- Protein: 1.3 g

246. Spinach and Endives Salad

5 MIN

0 MIN

4

- 2 endives, roughly shredded
- 1 tbsp. dill, chopped
- 1/4 cup lemon juice
- 1/4 cup olive oil
- 2 cups baby spinach
- 2 tomatoes, cubed
- 1 cucumber, sliced
- 1/2 cups walnuts, chopped

1. In a large bowl, combine the endives with the spinach and the other ingredients, toss and serve as a side dish.

- Calories: 238
- Carbohydrates: 8.4 g
- Fat: 22.3 g
- Fiber: 3.1 g
- Sodium: 24 mg
- Potassium: 506 mg
- Protein: 5.7 g

247. Basil Olives Mix

5 MIN

0 MIN

4

- 2 tbsp. olive oil
- 1 tbsp. balsamic vinegar
- A pinch of black pepper
- 4 cups corn
- 2 cups black olives, pitted and halved
- 1 red onion, chopped
- 1/2 cup cherry tomatoes halved
- 1 tbsp. basil, chopped
- 1 tbsp. jalapeno, chopped
- 2 cups romaine lettuce, shredded

1. Mix the corn with the olives, lettuce, and the other ingredients in a large bowl, toss well, divide between plates and serve as a side dish.

- Calories: 290
- Carbohydrates: 37.6 g
- Fat: 16.1 g
- Fiber: 7.4 g
- Sodium: 613 mg
- Potassium: 562 mg
- Protein: 6.2 g

248. Arugula Salad

INGREDIENTS

- 1/4 cup pomegranate seeds
- 5 cups baby arugula
- 6 tbsp. green onions, chopped
- 1 tbsp. balsamic vinegar
- 2 tbsp. olive oil
- 3 tbsp. pine nuts
- 1/2 shallot, chopped

DIRECTIONS

1. In a salad bowl, combine the arugula with the pomegranate and the other ingredients, toss and serve.

NUTRITIONS

- Calories: 120
- Carbohydrates: 4.2 g
- Fat: 11.6 g
- Fiber: 0.9 g
- Sodium: 9 mg
- Potassium: 163 mg
- Protein: 1.8 g

249. Spanish Rice

INGREDIENTS

- 2 cups brown rice
- 2 cups extra-virgin olive oil
- 2 cloves garlic, minced
- 1 onion, diced
- 2 tomatoes, diced
- 1 jalapeno, seeded and diced
- 1 tbsp. tomato paste
- 2/4 cups cilantro, chopped
- 3 cups Chicken broth, low-sodium

DIRECTIONS

1. Warm the oven to 375°F. Puree the tomatoes, onion, plus garlic using a blender or food processor. Measure out two cups of this vegetable puree to use and discard the excess.
2. Into a large oven-safe Dutch pan, heat the extra virgin olive oil over medium heat until hot and shimmering. Add in the jalapeno and rice to toast, cooking while occasionally stirring for two to three minutes.
3. Slowly stir the chicken broth into the rice, followed by the vegetable puree and tomato paste. Stir until combine and increase the heat to medium-high until the broth reaches a boil.
4. Cover the Dutch pan with an oven-safe lid, transfer the pot to the preheated oven, and bake for 1 hour and 15 minutes. Remove and stir the cilantro into the rice. Serve.

NUTRITIONS

- Calories: 265
- Carbohydrates: 40 g
- Fat: 3 g
- Sodium: 32 mg
- Potassium: 322 mg
- Protein: 5 g

250. Sweet Potatoes and Apples

15 MIN

COOKING TIME

40 MIN

SERVINGS

4

INGREDIENTS

- 2 cubes sweet potatoes, sliced into 1-inch
- 2 apples, cut into 1-inch cubes
- 3 tbsp. extra virgin olive oil, divided
- 1/4 tsp. black pepper, ground
- 1 tsp. cinnamon, ground
- 2 tbsp. maple syrup
- Cooking spray

DIRECTIONS

1. Warm the oven to425°F and grease a large baking sheet with non-stick cooking spray. Toss the cubed sweet potatoes with 2 tbsp. olive oil and black pepper until coated. Roast the potatoes for 20 minutes, stirring them once halfway through the process.
2. Meanwhile, toss the apples with the remaining tbsp. olive oil, cinnamon, and maple syrup until evenly coated. After the sweet potatoes have cooked for 20 minutes, add the apples to the baking sheet and toss the sweet potatoes and apples.
3. Return to the oven, then roast it for 20 more minutes, once again giving it a good stir halfway through. Once the potatoes and apples are caramelized from the maple syrup, remove them from the oven and serve hot.

NUTRITIONS

- Calories: 100
- Carbohydrates: 22 g
- Fat: 0 g
- Sodium: 38 mg
- Potassium: 341 mg
- Protein: 2 g

251. Roasted Turnips

PREPARATION TIME

15 MIN

COOKING TIME

30 MIN

SERVINGS

4

INGREDIENTS

- 2 cubes turnips, peels, and cut into ½-inch cubes
- 1/4 tsp. black pepper, ground
- 5 tsp. garlic powder
- 5 tsp. onion powder
- 1 tbsp. extra virgin olive oil

DIRECTIONS

1. Warm the oven to400°F and prepare a large baking sheet, setting it aside. Begin by trimming the top and bottom edges off of the turnips and peeling them if you wish. Slice them into 1/2-inch cubes.
2. Toss the turnips with the extra virgin olive oil and seasonings and then spread them out on the prepared baking sheet. Roast the turnips until tender, stirring them halfway through, about thirty minutes in total.

NUTRITIONS

- Calories: 50
- Carbohydrates: 5 g
- Fat: 4 g
- Protein: 1 g
- Sodium: 44 mg
- Potassium: 134 mg

252. No-Mayo Potato Salad

PREPARATION TIME

15 MIN

COOKING TIME

20 MIN

SERVINGS

2

INGREDIENTS

- 3 lb. red potatoes
- 1/2 cup extra virgin olive oil
- 5 tbsp. white wine vinegar, divided
- 2 tsp. Dijon mustard
- 1 cup red onion, sliced
- 5 tsp. black pepper, ground
- 2 tbsp. basil, fresh, chopped
- 2 tbsp. dill weed, fresh, chopped
- 2 tbsp. parsley, fresh, chopped
- Water

DIRECTIONS

1. Add the red potatoes to a large pot and cover them with water until the water level is two inches above the potatoes. Put the pot on high heat, then boil potatoes until they are tender when poked with a fork, about 15 to 20 minutes. Drain off the water.
2. Let the potatoes cool until they can easily be handled but are still warm, then cut them in half and put them in a large bowl. Stir in 3 tbsp. the white wine vinegar, giving the potatoes a good stir so that they can evenly absorb the vinegar.
3. Mix the rest of 2 tbsp. vinegar, extra virgin olive oil, Dijon mustard, and black pepper in a small bowl. Add this mixture to the potatoes and give them a good toss to thoroughly coat the potatoes.
4. Toss in the red onion and minced herbs. Serve at room temperature or chilled. Serve immediately or store in the fridge for up to four days.

NUTRITIONS

- Calories: 144
- Carbohydrates: 19 g
- Fat: 7 g

- Protein: 2 g
- Sodium: 46 mg
- Potassium: 814 mg

253. Zucchini Tomato Bake

PREPARATION TIME

15 MIN

COOKING TIME

30 MIN

SERVINGS

4

INGREDIENTS

- 10 oz. grape tomatoes, cut in half
- 2 Zucchini
- 5 cloves garlic, minced
- 1 tsp. Italian herb seasoning
- 1/4 black pepper, ground
- 1/3 cup parsley, fresh, chopped
- 5 cups Parmesan cheese, low-sodium, grated
- Cooking spray

DIRECTIONS

1. Warm the oven to 350°F and coat a large baking sheet with non-stick cooking spray. Mix the tomatoes, zucchini, garlic, Italian herb seasoning, Black pepper, and Parmesan cheese in a bowl.
2. Put the mixture out on the baking sheet and roast until the zucchini for 30 minutes. Remove, and garnish with parsley over the top before serving.

NUTRITIONS

- Calories: 35
- Carbohydrates: 4 g
- Fat: 2 g

- Protein: 2 g
- Sodium: 30 mg
- Potassium: 649 mg

Chapter 8
Desserts

254. Poached Pears

15 MIN

COOKING TIME

30 MIN

SERVINGS

4

INGREDIENTS

- 1/4 cup apple juice extract
- 1/2 cup fresh raspberries
- 1 cup of orange juice extract
- 1 tsp. cinnamon, ground
- 1 tsp. ground nutmeg
- 2 tbsp. orange zest
- 4 whole pears, peeled, destemmed, core removed

DIRECTIONS

1. In a bowl, combine the fruit juices, nutmeg, and cinnamon, and then stir evenly. In a shallow pan, pour the fruit juice mixture, and set to medium fire.
2. Adjust the heat to simmer for 30 minutes; turn pears frequently to maintain poaching, do not boil. Transfer poached pears to a serving bowl; garnish with orange zest and raspberries.

NUTRITIONS

- Calories: 140
- Carbohydrates: 34 g
- Fats: 0.5 g

- Proteins: 1 g
- Fibers: 2 g
- Sodium: 9 mg

255. Pumpkin With Chia Seeds Pudding

PREPARATION TIME

60 MIN

COOKING TIME

0 MIN

SERVINGS

4

INGREDIENTS

For the pudding:
- 1/2 cup organic chia seeds
- 1/4 cup raw maple syrup
- 1 1/4 cup low-fat milk
- 1 cup pumpkin puree extract

For the toppings:
- 1/4 cup organic sunflower seeds
- 1/4 cup coarsely chopped almonds
- 1/4 cup blueberries

DIRECTIONS

1. Add all the ingredients for the pudding in a bowl and mix until blended. Cover and store in a chiller for 1 hour. Remove from the chiller, transfer contents to a jar and add the ingredients for the toppings. Serve immediately.

NUTRITIONS

- Calories: 189
- Carbohydrates: 27 g
- Fats: 7 g

- Sodium: 42 mg
- Potassium: 311 mg
- Sugar: 18 g

- Fibers: 4 g
- Proteins: 5 g

256. Chocolate Truffles

15 MIN

0 MIN

24

For the truffles:
- 1/2 cup cacao powder
- 1/4 cup chia seeds
- 1/4 cup flaxseed meal
- 1/4 cup maple syrup
- 1 cup flour
- 2 tbsp. almond milk

For the coatings:
- Cacao powder
- Chia seeds
- Flour
- Shredded coconut, unsweetened

1. Place all the ingredients for the truffle in a blender; pulse until it is thoroughly blended; transfer contents to a bowl. Form into chocolate balls, then cover with the coating ingredients. Serve immediately.

- Calories: 70
- Carbohydrates: 14 g
- Fats: 1 g
- Sodium: 2 mg
- Fibers: 2 g
- Sugar: 11 g
- Proteins: 1 g

257. Grilled Pineapple Strips

15 MIN

5 MIN

6

- Vegetable oil
- Dash of iodized salt
- 1 pineapple
- 1 tbsp. lime juice extract
- 1 tbsp. olive oil
- 1 tbsp. raw honey
- 3 tbsp. brown sugar

1. Peel the pineapple, remove the eyes of the fruit, and discard the core. Slice lengthwise, forming six wedges. Mix the rest of the ingredients in a bowl until blended.
2. Brush the coating mixture on the pineapple (reserve some for basting). Grease an oven or outdoor grill rack with vegetable oil.
3. Place the pineapple wedges on the grill rack and heat for a few minutes per side until golden brownish, basting it frequently with a reserved glaze. Serve on a platter.

- Calories: 97
- Carbohydrates: 20 g
- Fats: 2 g
- Sodium: 2 mg
- Sugar: 17 g
- Fibers: 1 g
- Proteins: 1 g

258. Raspberry Peach Pancake

PREPARATION TIME

15 MIN

COOKING TIME

30 MIN

SERVINGS

4

INGREDIENTS

- 1/2 tsp. sugar
- 1/2 cup raspberries
- 1/2 cup fat-free milk
- 1/2 cup all-purpose flour
- 1/4 cup vanilla yogurt
- 1/8 tsp. iodized salt
- 1 tbsp. butter
- 2 medium peeled, thinly sliced peaches
- 3 lightly beaten organic eggs

DIRECTIONS

1. Preheat oven to 400°F. Toss peaches and raspberries with sugar in a bowl. Melt butter on a 9-inch round baking plate. Mix eggs, milk, plus salt in a small bowl until blended; whisk in the flour.
2. Remove the round baking plate from the oven, tilt to coat the bottom and sides with the melted butter; pour in the flour mixture.
3. Put it in the oven until it becomes brownish and puffed. Remove the pancake from the oven. Serve immediately with more raspberries and vanilla yogurt.

NUTRITIONS

- Calories: 199
- Carbohydrates: 25 g
- Fats: 7 g

- Sodium: 173 mg
- Cholesterol: 149 g
- Sugar: 11 g

- Fibers: 3 g
- Proteins: 9 g

259. Mango Rice Pudding

PREPARATION TIME

15 MIN

COOKING TIME

35 MIN

SERVINGS

4

INGREDIENTS

- 1/2 tsp. ground cinnamon
- 1/4 tsp. iodized salt
- 1 tsp. vanilla extract
- 1 cup long-grain uncooked brown rice
- 2 mediums ripe, peeled, cored mango
- 1 cup vanilla soymilk
- 2 tbsp. sugar
- 2 cups of water

DIRECTIONS

1. Bring saltwater to a boil in a saucepan to cook rice; after a few minutes, simmer covered for 30 to 35 minutes until the rice absorbs the water. Mash the mango with a mortar and pestle or stainless-steel fork.
2. Pour milk, sugar, cinnamon, and the mashed mango into the rice; cook uncovered on low heat, stirring frequently. Remove the mango rice pudding from the heat, then stir in the vanilla soymilk. Serve immediately.

NUTRITIONS

- Calories: 275
- Carbohydrates: 58 mg
- Fats: 3 g

- Sodium: 176 mg
- Sugar: 20 g
- Fibers: 3 g

260. Choco Banana Cake

15 MIN

COOKING TIME

30 MIN

SERVINGS

18

INGREDIENTS

- 1/2 cup semisweet dark chocolate
- 1/2 cup brown sugar
- 1/2 tsp. baking soda
- 1/4 cup unsweetened cocoa powder
- 1/4 cup canola oil
- 3/4 cup soymilk
- 1 large egg
- 1 egg white
- 1 large, ripe, mashed banana
- 1 tbsp. lemon juice extract
- 1 tsp. vanilla extract
- 2 cups all-purpose flour

DIRECTIONS

1. Preheat the oven to 350 °F. Coat a baking pan with a non-stick spray. Whisk brown sugar, flour, baking soda, and cocoa powder in a bowl.
2. In another bowl, whisk bananas, lemon juice extract, vanilla extract, oil, soymilk, egg, and egg white. Create a hole in the flour mixture's core or center, then pour in the banana mixture and mix in the dark chocolate.
3. Stir all the ingredients with a spoon until thoroughly blended; spoon the batter onto the baking pan. Place in the oven and bake for 25 to 30 minutes until the center springs back when pressed lightly using your fingertips.

NUTRITIONS

- Calories: 150
- Carbohydrates: 27 g
- Fats: 3 g

- Sodium: 52 mg
- Cholesterol: 12 mg
- Proteins: 3 g

261. Zesty Zucchini Muffins

PREPARATION TIME

15 MIN

COOKING TIME

30 MIN

SERVINGS

12

INGREDIENTS

- Vegetable oil cooking spray
- 1/2 cup of sugar
- 1/4 tsp. iodized salt
- 1/4 tsp. ground nutmeg
- 3/4 cup skim milk
- 1 cup shredded zucchini
- 1 tbsp. baking powder
- 1 large egg
- 2 tsp. grated lemon rind
- 2 cups of all-purpose flour
- 3 tbsp. vegetable oil

DIRECTIONS

1. Mix the flour, baking powder, sugar, salt, ground nutmeg, plus lemon rinds in a bowl. Create a well in the center of the flour batter. In another bowl, mix zucchini, milk, vegetable oil, and egg. Coat muffin cups with vegetable oil cooking spray.
2. Divide the batter equally into 12 muffin cups. Transfer the muffin cups to the baking pan, put them in a microwave oven, and bake at 400 °F for 30 minutes until light golden brown. Remove, then allow to cool on a wire rack before serving.

NUTRITIONS

- Calories: 169
- Carbohydrates: 29.1 g
- Fats: 4.8 g

- Sodium: 211.5 mg
- Potassium: 80.2 g
- Fibers: 2.5 g

- Sugar: 12.8 g
- Proteins: 0 g

262. Blueberry Oat Muffins

15 MIN

COOKING TIME

30 MIN

SERVINGS

12

INGREDIENTS

- 1/2 cup raw oatmeal
- 1/2 tsp. baking powder
- 1/2 tsp. iodized salt
- 1/2 cup dry milk
- 1/4 cup of vegetable oil
- 1/4 tsp. baking soda
- 1/3 cup sugar
- 1 1/2 cup flour
- 1 cup milk
- 1 cup blueberries
- 1 egg

DIRECTIONS

1. Preheat oven to 350 °F. Coat the muffin tins with vegetable oil. Mix or combine the flour, baking soda, baking powder, oats, sugar, and salt in a bowl. Mix milk, dry milk, egg, and vegetable oil in another bowl.
2. Pour the bowl of wet ingredients into the bowl of dry ingredients and mix partially. Add the blueberries and mix until the consistency turns lumpy. Scoop blueberry batter into the muffin tins.
3. Bake for 30 minutes until the muffins turn golden brown on the edges. Serve warm immediately or put it in an airtight container and store it in the refrigerator to chill.

NUTRITIONS

- Calories: 150
- Carbohydrates: 22 g
- Fats: 5 g

- Sodium: 180 mg
- Fibers: 1 g
- Proteins: 4 g

263. Banana Bread

PREPARATION TIME

15 MIN

COOKING TIME

60 MIN

SERVINGS

14

INGREDIENTS

- Vegetable oil cooking spray
- 1/2 cup brown rice flour
- 1/2 cup amaranth flour
- 1/2 cup tapioca flour
- 1/2 cup millet flour
- 1/2 cup quinoa flour
- 1/2 cup of raw sugar
- 3/4 cup egg whites
- 1/8 tsp. iodized salt
- 1 tsp. baking soda
- 2 tbsp. grapeseed oil
- 2 pieces of mashed banana

DIRECTIONS

1. Preheat oven to 350°F. Coat a loaf pan with a vegetable oil cooking spray, dust evenly with a bit of flour, iodized salt, and set aside. In a bowl, mix the brown rice flour, amaranth flour, tapioca flour, millet flour, quinoa flour, and baking soda.
2. Coat a separate bowl with vegetable oil, then mix eggs, sugar, and mashed bananas. Pour the bowl of wet ingredients into the bowl of dry ingredients and mix thoroughly. Scoop the mixture into the loaf pan. Bake for an hour.
3. To check the doneness, insert a toothpick in the center of the loaf pan; if you remove the toothpick and it has no batter sticking to it, remove the bread from the oven. Slice and serve immediately and store the remaining banana bread in a refrigerator to prolong shelf life.

NUTRITIONS

- Calories: 150
- Fats: 3 g
- Sodium: 150 mg

- Fibers: 2 g
- Sugar: 7 g
- Proteins: 4 g

264. Milk Chocolate Pudding

15 MIN

COOKING TIME

15 MIN

SERVINGS

4

INGREDIENTS

- 1/2 tsp. vanilla extract
- 1/3 cup chocolate chips
- 1/8 tsp. salt
- 2 cups nonfat milk
- 2 tbsp. cocoa powder
- 2 tbsp. sugar
- 3 tbsp. cornstarch

DIRECTIONS

1. Mix cocoa powder, cornstarch, sugar, and salt in a saucepan and whisk in milk; frequently stir over medium heat.
2. Remove, put the chocolate chips and vanilla extract, stir until the chocolate chips and vanilla melt into the pudding. Pour contents into serving bowls and store in a chiller. Serve chilled.

NUTRITIONS

- Calories: 197
- Carbohydrates: 9 g
- Fats: 5 g
- Sodium: 5 mg
- Proteins: 0.5 g

265. Minty Lime and Grapefruit Yogurt Parfait

PREPARATION TIME

15 MIN

COOKING TIME

0 MIN

SERVINGS

46

INGREDIENTS

- A handful of torn mint leaves
- 2 tsp. grated lime zest
- 2 tbsp. lime juice extract
- 3 tbsp. raw honey
- 4 large red grapefruits
- 4 cups reduced-fat plain yogurt

DIRECTIONS

1. Cut the top and lower part of the red grapefruits and stand the fruit upright on a cutting board. Discard the peel with a knife and slice along the membrane of each segment to remove the skin.
2. Mix yogurt, lime juice extract, and lime zest in a bowl. Layer half of the grapefruit and yogurt mixture into 6 parfait glasses; add another layer until the glass is filled and then drizzle with honey and top with mint leaves. Serve immediately.

NUTRITIONS

- Calories: 207
- Carbohydrates: 39 mg
- Fats: 3 g
- Sodium: 115 mg
- Cholesterol: 10 mg
- Sugar: 36 g
- Fibers: 3 g

266. Peach Tarts

15 MIN

COOKING TIME

55 MIN

SERVINGS

8

INGREDIENTS

Tart Ingredients:
- 1/4 cup softened butter
- 1/4 tsp. ground nutmeg
- 1 cup all-purpose flour
- 3 tbsp. sugar

Filling ingredients:
- 1/4 tsp. ground cinnamon
- 1/4 cup coarsely chopped almonds
- 1/8 tsp. almond extract
- 1/3 cup sugar
- 2 lb. peaches medium, peeled, thinly sliced

DIRECTIONS

1. Preheat oven to 375 °F. Mix butter, nutmeg, and sugar in a bowl until light and fluffy. Add and beat in flour until well-blended. Place the batter on an ungreased fluted tart baking pan and press firmly on the bottom and topsides.
2. Put it in the medium rack of the preheated oven and bake for about 10 minutes until it turns to a crust. In a bowl, coat peaches with sugar, flour, cinnamon, almond extract, and almonds.
3. Open the oven, put the tart crust on the lower rack of the oven, and pour in the peach filling; bake for about 40 to 45 minutes. Remove, cool, and serve; or cover with a cling wrap and refrigerate to serve chilled.

NUTRITIONS

- Calories: 222
- Carbohydrates: 36 g
- Fats: 8 g
- Sodium: 46 mg
- Cholesterol: 15 mg
- Sugar: 21 g
- Fibers: 3 g
- Proteins: 4 g

267. Raspberry Nuts Parfait

PREPARATION TIME

15 MIN

COOKING TIME

10 MIN

SERVINGS

1

INGREDIENTS

- 1/4 cup frozen raspberries
- 1/4 cup frozen blueberries
- 1/4 cup toasted, thinly sliced nuts
- 1 cup nonfat, plain Greek yogurt
- 2 tsp. raw honey

DIRECTIONS

1. First, layer Greek yogurt in a parfait glass; add berries; layer yogurt again, top with nuts and more berries; drizzle with honey. Serve chilled.

NUTRITIONS

- Calories: 378
- Carbohydrates: 35 g
- Fats: 15 g
- Sodium: 83 mg
- Fibers: 6 g
- Sugar: 25 g
- Proteins: 30 g

268. Strawberry Bruschetta

15 MIN

COOKING TIME

0 MIN

SERVINGS

12

INGREDIENTS

- 1 loaf sliced Ciabatta bread
- 8 oz. goat cheese
- 1 cup basil leaves
- 2 containers of strawberries, sliced
- 5 tbsp. balsamic glaze

DIRECTIONS

1. Wash and slice strawberries; set aside. Wash and chop the basil leaves; set aside. Slice the ciabatta bread and spread some goat cheese evenly on each slice; add strawberries, balsamic glaze, and top with basil leaves. Serve on a platter.

NUTRITIONS

- Calories: 80
- Carbohydrates: 12 g
- Fats: 2 g

- Sodium: 59 mg
- Proteins: 3 g

269. Vanilla Cupcakes With Cinnamon-Fudge Frosting

PREPARATION TIME

10 MIN

COOKING TIME

18 MIN

SERVINGS

1 DOZEN

INGREDIENTS

- 1 1/2 cups white whole-wheat flour
- 3/4 cup sugar
- 3/4 tsp. sodium-free baking powder
- 1/2 tsp. sodium-free baking soda
- 1 cup nondairy milk
- 6 tbsp. canola oil
- 1 tbsp. apple cider vinegar
- 1 tbsp. pure vanilla extract

Frosting:
- 2 cups powdered sugar
- 1/3 cup unsweetened cocoa powder
- 4 tbsp. non-hydrogenated vegetable shortening
- 4 tbsp. nondairy milk
- 1 tsp. ground cinnamon
- 1 tsp. pure vanilla extract

DIRECTIONS

1. Heat oven to 350°F. Line a 12 muffin tin with paper liners and put aside. Mix or combine the flour, sugar, baking powder, and baking soda into a mixing bowl. Add the remaining batter ingredients and stir just until combined.
2. Split the batter evenly between the muffin cups, then bake for 18 minutes. Remove, then put on a wire rack to cool. Beat until fluffy the frosting ingredients into a mixing bowl. Frost cupcakes. Serve immediately.

NUTRITIONS

- Calories: 347
- Carbohydrates: 60 g
- Fat: 7 g

- Sodium: 46 mg
- Fiber: 4 g
- Sugar: 3 g

- Protein: 13 g

270. Chocolate Cupcakes With Vanilla Frosting

15 MIN

20 MIN

12

INGREDIENTS

- 1 1/2 cups white whole-wheat flour
- 1 cup of sugar
- 2 tsp. sodium-free baking soda
- 1/4 cup unsweetened cocoa powder
- 1 cup of water
- 4 tbsp. canola oil
- 4 tbsp. unsweetened applesauce
- 1 tbsp. pure vanilla extract
- 1 tsp. distilled white vinegar

Frosting:
- 1 1/2 cups powdered sugar
- 4 tbsp. non-hydrogenated vegetable shortening
- 2 1/2 tbsp. nondairy milk
- 1 tbsp. pure vanilla extract

DIRECTIONS

1. Warm oven to 350°F. Prepare a 12 muffins tin with paper liners and set it aside. Measure the flour, sugar, and baking soda into a mixing bowl and whisk well to combine. Put the rest of the batter ingredients and stir just until combined.
2. Divide the batter evenly into the muffin cups. Bake for 20 minutes or until a toothpick inserted in the center of the cupcakes comes out clean.
3. Remove, then put on a wire rack to cool. Mix the frosting ingredients into a clean mixing bowl, then frost cupcakes. Serve immediately.

NUTRITIONS

- Calories: 272
- Carbohydrates: 45 g
- Fat: 9 g
- Sodium: 2 mg
- Fiber: 1 g
- Sugar: 32 g
- Protein: 2 g

271. Chocolate Chip Banana Muffin Top Cookies

15 MIN

15 MIN

16

INGREDIENTS

- 1 cup quick oats
- 1 cup white whole-wheat flour
- 1/4 cup sugar
- 1 tbsp. sodium-free baking powder
- 1 tsp. ground cinnamon
- 3 ripe medium bananas, mashed
- 4 tbsp. canola oil
- 1 tbsp. pure vanilla extract
- 3/4 cup chocolate chips

DIRECTIONS

1. Preheat oven to 350°F. Put aside a baking sheet with parchment paper. Measure the oats, flour, sugar, baking powder, and cinnamon into a mixing bowl and whisk. Put the rest of the ingredients and stir just until combined.
2. Using a medium-sized ice cream scoop, scoop the batter onto the prepared baking sheet, leaving an inch or two between cookies. Bake for 15 minutes. Remove, then put on a wire rack to cool. Serve immediately.

NUTRITIONS

- Calories: 150
- Carbohydrates: 23 g
- Fat: 6 g
- Sodium: 0 mg
- Fiber: 1 g
- Sugar: 10 g
- Protein: 2 g

272. Lemon Cookies

15 MIN

COOKING TIME

10 MIN

SERVINGS

36

INGREDIENTS

- 2 1/2 cups white whole-wheat flour
- 1 1/2 cups sugar
- 1 tbsp. sodium-free baking powder
- 3/4 cup canola oil
- 2 large lemons, juice, and grated zest
- 1 tbsp. pure vanilla extract

DIRECTIONS

1. Preheat oven to 350°F. Mix the flour, sugar, plus baking powder into a mixing bowl. Put the rest of the ingredients and stir to form a stiff dough.
2. Drop by rounded tbsp. onto an ungreased baking sheet. Bake for 10 minutes. Remove, then let cool on sheet for a few minutes before transferring to a wire rack to cool fully. Serve immediately.

NUTRITIONS

- Calories: 106
- Carbohydrates: 15 g
- Fat: 5 g
- Sodium: 0 mg
- Fiber: 0 g
- Sugar: 8 g
- Protein: 1 g

273. Peanut Butter Chocolate Chip Blondies

PREPARATION TIME

15 MIN

COOKING TIME

20 MIN

SERVINGS

24

INGREDIENTS

- 1/4 cup salt-free peanut butter
- 3/4 cup light brown sugar
- 1/2 cup unsweetened applesauce
- 1/4 cup canola oil
- 2 egg whites
- 1 tbsp. pure vanilla extract
- 2 tsp. sodium-free baking powder
- 1 cup unbleached all-purpose flour
- 1/2 cup white whole-wheat flour
- 1/2 cup semisweet chocolate chips

DIRECTIONS

1. Preheat oven to 400°F. Oiled and flour a 9-inch × 13-inch baking pan and set aside. Measure the peanut butter, sugar, applesauce, oil, egg whites, and vanilla into a mixing bowl and stir well to combine.
2. Add the baking powder and mix. Gradually add in the flours, stirring well. Fold in the chocolate chips. Spread batter in prepared pan and smooth to even.
3. Bake for 20 minutes. Remove, then let it cool. Cool before cutting into bars and serving.

NUTRITIONS

- Calories: 18
- Carbohydrates: 17 g
- Fat: 5 g
- Sodium: 7 mg
- Fiber: 1 g
- Sugar: 10 g
- Protein: 2 g

274. Ginger Snaps

15 MIN

COOKING TIME

10 MIN

SERVINGS

18

INGREDIENTS

- 4 tbsp. unsalted butter
- 1/2 cup light brown sugar
- 2 tbsp. molasses
- 1 egg white
- 2 1/2 tsp. ground ginger
- 1/4 tsp. ground allspice
- 1 tsp. sodium-free baking soda
- 1/2 cup unbleached all-purpose flour
- 12 cup white whole-wheat flour
- 1 tbsp. sugar

DIRECTIONS

1. Warm oven to 375°F. Put aside a baking sheet with parchment paper. Put the butter, sugar, plus molasses into a mixing bowl and beat well.
2. Mix the egg white, ginger, and allspice. Mix in the baking soda, then put the flours, then beat.
3. Roll the dough into small balls. Put the balls on a prepared baking sheet and press down using a glass dipped in the tablespoon sugar.
4. Once the glass presses on the dough, it will moisten sufficiently to coat with sugar. Bake for 10 minutes. Let it cool, then serve.

NUTRITIONS

- Calories: 81
- Carbohydrates: 14 g
- Fat: 2 g

- Sodium: 6 mg
- Fiber: 0 g
- Sugar: 8 g

- Protein: 1 g

275. Carrot Cake Cookies

PREPARATION TIME

15 MIN

COOKING TIME

12 MIN

SERVINGS

36

INGREDIENTS

- 3 medium carrots, shredded
- 1 1/2 cups white whole-wheat flour
- 3/4 cup oat flour
- 3/4 cup light brown sugar
- 1 egg white
- 1/3 cup canola oil
- 1 tbsp. pure vanilla extract
- 1 tsp. sodium-free baking powder
- 1 1/2 tsp. ground cinnamon
- 1/2 tsp. ground nutmeg
- 1/4 tsp. ground ginger
- 1/8 tsp. ground cloves

DIRECTIONS

1. Preheat oven to 375°F. Prepare and line a baking sheet with parchment paper and set it aside. Place all the ingredients into a mixing bowl and stir well to combine. The dough will be quite sticky.
2. Put onto a lined baking sheet. Bake for 12 minutes. Remove, then transfer cookies to a wire rack to cool. Store in an airtight container.

NUTRITIONS

- Calories: 67
- Carbohydrates: 10 g
- Fat: 2 g

- Sodium: 7 mg
- Fiber: 0 g
- Sugar: 4 g

- Protein: 1 g

276. Chewy Pumpkin Oatmeal Raisin Cookies

15 MIN

COOKING TIME

16 MIN

SERVINGS

48

INGREDIENTS

- 1 cup pumpkin purée
- 1 2/3 cups sugar
- 2 tbsp. molasses
- 1 1/2 tsp. pure vanilla extract
- 2/3 cup canola oil
- 1 tbsp. ground flaxseed
- 2 tsp. Ener-G Baking Soda Substitute
- 1 tsp. ground cinnamon
- 1/2 tsp. ground nutmeg
- 1 cup unbleached all-purpose flour
- 1 cup white whole-wheat flour
- 1 1/3 cups rolled or quick oats
- 1 cup seedless raisins

DIRECTIONS

1. Preheat oven to 350°F. Spray 2 baking sheets lightly with oil and set aside. Measure the ingredients into a large mixing bowl and stir using a rubber spatula.
2. Scoop batter out by tablespoon—a small retractable ice cream scoop works wonderfully here—and place on the prepared baking sheets.
3. Put sheets on the middle rack in the oven and bake for 16 minutes. Remove, then transfer cookies to a wire rack to cool. Repeat process with remaining batter. Cool, and serve.

NUTRITIONS

- Calories: 97
- Carbohydrates: 16 g
- Fat: 3 g

- Sodium: 1 mg
- Fiber: 0.6 g
- Sugar: 9 g

- Protein: 1 g

277. Easy Apple Crisp

PREPARATION TIME

15 MIN

COOKING TIME

25 MIN

SERVINGS

8

INGREDIENTS

- 6 medium apples
- 1 tbsp. lemon juice
- 1/3 cup sugar
- 1/2 cup rolled or quick oats
- 1/2 cup white whole-wheat flour
- 1/2 cup light brown sugar
- 1 tbsp. pure vanilla extract
- 1 tsp. ground cinnamon
- 1/2 tsp. ground ginger
- 3 tbsp. unsalted butter

DIRECTIONS

1. Preheat oven to 425°F. Take out a 2-quart baking pan and set it aside. Slice each apple into 16 wedges. Put into a mixing bowl, place the lemon juice and sugar, and toss well to coat.
2. Turn batter out into the baking pan, then set aside. Place the oats, flour, sugar, vanilla, and spices into a mixing bowl and stir to combine.
3. Slice the butter into the mixture using your hands and process until a wet crumb has formed. Sprinkle mixture over the fruit. Bake for 25 minutes. Remove, then let it cool and serve.

NUTRITIONS

- Calories: 232
- Carbohydrates: 46 g
- Fat: 5 g

- Sodium: 5 mg
- Fiber: 2 g
- Sugar: 34 g

- Protein: 2 g

278. Mango Crumble

15 MIN

COOKING TIME

25 MIN

SERVINGS

8

INGREDIENTS

- 2 barely ripe mangoes
- 2 tbsp. light brown sugar
- 1 tbsp. cornstarch
- 1 1/2 tsp. minced fresh ginger
- 1/2 cup unbleached all-purpose flour
- 1/2 cup white whole-wheat flour
- 1/2 cup sugar
- 1 tsp. ground cinnamon
- 1/4 tsp. ground ginger
- 3 tbsp. unsalted butter

DIRECTIONS

1. Preheat oven to 375°F. Take out an 8-inch square baking pan and set it aside. Peel mangoes and cut into 1-inch chunks. Place in a mixing bowl.
2. Add the brown sugar, cornstarch, and minced ginger and toss to coat. Put the batter out into the baking pan and spread to even. In another bowl, whisk the flours, sugar, cinnamon, and ginger.
3. Slice the butter into pieces, and put it in the bowl. Work the butter into the mixture using your hands until it resembles damp sand and sticks when squeezed. Sprinkle mixture evenly over the fruit.
4. Bake for 25 minutes, until the fruit is tender. Remove, and put on a wire rack to cool. Serve warm or cool.

NUTRITIONS

- Calories: 190
- Carbohydrates: 37 g
- Fat: 5 g
- Sodium: 3 mg
- Fiber: 2 g
- Sugar: 23 g
- Protein: 3 g

279. Homemade Banana Ice Cream

PREPARATION TIME

5 MIN

COOKING TIME

0 MIN

SERVINGS

4

INGREDIENTS

- 4 ripe bananas

DIRECTIONS

1. Place bananas in the freezer and freeze until solid. Remove bananas from the freezer, peel them, and slice into chunks. Pulse chunks them into a blender or food processor. Scoop mixture out and serve immediately.

NUTRITIONS

- Calories: 105
- Carbohydrates: 26 g
- Fat: 0 g
- Sodium: 1 mg
- Fiber: 3 g
- Sugar: 14 g
- Protein: 1 g

280. Glazed Pears With Hazelnuts

15 MIN

COOKING TIME

20 MIN

SERVINGS

4

INGREDIENTS

- 4 pears, peeled, cored, and quartered lengthwise
- 1 cup apple juice
- 1 tbsp. grated fresh ginger
- 1/2 cup pure maple syrup
- 1/4 cup chopped hazelnuts

DIRECTIONS

1. Put the pears in a pot, then pour in the apple juice. Bring to a boil over medium-high heat, then reduce the heat to medium-low. Stir constantly.
2. Cover and simmer for an additional 15 minutes or until the pears are tender.
3. Meanwhile, combine the ginger and maple syrup in a saucepan. Bring to a boil over medium-high heat. Stir frequently. Turn off the heat and transfer the syrup to a small bowl and let sit until ready to use.
4. Transfer the pears to a large serving bowl with a slotted spoon, then top the pears with syrup. Spread the hazelnuts over the pears and serve immediately.

NUTRITIONS

- Calories: 287
- Carbohydrates: 66.9 g
- Fat: 3.1 g

- Protein: 2.2 g

281. Lemony Blackberry Granita

15 MIN

COOKING TIME

0 MIN

SERVINGS

4

INGREDIENTS

- 1 lb. (454 g.) fresh blackberries
- 1 tsp. chopped fresh thyme
- 1/4 cup freshly squeezed lemon juice
- 1/2 cup raw honey
- 1/2 cup water

DIRECTIONS

1. Put all the ingredients in a food processor, then pulse to purée. Pour the mixture through a sieve into a baking dish. Discard the seeds that remain in the sieve.
2. Put the baking dish in the freezer for 2 hours. Remove the dish from the refrigerator and stir to break any frozen parts.
3. Return the dish back to the freezer for an hour, then stir to break any frozen parts again. Return the dish to the freezer for 4 hours until the granita is completely frozen.
4. Remove it from the freezer and mash to serve.

NUTRITIONS

- Calories: 183
- Carbohydrates: 45.9 g
- Fat: 1.1 g

- Protein: 2.2 g

Chapter 9

Appetizer /Snack Recipes

282. Cucumber Sandwich Bites

INGREDIENTS

- 1 cucumber, sliced
- 8 slices whole wheat bread
- 2 tbsp. cream cheese, soft
- 1 tbsp. chives, chopped
- 1/4 cup avocado, peeled, pitted, and mashed
- 1 tsp. mustard
- Salt and black pepper to the taste

DIRECTIONS

1. Spread the mashed avocado on each bread slice, also spread the rest of the ingredients except the cucumber slices.
2. Divide the cucumber slices into the bread slices, cut each slice in thirds, arrange on a platter and serve as an appetizer.

NUTRITIONS

- Calories: 187
- Carbohydrates: 4.5 g
- Fat: 12.4 g

- Protein: 8.2 g

283. Yogurt Dip

INGREDIENTS

- 2 cups Greek yogurt
- 2 tbsp. pistachios, toasted and chopped
- A pinch of salt and white pepper
- 2 tbsp. mint, chopped
- 1 tbsp. kalamata olives, pitted and chopped
- 1/4 cup za'atar spice
- 1/4 cup pomegranate seeds
- 1/3 cup olive oil

DIRECTIONS

1. Mix the yogurt with the pistachios and the rest of the ingredients, whisk well, divide into small cups and serve with pita chips on the side.

NUTRITIONS

- Calories: 294
- Fat: 18 g
- Carbohydrates: 2 g

- Protein: 10 g

284. Tomato Bruschetta

10 MIN

10 MIN

6

INGREDIENTS

- 1 baguette, sliced
- 1/3 cup basil, chopped
- 6 tomatoes, cubed
- 2 garlic cloves, minced
- A pinch of salt and black pepper
- 1 tsp. olive oil
- 1 tbsp. balsamic vinegar
- 1/2 tsp. garlic powder
- Cooking spray

DIRECTIONS

1. Situate the baguette slices on a baking sheet lined with parchment paper, grease with cooking spray. Bake for 10 minutes at 400°F.
2. Combine the tomatoes with the basil and the remaining ingredients, toss well and leave aside for 10 minutes. Divide the tomato mix on each baguette slice, arrange them all on a platter and serve.

NUTRITIONS

- Calories: 162
- Carbohydrates: 29 g
- Fat: 4 g

- Protein: 4 g

285. Olives and Cheese Stuffed Tomatoes

10 MIN

0 MIN

4

INGREDIENTS

- 24 cherry tomatoes, top cut off, and insides scooped out
- 2 tbsp. olive oil
- 1/4 tsp. red pepper flakes
- 1/2 cup feta cheese, crumbled
- 2 tbsp. black olive paste
- 1/4 cup mint, torn

DIRECTIONS

1. In a bowl, mix the olives paste with the rest of the ingredients except the cherry tomatoes and whisk well. Stuff the cherry tomatoes with this mix, arrange them all on a platter, and serve as an appetizer.

NUTRITIONS

- Calories: 136
- Carbohydrates: 5.6 g
- Fat: 8.6 g

- Protein: 5.1 g

286. Pepper Tapenade

10 MIN

COOKING TIME

0 MIN

SERVINGS

4

INGREDIENTS

- 7 oz. roasted red peppers, chopped
- 1/2 cup parmesan, grated
- 1/3 cup parsley, chopped
- 14 oz. canned artichokes, drained and chopped
- 3 tbsp. olive oil
- 1/4 cup capers, drained
- 1 1/2 tbsp. lemon juice
- 2 garlic cloves, minced

DIRECTIONS

1. In your blender, combine the red peppers with the parmesan and the rest of the ingredients and pulse well. Divide into cups and serve as a snack.

NUTRITIONS

- Calories: 200
- Carbohydrates: 12.4 g
- Fat: 5.6 g

- Protein: 4.6 g

287. Coriander Falafel

PREPARATION TIME

10 MIN

COOKING TIME

10 MIN

SERVINGS

8

INGREDIENTS

- 1 cup canned garbanzo beans
- 1 bunch parsley leaves
- 1 yellow onion, chopped
- 5 garlic cloves, minced
- 1 tsp. coriander, ground
- A pinch of salt and black pepper
- 1/4 tsp. cayenne pepper
- 1/4 tsp. baking soda
- 1/4 tsp. cumin powder
- 1 tsp. lemon juice
- 3 tbsp. tapioca flour
- Olive oil for frying

DIRECTIONS

1. In your food processor, combine the beans with the parsley, onion, and the rest of the ingredients except the oil and the flour and pulse well.
2. Transfer the mix to a bowl, add the flour, stir well, shape 16 balls out of this mix and flatten them a bit.
3. Preheat pan over medium-high heat, add the falafels, cook them for 5 minutes on both sides, put in paper towels, drain excess grease, arrange them on a platter and serve as an appetizer.

NUTRITIONS

- Calories: 122
- Carbohydrates: 12.3 g
- Fat: 6.2 g

- Protein: 3.1 g

288. Red Pepper Hummus

10 MIN

COOKING TIME

0 MIN

SERVINGS

6

INGREDIENTS

- 6 oz. roasted red peppers, peeled and chopped
- 16 oz. canned chickpeas, drained and rinsed
- 1/4 cup Greek yogurt
- 3 tbsp. tahini paste
- Juice of 1 lemon
- 3 garlic cloves, minced
- 1 tbsp. olive oil
- A pinch of salt and black pepper
- 1 tbsp. parsley, chopped

DIRECTIONS

1. In your food processor, combine the red peppers with the rest of the ingredients except the oil and the parsley and pulse well. Add the oil, pulse again, divide into cups, sprinkle the parsley on top, and serve as a party spread.

NUTRITIONS

- Calories: 255
- Carbohydrates: 17.4 g
- Fat: 11.4 g

- Protein: 6.5 g

289. White Bean Dip

PREPARATION TIME

10 MIN

COOKING TIME

0 MIN

SERVINGS

4

INGREDIENTS

- 15 oz. canned white beans, drained and rinsed
- 6 oz. canned artichoke hearts, drained and quartered
- 4 garlic cloves, minced
- 1 tbsp. basil, chopped
- 2 tbsp. olive oil
- Juice of 1/2 lemon
- Zest of 1/2 lemon, grated
- Salt and black pepper to the taste

DIRECTIONS

1. In your food processor, combine the beans with the artichokes and the rest of the ingredients except the oil and pulse well. Add the oil gradually, pulse the mix again, divide into cups and serve as a party dip.

NUTRITIONS

- Calories: 27
- Carbohydrates: 18.5 g
- Fat: 11.7 g

- Protein: 16.5 g

290. Hummus With Ground Lamb

INGREDIENTS

- 10 oz. hummus
- 12 oz. lamb meat, ground
- 1/2 cup pomegranate seeds
- 1/4 cup parsley, chopped
- 1 tbsp. olive oil
- Pita chips for serving

DIRECTIONS

1. Preheat pan over medium-high heat, cook the meat, and brown for 15 minutes stirring often. Spread the hummus on a platter, spread the ground lamb all over, also spread the pomegranate seeds and the parsley, and serve with pita chips as a snack.

NUTRITIONS

- Calories: 133
- Carbohydrates: 6.4 g
- Fat: 9.7 g
- Protein: 5.4 g

291. Eggplant Dip

INGREDIENTS

- 1 eggplant, poked with a fork
- 2 tbsp. tahini paste
- 2 tbsp. lemon juice
- 2 garlic cloves, minced
- 1 tbsp. olive oil
- Salt and black pepper to the taste
- 1 tbsp. parsley, chopped

DIRECTIONS

1. Put the eggplant in a roasting pan, bake at 400°F for 40 minutes, cool down, peel, and transfer to your food processor.
2. Blend the rest of the ingredients except the parsley, pulse well, divide into small bowls and serve as an appetizer with the parsley sprinkled on top.

NUTRITIONS

- Calories: 121
- Carbohydrates: 1.4 g
- Fat: 4.3 g
- Protein: 4.3 g

292. Veggie Fritters

10 MIN

COOKING TIME

10 MIN

SERVINGS

8

INGREDIENTS

- 2 garlic cloves, minced
- 2 yellow onions, chopped
- 4 scallions, chopped
- 2 carrots, grated
- 2 tsp. cumin, ground
- 1/2 tsp. turmeric powder
- Salt and black pepper to the taste
- 1/4 tsp. coriander, ground
- 2 tbsp. parsley, chopped
- 1/4 tsp. lemon juice
- 1/2 cup almond flour
- 2 beets, peeled and grated
- 2 eggs, whisked
- 1/4 cup tapioca flour
- 3 tbsp. olive oil

DIRECTIONS

1. In a bowl, combine the garlic with the onions, scallions, and the rest of the ingredients except the oil, stir well and shape medium fritters out of this mix.
2. Preheat pan over medium-high heat, place the fritters, cook for 5 minutes on each side, arrange on a platter and serve.

NUTRITIONS

- Calories: 209
- Carbohydrates: 4.4 g
- Fat: 11.2 g
- Protein: 4.8 g

293. Bulgur Lamb Meatballs

PREPARATION TIME

10 MIN

COOKING TIME

15 MIN

SERVINGS

6

INGREDIENTS

- 1 1/2 cups Greek yogurt
- 1/2 tsp. cumin, ground
- 1 cup cucumber, shredded
- 1/2 tsp. garlic, minced
- A pinch of salt and black pepper
- 1 cup bulgur
- 2 cups water
- 1 lb. lamb, ground
- 1/4 cup parsley, chopped
- 1/4 cup shallots, chopped
- 1/2 tsp. allspice, ground
- 1/2 tsp. cinnamon powder
- 1 tbsp. olive oil

DIRECTIONS

1. Mix the bulgur with the water, cover the bowl, leave aside for 10 minutes, drain and transfer to a bowl.
2. Add the meat, the yogurt, and the rest of the ingredients except the oil, stir well and shape medium meatballs out of this mix.
3. Preheat pan over medium-high heat, place the meatballs, cook them for 7 minutes on each side, arrange them all on a platter and serve as an appetizer.

NUTRITIONS

- Calories: 300
- Carbohydrates: 22.6 g
- Fat: 9.6 g
- Protein: 6.6 g

294. Cucumber Bites

PREPARATION TIME

10 MIN

COOKING TIME

0 MIN

SERVINGS

12

INGREDIENTS

- 1 English cucumber, sliced into 32 rounds
- 10 oz. hummus
- 16 cherry tomatoes, halved
- 1 tbsp. parsley, chopped
- 1 oz. feta cheese, crumbled

DIRECTIONS

1. Spread the hummus on each cucumber round, divide the tomato halves on each, sprinkle the cheese and parsley on to and serve as an appetizer.

NUTRITIONS

- Calories: 162
- Carbohydrates: 6.4 g
- Fat: 3.4 g
- Protein: 2.4 g

295. Stuffed Avocado

PREPARATION TIME

10 MIN

COOKING TIME

0 MIN

SERVINGS

2

INGREDIENTS

- 1 avocado, halved and pitted
- 10 oz. canned tuna, drained
- 2 tbsp. sun-dried tomatoes, chopped
- 1 1/2 tbsp. basil pesto
- 2 tbsp. black olives, pitted and chopped
- Salt and black pepper to the taste
- 2 tsp. pine nuts, toasted and chopped
- 1 tbsp. basil, chopped

DIRECTIONS

1. Mix the tuna with the sun-dried tomatoes and the rest of the ingredients except the avocado and stir. Stuff the avocado halves with the tuna mix and serve as an appetizer.

NUTRITIONS

- Calories: 233
- Carbohydrates: 11.4 g
- Fat: 9 g
- Protein: 5.6 g

296. Wrapped Plums

5 MIN

COOKING TIME

0 MIN

SERVINGS

8

INGREDIENTS

- 2 oz. prosciutto, cut into 16 pieces
- 4 plums, quartered
- 1 tbsp. chives, chopped
- A pinch of red pepper flakes, crushed

DIRECTIONS

1. Wrap each plum quarter in a prosciutto slice, arrange them all on a platter, sprinkle the chives and pepper flakes all over, and serve.

NUTRITIONS

- Calories: 30
- Carbohydrates: 4 g
- Fat: 1 g

- Protein: 2 g

297. Marinated Feta and Artichokes

PREPARATION TIME

10 MIN + 4H INACTIVE TIME

COOKING TIME

10 MIN

SERVINGS

2

INGREDIENTS

- 4 oz. traditional Greek feta, cut into 1/2-inch cubes
- 4 oz. drained artichoke hearts, quartered lengthwise
- 1/3 cup extra-virgin olive oil
- Zest and juice of 1 lemon
- 2 tbsp. roughly chopped fresh rosemary
- 2 tbsp. roughly chopped fresh parsley
- 1/2 tsp. black peppercorns

DIRECTIONS

1. In a glass bowl combine the feta and artichoke hearts. Add the olive oil, lemon zest and juice, rosemary, parsley, and peppercorns, and toss gently to coat, being sure not to crumble the feta.
2. Cool for 4 hours, or up to 4 days. Take out of the refrigerator 30 minutes before serving.

NUTRITIONS

- Calories: 235
- Carbohydrates: 1 g
- Fat: 23 g

- Protein: 4 g

298. Tuna Croquettes

40 MIN

COOKING TIME

25 MIN

SERVINGS

36

INGREDIENTS

- 6 tbsp. extra-virgin olive oil, plus 1 to 2 cups
- 5 tbsp. almond flour, plus 1 cup, divided
- 1 1/4 cups heavy cream
- 1 (4 oz.) can olive oil-packed yellowfin tuna
- 1 tbsp. chopped red onion
- 2 tsp. minced capers
- 1/2 tsp. dried dill
- 1/4 tsp. freshly ground black pepper
- 2 large eggs
- 1 cup panko breadcrumbs (or a gluten-free version)

DIRECTIONS

1. In a large skillet, warm up 6 tbsp. olive oil over medium-low heat. Add 5 tbsp. almond flour and cook, stirring constantly, until a smooth paste forms and the flour browns slightly, 2 to 3 minutes.
2. Select the heat to medium-high and gradually mix in the heavy cream, whisking constantly until completely smooth and thickened, another 4 to 5 minutes. Remove and add in the tuna, red onion, capers, dill, and pepper.
3. Transfer the mixture to an 8-inch square baking dish that is well coated with olive oil and set aside at room temperature.
4. Wrap and cool for 4 hours or up to overnight. To form the croquettes, set out three bowls. In one, beat together the eggs.
5. In another, add the remaining almond flour. In the third, add the panko. Line a baking sheet with parchment paper.
6. Scoop about a tbsp. of cold prepared dough into the flour mixture and roll to coat. Shake off excess and, using your hands, roll into an oval.
7. Dip the croquette into the beaten egg, then lightly coat in panko. Set on the lined baking sheet and repeat with the remaining dough.
8. In a small saucepan, warm up the remaining 1 to 2 cups of olive oil, over medium-high heat.
9. Once the oil is heated, fry the croquettes 3 or 4 at a time, depending on the size of your pan, removing with a slotted spoon when golden brown.
10. You will need to adjust the temperature of the oil occasionally to prevent burning. If the croquettes get dark brown very quickly, lower the temperature.

NUTRITIONS

- Calories: 245
- Carbohydrates: 1 g
- Fat: 22 g
- Protein: 6 g

299. Smoked Salmon Crudites

PREPARATION TIME

10 MIN

COOKING TIME

15 MIN

SERVINGS

4

INGREDIENTS

- 6 oz. smoked wild salmon
- 2 tbsp. Roasted Garlic Aioli
- 1 tbsp. Dijon mustard
- 1 tbsp. chopped scallions, green parts only
- 2 tsp. chopped capers
- 1/2 tsp. dried dill
- 4 endive spears or hearts of romaine
- 1/2 English cucumber, cut into 1/4-inch-thick rounds

DIRECTIONS

1. Roughly cut the smoked salmon and transfer in a small bowl. Add the aioli, Dijon, scallions, capers, and dill and mix well.
2. Top endive spears and cucumber rounds with a spoonful of smoked salmon mixture and enjoy chilled.

NUTRITIONS

- Calories: 92
- Carbohydrates: 1 g
- Fat: 5 g
- Protein: 9 g

300. Citrus-Marinated Olives

4 HOURS

0 MIN

2

- 2 cups mixed green olives with pits
- 1/4 cup red wine vinegar
- 1/4 cup extra-virgin olive oil
- 4 garlic cloves, finely minced
- Zest and juice of 1 large orange
- 1 tsp. red pepper flakes
- 2 bay leaves
- 1/2 tsp. ground cumin
- 1/2 tsp. ground allspice

1. Incorporate the olives, vinegar, oil, garlic, orange zest and juice, red pepper flakes, bay leaves, cumin, and allspice and mix well.
2. Seal and chill for 4 hours or up to a week to allow the olives to marinate, tossing again before serving.

- Calories: 133
- Carbohydrates: 2 g
- Fat: 14 g

- Protein: 1 g

301. Olive Tapenade With Anchovies

1H 10 MIN

0 MIN

2

- 2 cups pitted Kalamata olives or other black olives
- 2 anchovy fillets, chopped
- 2 tsp. chopped capers
- 1 garlic clove, finely minced
- 1 cooked egg yolk
- 1 tsp. Dijon mustard
- 1/4 cup extra-virgin olive oil
- Seedy Crackers, Versatile Sandwich Round, or vegetables, for serving (optional)

1. Rinse the olives in cold water and drain well. In a food processor, blender, or a large jar (if using an immersion blender) place the drained olives, anchovies, capers, garlic, egg yolk, and Dijon.
2. Process until it forms a thick paste. While running, gradually stream in the olive oil. Handover to a small bowl, cover, and refrigerate for at least 1 hour to let the flavors develop.
3. Serve with Seedy Crackers, atop a Versatile Sandwich Round, or with your favorite crunchy vegetables.

- Calories: 179
- Carbohydrates: 2 g
- Fat: 19 g

- Protein: 2 g

302. Roasted Vegetable Soup

PREPARATION TIME

15 MIN

COOKING TIME

20 MIN

SERVINGS

2

INGREDIENTS

- 1 tbsp. olive oil
- 5 garlic cloves, peeled
- 1/3 lb. Potatoes diced (1 cm thick)
- 2 yellow bell peppers, diced
- 1/2 tsp. fresh rosemary, finely chopped
- 1 carrot, halved lengthwise and cut into 1 cm piece
- 1 red onion, in chunks
- 2/5 quarts carrot juice
- 1/3 lb. Italian tomatoes, diced
- 1 tsp. fresh tarragon
- Salt and pepper, to taste

DIRECTIONS

1. Preheat oven to 400°F.
2. In a baking tray place potatoes, peppers, garlic, carrot, onion, and tomatoes. Drizzle with olive oil and roast for 10 to 15 minutes.
3. In a saucepan add carrot juice, tarragon; let boil a little.
4. Add all roasted vegetables and stir well. Let it simmer for a few minutes.
5. Season with salt, pepper, and rosemary. Mix well.
6. Serve and enjoy.

NUTRITIONS

- Calories: 318
- Carbohydrates: 60 g
- Fat: 97 g

- Protein: 1.7 g

303. Mediterranean Tomato Soup

PREPARATION TIME

5 MIN

COOKING TIME

30 MIN

SERVINGS

2

INGREDIENTS

- 2 red bell peppers, unseeded, chopped
- 2 medium onions, chopped
- 2–3 garlic cloves, minced
- 7–8 tomatoes, chopped
- 2/5 quarts chicken broth
- Salt and pepper, to taste
- 3 tbsp. olive oil
- 1 tbsp. vinegar

DIRECTIONS

1. Heat oil in a saucepan and cook onion, garlic, and bell peppers for 5 to 6 minutes or until bell peppers is roasted well.
2. Add tomatoes, salt, pepper, and vinegar; stir fry for 4-5 minutes.
3. Add chicken broth and cover with lid. Let it cook for about 20 minutes on low heat.
4. When tomatoes are cooked well, puree the soup with the help of an electric beater.
5. Simmer for 1 to 2 minutes.
6. Add to a serving dish and top with desired herbs.
7. Serve and enjoy.

NUTRITIONS

- Calories: 318
- Carbohydrates: 60 g
- Fat: 97 g

- Protein: 1.7 g

304. Tomato and Cabbage Puree Soup

5 MIN

COOKING TIME

30 MIN

SERVINGS

2

INGREDIENTS

- 2/3 lb. Tomatoes, chopped
- 3–4 garlic cloves, minced
- 1/5 lb. Cabbage, chopped
- 4 tbsp. olive oil
- 1 red onion, chopped
- Salt and pepper, to taste
- Spice mix of choice
- 4-quarts of vegetable broth

DIRECTIONS

1. Heat oil in a saucepan and cook onion, garlic, and cabbage for about 4 to 5 minutes. Make sure that cabbage is nicely softened.
2. Add tomatoes and stir fry until liquid is reduced and tomatoes are dissolved.
3. Add salt, pepper, spice mix, and vegetable broth.
4. Cover the saucepan with a lid and let the mixture cook on low flame for about 30 minutes.
5. Puree the soup with the help of an electric beater.
6. Serve and enjoy.

NUTRITIONS

- Calories: 218
- Carbohydrates: 220 g
- Fat: 15 g

- Protein: 2 g

305. Karen's Apple Kugel

PREPARATION TIME

15 MIN

COOKING TIME

25 MIN

SERVINGS

8

INGREDIENTS

- 3 sheets unsalted matzo
- 2 cups of water
- 4 tart green apples
- 1 tbsp. freshly squeezed lemon juice
- 3 tbsp. unsalted butter, melted
- 1/4 cup brown sugar
- 1/2 cup seedless raisins
- 3 egg whites
- 1 1/2 tsp. ground cinnamon

DIRECTIONS

1. Preheat oven to 400°F. Take out an 8" × 11" baking dish and set it aside. Place the matzo in an 8-inch square baking pan. Pour the water into the pan and set it aside to rehydrate.
2. Peel apples, core, and cut into quarters. Cut each quarter crosswise into thirds and then lengthwise into slices no more than 1/4 inch thick. Transfer apples to a mixing bowl.
3. Check on the matzo. When soft, drain the matzo and squeeze out excess water. Place matzo into the mixing bowl. Put the rest of the ingredients and stir well to combine.
4. Pour mixture into the 8" × 11" baking dish. Bake for 25 minutes. Remove from the oven. Set on a wire rack to cool. Cut into portions and serve warm or cool.

NUTRITIONS

- Calories: 181
- Carbohydrates: 34 g
- Fat: 4 g

- Sodium: 24 mg
- Fiber: 2 g
- Sugar: 21 g

- Protein: 3 g

306. Peach Cobbler

PREPARATION TIME

15 MIN

COOKING TIME

25 MIN

SERVINGS

8

INGREDIENTS

- 6 ripe peaches, peeled and sliced
- 3 tbsp. sugar
- Juice of 1 fresh lemon
- 1 1/4 cups unbleached all-purpose flour
- 1/2 cup white whole-wheat flour
- 2/3 cup sugar
- 1 tsp. sodium-free baking powder
- 4 tbsp. unsalted butter, melted and cooled
- 1 egg white
- 1/2 cup low-fat milk
- 1 tbsp. pure vanilla extract

DIRECTIONS

1. Preheat oven to 425°F. Take out a 9-inch × 13-inch baking dish and set it aside. Put the sliced peaches into a mixing bowl, put sugar plus lemon juice, and toss well to coat. Transfer to the baking dish. Set aside.
2. Mix the flours, sugar, plus baking powder into a mixing bowl. Add the melted butter, egg white, milk, and vanilla and stir well to combine. Scoop batter over sliced peaches.
3. Put baking dish on middle rack in the oven, then bake for 25 minutes. Remove dish from oven and place on a wire rack to cool. Serve warm or cool.

NUTRITIONS

- Calories: 273
- Carbohydrates: 50 g
- Fat: 6 g

- Sodium: 15 mg
- Fiber: 3 g
- Sugar: 28 g

- Protein: 5 g

307. Blueberry Pudding Cake

PREPARATION TIME

15 MIN

COOKING TIME

25 MIN

SERVINGS

6

INGREDIENTS

- 3 cups blueberries
- 3/4 cup sugar, divided
- 1 tbsp. freshly squeezed lemon juice
- 6 tbsp. unsalted butter, softened
- 2 tsp. pure vanilla extract
- 1 tsp. freshly grated lemon zest
- 1 egg white
- 1 1/2 tsp. sodium-free baking powder
- 2 tbsp. low-fat milk
- 2/3 cup white whole-wheat flour

DIRECTIONS

1. Preheat oven to 400°F. Oiled an 8-inch square baking pan lightly with oil and set aside. Place blueberries into a mixing bowl. Add 1/4 cup sugar and the lemon juice and toss well to coat.
2. Pour berries into the prepared baking pan, place on the middle rack in the oven, and bake for 5 minutes. Remove from the oven and set aside. Place the butter and remaining 1/2 cup sugar into a mixing bowl and beat to combine.
3. Add the vanilla, lemon zest, and egg white and mix well. Add the baking powder and milk and stir. Gradually add in the flour, mixing until combined.
4. Pour batter over the cooked blueberries. Bake for 20 minutes, until golden brown. Serve warm or cool.

NUTRITIONS

- Calories: 300
- Carbohydrates: 46 g
- Fat: 12 g

- Sodium: 14 mg
- Fiber: 2 g
- Sugar: 32 g

- Protein: 2 g

308. Vegan Rice Pudding

15 MIN

COOKING TIME

20 MIN

SERVINGS

8

INGREDIENTS

- 1-quart vanilla nondairy milk
- 1 cup basmati or jasmine rice, rinsed
- 1/4 cup sugar
- 1 tsp. pure vanilla extract
- 1/8 tsp. pure almond extract
- 1/2 tsp. ground cinnamon
- 1/8 tsp. ground cardamom

DIRECTIONS

1. Mix all of the ingredients into a saucepan and stir well to combine. Bring to a boil over medium-high heat. Adjust heat to low and simmer, stirring very frequently, about 15 to 20 minutes. Remove from heat and cool. Serve sprinkled with additional ground cinnamon if desired.

NUTRITIONS

- Calories: 148
- Carbohydrates: 26 g
- Fat: 2 g
- Sodium: 48 mg
- Fiber: 1 g
- Sugar: 10 g
- Protein: 4 g

309. Beetroot and Berry Smoothie

PREPARATION TIME

5 MIN

COOKING TIME

0 MIN

SERVINGS

1

INGREDIENTS

- 1/2 cup pineapple juice
- 1/2 cup low-fat vanilla yogurt
- 1/2 cup frozen strawberries
- 1/4 cup frozen blueberries
- 1/4 cup beetroot (peeled, washed, and sliced)

DIRECTIONS

1. Combine all the ingredients in a blender and blend until you obtain a smooth puree. Serve cold.

NUTRITIONS

- Calories: 218
- Carbohydrates: 40.7 g
- Fat: 1.9 g
- Protein: 8.4 g
- Sodium: 121 mg

310. Berry Blast

15 MIN

COOKING TIME

40 MIN

SERVINGS

1

INGREDIENTS

- 4 cups blueberries (2 cups fresh and 2 cups frozen)
- 1 cup rolled oats
- 1 tsp. cinnamon
- 2 tbsp. all-purpose flour
- 2 tsp. unsalted butter
- 1 tbsp. maple syrup
- Cooking spray

DIRECTIONS

1. Coat a pie pan with cooking spray and set it aside. Put the blueberries on the pie plate. Preheat the oven to 250°F.
2. Combine the flour, butter, oats, maple syrup, and cinnamon in a large mixing bowl and whisk until you obtain a grainy mixture.
3. Transfer the oats mixture to the pie pan and bake for forty minutes until the mixture is golden brown. Serve warm.

NUTRITIONS

- Calories: 824
- Carbohydrates: 166.6 g
- Fat: 15.2 g

- Protein: 16.9 g
- Sodium: 65 mg

311. Oats and Fruit Bar Cracker

PREPARATION TIME

15 MIN

COOKING TIME

0 MIN

SERVINGS

3

INGREDIENTS

- 1 cup quinoa
- 1 cup oats
- 1/2 cup figs (dried)
- 1/2 cup honey
- 1/2 cup almonds (chopped)
- 1/2 cup apricots (dried)
- 1/2 cup wheat germ
- 1/2 cup pineapple (dried and chopped)
- 1 tbsp. cornstarch

DIRECTIONS

1. Mix the ingredients in a mixing bowl until you obtain a well-balanced mixture. Put the batter on a baking tray or plate and flatten it. Ensure that the mixture is at least one inch thick. Let it cool before you cut it into pieces and serve.

NUTRITIONS

- Calories: 766
- Carbohydrates: 144.2 g
- Fat: 15.7 g

- Protein: 22.2 g
- Sodium: 12 mg

312. Colorful Pops

15 MIN

0 MIN

6

- 2 cups of watermelon, strawberries, and cantaloupe (diced)
- 2 cups pure apple juice
- 2 cups fresh blueberries
- 6 craft sticks
- 6 paper cups

1. Mix all the fruit in a mixing bowl. Divide the fruit salad into the paper cups and pour the apple juice. Ensure that the apple juice only covers half the paper cup. Deep-freeze the cups for an hour or until they are partially frozen.
2. Remove the cups and add the sticks to the cups, and deep freeze for one more hour. Serve them as colorful pops!

- Calories: 83
- Carbohydrates: 20.8 g
- Fat: 0.2 g

- Protein: 0.7 g
- Sodium: 8 mg

313. Pumpkin Pie Recipe

15 MIN

50 MIN

2

- 1 cup ginger snaps
- 8 oz. canned pumpkin
- 1/4 cup egg whites
- 1/4 cup erythritol
- 1 tsp. pumpkin pie spice
- 6 oz. evaporated skim milk
- Cooking spray

1. Preheat the oven to 300°F. Oiled a glass pie pan with cooking spray. Crumble the ginger snaps and pat them into the glass pan. Mix the rest of the ingredients in a mixing bowl and pour it into the prepared glass pie pan.
2. Bake the dish for 50 minutes or until a knife inserted in the center comes out clean. Transfer the pie pan into the refrigerator and allow it to cool. Serve cold.

- Calories: 792
- Carbohydrates: 172.7 g
- Fat: 16.6 g

- Protein: 20 g
- Sodium: 1181 mg

314. Walnut and Oatmeal Chocolate Chip Cookies

15 MIN

COOKING TIME

20 MIN

SERVINGS

4

INGREDIENTS

- 1 cup rolled oats
- 1/4 cup all-purpose flour
- 1/4 cup whole-wheat pastry flour
- 1/2 tsp. ground cinnamon
- 1/4 tsp. baking soda
- 1/4 tsp. salt
- 1/4 tsp. tahini
- 2 tbsp. unsalted butter (cubed)
- 1/2 cup erythritol
- 1/2 cup maple syrup
- 2 eggs (one whole and one egg white)
- 1/2 tbsp. vanilla extract
- 1/2 cup bittersweet chocolate chips
- 1/4 cup chopped walnuts

DIRECTIONS

1. Place racks in the oven's upper and lower parts and preheat the oven to 300°F. Prepare or arrange two lined baking sheets with parchment paper. Combine the oats, whole-wheat flour, all-purpose flour, baking soda, cinnamon, and salt in a bowl and whisk.
2. Beat butter and tahini in a large mixing bowl and blend until you obtain a paste. Add maple syrup and granulated sugar to the bowl and continue to beat until you get a well-combined mixture. Note that the mixture will still be slightly grainy.
3. Now, add the vanilla extract, egg white, and whole egg to the bowl and continue to whisk until you obtain a well-combined mixture.
4. Stir in the oat mixture, chocolate chips, and walnuts into the bowl. Wet your hands slightly, roll one tbsp. of the batter into a small ball, and place it on the baking sheet. Flatten the ball out but ensure that the sides do not crack. Continue with the remaining batter and leave at least a two-inch space between each cookie.
5. Bake the cookies for twenty minutes or until golden brown. Cool the cookies for two minutes before you transfer them onto the wire rack to cool completely.

NUTRITIONS

- Calories: 530
- Carbohydrates: 98.6 g
- Fat: 14.8 g
- Protein: 10.6 g
- Sodium: 280 mg

315. Blueberry Waffles

PREPARATION TIME

15 MIN

COOKING TIME

15 MIN

SERVINGS

8

INGREDIENTS

- 2 cups whole wheat flour
- 1 tbsp. baking powder
- 1 tsp. ground cinnamon 2 tbsp. sugar
- 2 large eggs
- 3 tbsp. unsalted butter, melted
- 3 tbsp. nonfat plain Greek yogurt
- 1 1/2 cups 1% milk
- 2 tsp. vanilla extract
- 4 oz. blueberries
- Nonstick cooking spray
- 1/2 cup maple almond butter

DIRECTIONS

1. Preheat waffle iron. Mix the flour, baking powder, cinnamon, plus sugar in a large bowl. Mix the eggs, melted butter, yogurt, milk, and vanilla in a small bowl. Combine well.
2. Put the wet ingredients into the dry mix and whisk until well combined. Do not over whisk; it's okay if the mixture has some lumps. Fold in the blueberries.
3. Oiled the waffle iron with cooking spray, then cook 1/3 cup of the batter until the waffles are lightly browned and slightly crisp. Repeat with the rest of the batter.
4. Place 2 waffles in each of 4 storage containers. Store the almond butter in 4 condiment cups. To serve, top each warm waffle with 1 tbsp. of maple almond butter.

NUTRITIONS

- Calories: 647
- Carbohydrates: 67 g
- Fat: 37 g
- Protein: 22 g
- Sodium: 156 mg

316. Apple Pancakes

15 MIN

COOKING TIME

5 MIN

SERVINGS

16

INGREDIENTS

- 1/4 cup extra-virgin olive oil, divided
- 1 cup whole wheat flour
- 2 tsp. baking powder
- 1 tsp. baking soda
- 1 tsp. ground cinnamon
- 1 cup 1% milk
- 2 large eggs
- 1 medium Gala apple, diced
- 2 tbsp. maple syrup
- 1/4 cup chopped walnuts

DIRECTIONS

1. Set aside 1 tsp. oil to use for greasing a griddle or skillet. In a large bowl, stir the flour, baking powder, baking soda, cinnamon, milk, eggs, apple, and the remaining oil.
2. Warm griddle or skillet on medium-high heat and coat with the reserved oil. Working in batches, pour in about 1/4 cup of the batter for each pancake. Cook until browned on both sides.
3. Place 4 pancakes into each of 4 medium storage containers and the maple syrup in 4 small containers. Put each serving with 1 tbsp. walnuts and drizzle with 1/2 tbsp. maple syrup.

NUTRITIONS

- Calories: 378
- Carbohydrates: 39 g
- Fat: 22 g

- Protein: 10 g
- Sodium: 65 mg

317. Super-Simple Granola

PREPARATION TIME

15 MIN

COOKING TIME

25 MIN

SERVINGS

8

INGREDIENTS

- 1/4 cup extra-virgin olive oil
- 1/4 cup honey
- 1/2 tsp. ground cinnamon
- 1/2 tsp. vanilla extract
- 1/4 tsp. salt
- 2 cups rolled oats
- 1/2 cup chopped walnuts
- 1/2 cup slivered almonds

DIRECTIONS

1. Preheat the oven to 350°F. Mix the oil, honey, cinnamon, vanilla, and salt in a large bowl. Add the oats, walnuts, and almonds. Stir to coat. Put the batter out onto the prepared sheet pan. Bake for 20 minutes. Let cool.

NUTRITIONS

- Calories: 254
- Carbohydrates: 25 g
- Fat: 16 g

- Fiber: 3.5 g
- Protein: 5 g
- Potassium: 163 mg

- Sodium: 73 mg

318. Savory Yogurt Bowls

15 MIN

COOKING TIME

0 MIN

SERVINGS

4

INGREDIENTS

- 1 medium cucumber, diced
- 1/2 cup pitted Kalamata olives, halved
- 2 tbsp. fresh lemon juice
- 1 tbsp. extra-virgin olive oil
- 1 tsp. dried oregano
- 1/4 tsp. freshly ground black pepper
- 2 cups nonfat plain Greek yogurt
- 1/2 cup slivered almonds

DIRECTIONS

1. In a small bowl, mix the cucumber, olives, lemon juice, oil, oregano, and pepper. Divide the yogurt evenly among 4 storage containers. Top with the cucumber-olive mix and almonds.

NUTRITIONS

- Calories: 240
- Carbohydrates: 10 g
- Fat: 16 g

- Protein: 16 g
- Potassium: 353 mg
- Sodium: 350 mg

319. Energy Sunrise Muffins

PREPARATION TIME

15 MIN

COOKING TIME

25 MIN

SERVINGS

16

INGREDIENTS

- Nonstick cooking spray
- 2 cups whole wheat flour
- 2 tsp. baking soda
- 2 tsp. ground cinnamon
- 1 tsp. ground ginger
- 1/4 tsp. salt
- 3 large eggs
- 1/2 cup packed brown sugar
- 1/3 cup unsweetened applesauce
- 1/4 cup honey
- 1/4 cup vegetable or canola oil
- 1 tsp. grated orange zest
- Juice of 1 medium orange
- 2 tsp. vanilla extract
- 2 cups shredded carrots
- 1 large apple, peeled and grated
- 1/2 cup golden raisins
- 1/2 cup chopped pecans
- 1/2 cup unsweetened coconut flakes

DIRECTIONS

If you can place two 12-cup muffin tins side by side in the oven, then leave a rack in the middle, then preheat the oven to 350°F.

1. Coat 16 cups of the muffin tins with cooking spray or line with paper liners. Mix the flour, baking soda, cinnamon, ginger, and salt in a large bowl. Set aside.
2. Mix the eggs, brown sugar, applesauce, honey, oil, orange zest, orange juice, and vanilla until combined in a medium bowl. Add the carrots and apple and whisk again.
3. Mix the dry and wet ingredients with a spatula. Fold in the raisins, pecans, and coconut. Mix everything once again, just until well combined. Put the batter into the prepared muffin cups, filling them to the top.
4. Bake for 20 to 25 minutes, or until a wooden toothpick inserted into the middle of the center muffin comes out clean (switching racks halfway through if baking on 2 racks). Cool for 5 minutes in the tins, then transfers to a wire rack to cool for an additional 5 minutes. Cool completely before storing in containers.

NUTRITIONS

- Calories: 292
- Carbohydrates: 42 g
- Fat: 14 g

- Protein: 5 g
- Sodium: 84 mg

320. Spinach, Egg, and Cheese Breakfast Quesadillas

PREPARATION TIME

15 MIN

COOKING TIME

15 MIN

SERVINGS

4

INGREDIENTS

- 1 1/2 tbsp. extra-virgin olive oil
- 1/2 medium onion, diced
- 1 medium red bell pepper, diced
- 4 large eggs
- 1/8 tsp. salt
- 1/8 tsp. freshly ground black pepper
- 4 cups baby spinach
- 1/2 cup crumbled feta cheese
- Nonstick cooking spray
- 4 (6-inch) whole-wheat tortillas, divided
- 1 cup shredded part-skim low-moisture mozzarella cheese, divided

DIRECTIONS

1. Warm-up oil over medium heat in a large skillet. Add the onion and bell pepper and sauté for about 5 minutes, or until soft.
2. Mix the eggs, salt, and black pepper in a medium bowl. Stir in the spinach and feta cheese. Put the egg batter in the skillet and scramble for about 2 minutes, or until the eggs are cooked. Remove from the heat.
3. Coat a clean skillet with cooking spray and add 2 tortillas. Place one-quarter of the spinach-egg mixture on one side of each tortilla. Sprinkle each with 1/4 cup of mozzarella cheese. Fold the other halves of the tortillas down to close the quesadillas and brown for about 1 minute.
4. Turn over and cook again in a minute on the other side. Repeat with the remaining 2 tortillas and 1/2 cup of mozzarella cheese. Cut each quesadilla in half or wedges. Divide among 4 storage containers or reusable bags.

NUTRITIONS

- Calories: 453
- Carbohydrates: 28 g
- Fat: 28 g
- Fiber: 4.5 g
- Protein: 23 g
- Potassium: 205 mg
- Sodium: 837 mg

321. Simple Cheese and Broccoli Omelets

PREPARATION TIME

15 MIN

COOKING TIME

10 MIN

SERVINGS

4

INGREDIENTS

- 3 tbsp. extra-virgin olive oil, divided
- 2 cups chopped broccoli
- 8 large eggs
- 1/4 cup 1% milk
- 1/2 tsp. freshly ground black pepper
- 8 tbsp. shredded reduced-fat Monterey Jack cheese, divided

DIRECTIONS

1. In a nonstick skillet, heat 1 tbsp. oil over medium-high heat. Add the broccoli and sauté, occasionally stirring, for 3 to 5 minutes, or until the broccoli turns bright green. Scrape into a bowl.
2. Mix the eggs, milk, plus pepper in a small bowl. Wipe out the skillet and heat 1/2 tbsp. oil. Add one-quarter of the egg mixture and tilt the skillet to ensure an even layer. Cook for 2 minutes and then add 2 tbsp. cheese and one-quarter of the broccoli. Use a spatula to fold into an omelet.
3. Repeat step 3 with the remaining 1 1/2 tbsp. oil, remaining egg mixture, 6 tbsp. cheese, and remaining broccoli to make a total of 4 omelets. Divide into 4 storage containers.

NUTRITIONS

- Calories: 292
- Carbohydrates: 4 g
- Fat: 23 g
- Fiber: 1 g
- Protein: 18 g
- Potassium: 308 mg
- Sodium: 282 mg

322. Creamy Avocado and Egg Salad Sandwiches

15 MIN

COOKING TIME

15 MIN

SERVINGS

4

INGREDIENTS

- 2 small avocados, halved and pitted
- 2 tbsp. nonfat plain Greek yogurt
- Juice of 1 large lemon
- 1/4 tsp. salt
- 1/2 tsp. freshly ground black pepper
- 8 large eggs, hardboiled, peeled, and chopped
- 3 tbsp. finely chopped fresh dill
- 3 tbsp. finely chopped fresh parsley
- 8 whole wheat bread slices (or your choice)

DIRECTIONS

1. Scoop the avocados into a large bowl and mash. Mix in the yogurt, lemon juice, salt, and pepper. Add the eggs, dill, and parsley and combine.
2. Store the bread and salad separately in 4 reusable storage bags and 4 containers and assemble the night before or serving. To serve, divide the mixture evenly among 4 of the bread slices and top with the other slices to make sandwiches.

NUTRITIONS

- Calories: 488
- Carbohydrates: 48 g
- Fat: 22 g

- Fiber: 8 g
- Protein: 23 g
- Potassium: 469 mg

- Sodium: 597 mg

323. Breakfast Hash

PREPARATION TIME

15 MIN

COOKING TIME

25 MIN

SERVINGS

4

INGREDIENTS

- Nonstick cooking spray
- 2 large sweet potatoes, 1/2-inch cubes
- 1 scallion, finely chopped
- 1/4 tsp. salt
- 1/2 tsp. freshly ground black pepper
- 8 oz. extra-lean ground beef (96% or leaner)
- 1 medium onion, diced
- 2 garlic cloves, minced
- 1 red bell pepper, diced
- 1/4 tsp. ground cumin
- 1/4 tsp. paprika
- 2 cups coarsely chopped kale leaves
- 3/4 cup shredded reduced-fat Cheddar cheese
- 4 large eggs

DIRECTIONS

1. Oiled a large skillet with cooking spray and heat over medium heat. Add the sweet potatoes, scallion, salt, and pepper. Sauté for 10 minutes, stirring often.
2. Add the beef, onion, garlic, bell pepper, cumin, and paprika. Sauté, frequently stirring, for about 4 minutes, or until the meat browns. Add the kale to the skillet and stir until wilted. Sprinkle with the Cheddar cheese.
3. Make four wells in the hash batter and crack an egg into each. Cover and let the eggs cook until the white is fully cooked and the yolk is to your liking. Divide into 4 storage containers.

NUTRITIONS

- Calories: 323
- Carbohydrates: 23 g
- Fat: 15 g

- Fiber: 4 g
- Protein: 25 g
- Potassium: 676 mg

- Sodium: 587 mg

324. Hearty Breakfast Casserole

15 MIN

30 MIN

4

INGREDIENTS

- Nonstick cooking spray
- 1 large green bell pepper, diced
- 8 oz. cremini mushrooms, diced
- 1/2 medium onion, diced
- 3 garlic cloves, minced
- 1 large sweet potato, grated
- 1 cup baby spinach
- 12 large eggs
- 3 tbsp. 1% milk
- 1 tsp. mustard powder
- 1 tsp. paprika
- 1 tsp. freshly ground black pepper
- 1/2 tsp. salt
- 1/2 cup shredded reduced-fat Colby-Jack cheese

DIRECTIONS

1. Preheat the oven to 350°F. Oiled at a 9-by-13-inch baking dish with cooking spray. Coat a large skillet with cooking spray and heat over medium heat. Add the bell pepper, mushrooms, onion, garlic, and sweet potato.
2. Sauté, frequently stirring, for 3 to 4 minutes, or until the onion is translucent. Add the spinach and continue to sauté while stirring, until the spinach has wilted. Remove, then set aside to cool slightly.
3. Mix the eggs, milk, mustard powder, paprika, black pepper, and salt in a large bowl. Add the sautéed vegetables. Put the batter into the prepared baking dish.
4. Bake for 30 minutes. Remove from the oven, sprinkle with the Colby-Jack cheese, return to the oven, and bake again for 5 minutes to melt the cheese. Divide into 4 storage containers.

NUTRITIONS

- Calories: 378
- Carbohydrates: 17 g
- Fat: 25 g
- Fiber: 3 g
- Protein: 26 g
- Potassium: 717 mg
- Sodium: 658 mg

325. Creamy Apple-Avocado Smoothie

15 MIN

0 MIN

2

INGREDIENTS

- 1/2 medium avocado, peeled and pitted
- 1 medium apple, chopped
- 1 cup baby spinach leaves
- 1 cup nonfat vanilla Greek yogurt
- 1/2 to 1 cup of water
- 1 cup ice
- Freshly squeezed lemon juice (optional)

DIRECTIONS

1. Blend all of the ingredients using a blender, and blend until smooth and creamy. Put a squeeze of lemon juice on top if desired, and serve immediately.

NUTRITIONS

- Calories: 200
- Carbohydrates: 27 g
- Fat: 7 g
- Sodium: 56 mg
- Potassium: 378 mg
- Fiber: 5 g
- Sugar: 20 g
- Protein: 10 g

Chapter 10
Measurement Conversion Chart

VOLUME EQUIVALENTS(DRY)

US STANDARD	METRIC (APPROXIMATE)
1/8 teaspoon	0.5 mL
1/4 teaspoon	1 mL
1/2 teaspoon	2 mL
3/4 teaspoon	4 mL
1 teaspoon	5 mL
1 tablespoon	15 mL
1/4 cup	59 mL
1/2 cup	118 mL
3/4 cup	177 mL
1 cup	235 mL
2 cups	475 mL
3 cups	700 mL
4 cups	1 L

VOLUME EQUIVALENTS(LIQUID)

US STANDARD	US STANDARD (OUNCES)	METRIC (APPROXIMATE)
2 tablespoons	1 fl.oz.	30 mL
1/4 cup	2 fl.oz.	60 mL
1/2 cup	4 fl.oz.	120 mL
1 cup	8 fl.oz.	240 mL
1 1/2 cup	12 fl.oz.	355 mL
2 cups or 1 pint	16 fl.oz.	475 mL
4 cups or 1 quart	32 fl.oz.	1 L
1 gallon	128 fl.oz.	4 L

TEMPERATURES EQUIVALENTS

FAHRENHEIT(F)	CELSIUS(C) (APPROXIMATE)
225 °F	107 °C
250 °F	120 °C
275 °F	135 °C
300 °F	150 °C
325 °F	160 °C
350 °F	180 °C
375 °F	190 °C
400 °F	205 °C
425 °F	220 °C
450 °F	235 °C
475 °F	245 °C
500 °F	260 °C

WEIGHT EQUIVALENTS

US STANDARD	METRIC (APPROXIMATE)
1 ounce	28 g
2 ounces	57 g
5 ounces	142 g
10 ounces	284 g
15 ounces	425 g
16 ounces (1 pound)	455 g
1.5 pounds	680 g
2 pounds	907 g

SHOPPING LIST

DASH DIET SHOPPING LIST PHASE 1

MEAT AND FISH

Chicken

Fatty fish

Herrings

Mackerel

Salmon

Sardines

Tuna

Lean beef

Turkey

DAIRY AND EGGS

Cheese

Eggs

Low-fat yogurt

Milk

Yogurt

VEGETABLES

Avocados

Bell Peppers

Carrots

Cucumber

Garlic

Kale

Lettuce

Onions

Seeds

Chia seeds

Linseed

Pumpkin

Sunflower

Spinach

Tomatoes

Zucchiniicourgettes

SNACKS

Almonds

Brazil nuts

Cashew nuts

Pistachios

Walnuts

PHASE 2, ADD

FRUIT

Apples

Blueberries

Grapes

Kiwi

Oranges

Raspberries

Strawberries

Vegetables

LEGUMES

Chickpeas

Black beans

Black-eyed peas

Red kidney beans

Potatoes

Sweet potatoes

GRAINS

Brown rice

Buckwheat

Bulgar wheat

Couscous

Pearl barley

Wholegrain pasta

Wholewheat bread

SNACKS

Chocolate

Conclusion

The DASH diet is well-supported by scientific research, and many find it easy to follow because it doesn't require counting calories or measuring portions.

The DASH diet is a way of eating that helps you reach and maintain a healthy weight, improves your overall health, and lowers your blood pressure.

The DASH diet is rich in fruits and vegetables, whole grains, low-fat dairy products, and lean meats. You'll get plenty of fiber from the fruit, whole grains, vegetables, and legumes. And a lot of good fats are found in nuts, seeds, and fatty fish.

The DASH diet limits sugars, sweets, and fats. It also recommends that you limit sodium.

Here is how a typical day's menu might look for someone who is following the DASH diet

· Breakfast Whole-wheat toast with peanut butter and banana slices

· Snack Apple

· Lunch Whole-grain pita pocket stuffed with tuna salad

· Snack Celery sticks with peanut butter Dinner Grilled salmon, brown rice, broccoli

In addition to following the menu guidelines above, it's also important to eat smaller portions and snacks less often when you're trying to lose weight.

If you follow the DASH diet, choose low-fat or fat-free dairy products often.

The DASH diet is an innovative approach to weight loss. By following the menu guidelines and carefully planning your meals, you will be able to lose weight in a safe and healthy manner.

The DASH diet is used with a combination of other lifestyle changes exercise, weight control, and smoking cessation. It's also proven to help people with high blood pressure, such as systolic blood pressure or diastolic blood pressure (when arteries relax between heartbeats), who aren't following a specific diet plan.

When you follow the DASH diet, you may notice an increase in your daily calorie consumption. That's because the DASH diet uses foods from different food groups and allows you to choose a variety of nutrient-rich foods.

WATCH YOUR WEIGHT

It's also important to watch your weight, and not only while you're on the DASH diet. You'll need to continue to exercise regularly as well.

Other low-fat diets may seem like a good choice for losing weight and lowering blood pressure at first glance. However, they can pose certain risks for people with certain health conditions, including high blood pressure. As long as the DASH diet is followed carefully and the sodium levels remain for a healthy range, it's considered a safe and effective way to lose weight if combined with a regular physical activity.

For example, the National Institutes of Health (NIH) recommends that adults consume 1mg to 2,300 mg of sodium a day. However, most people consume five times that much sodium every day.

The DASH diet emphasizes fruits, vegetables, and whole grains and includes low-fat or fat-free dairy products. The diet also limits the amount of sugar you can consume each day. It doesn't recommend avoiding healthy fats found in nuts, seeds, and fatty fish. And it allows for small portions of red meat and sweets every once in a while.

Index of Recipes

Printed in Great Britain
by Amazon